MEDICINE TRACKS

A Memoir

Donell Barlow

Cover illustration by Emma Noyes. Cover design by Anna Morgan.

This book is a work of memoir and creative nonfiction, and it should be read as such. In many instances, dialogue and identifying details have been fictionalized. Names, characters, places, and incidents have often been altered for literary effect or changed to protect the privacy of people involved.

Donell Barlow
Visit my website at www.DonellBarlow.com

Printed in the United States of America

First Printing: Aug 2018
Independently Published

ISBN 978-1718-003-12-5

This book is dedicated to the loving memory of my father,
Don Barlow.

Contents

Acknowledgements

I want to begin by thanking and being grateful for:

My incredibly supportive friends Kyla Hotchkiss, Lindsey Brown, Haley Young, Coco Noelle, and Britney Weaver.

My teachers who took me under their wing and gave me the medicine I needed, including Gerald Savage, Alex Turtle, and Tony Redhouse.

The women who became my mother figures after I lost mine, one of those being my late sister, Laura Jordan.

The authors whose words spoke to me during this transition of healing, including Jamie Sams, Caroline Myss, Adyashanti, and Ana Forrest.

I want to thank all of those who contributed to my growth, whether their actions came from pain or love.

CHAPTER 1
Elder Medicine

I HAD BEEN PATIENTLY WAITING for this moment for the last three and half years. It felt surreal to be in this sacred space, and I wondered if at any moment I would wake up from this dream.

Today was my welcoming ceremony in New Zealand. Upon arrival I would be welcomed by the Mana Whenua, which means a sense of belonging, as well as territorial rights to that specific area of land for the local Māori tribe. This greeting would offer a new healing to my spirit. This place was like nothing I had ever seen before. The ancestral house (marae) and its entrance gates were the boldest red in color, adorned in the most intricate carvings, each one unique and representing their ancestors and their history. Some of the eyes of the carvings appeared to be abalone shells, which are called pāua by the Māori of New Zealand. It felt so familiar to how my ancestors used these shells for ceremony and adornment. I was in complete awe of this sacred space, and we hadn't even gone inside yet.

My guide Tina ushered me over. "It's time, we are ready for you," she said. Tina had the most beautiful long black wavy hair, with a few grey strands showing her wisdom. I couldn't help but notice her amazing traditional tattoos down her legs. This commonality between our ancestral ink designs felt familiar and was just another reason to feel so at home here. To say I'm covered in tattoos is putting it mildly; if it were back in the turn of the twentieth century, I could have made a living as the "tattooed lady" in the circus.

Tina's energy and presence reassured me that this event would be incredibly special and something I would never forget. Before entering the gate, she went over the protocol of what would happen before I could enter the marae.

"Wait here until my Auntie makes the call for us to come forward," Tina explained. "And I will answer her. Then we will proceed to wait under the gate." She explained the rest of the ceremony in detail before each step.

"A Māori warrior will come forward, and perform his Haka Pōwhiri, a traditional dance of welcome. This dance was originally intended to intimidate the opposition before battle. By performing a series of vigorous movements, accompanied with fierce facial expressions. When he is done he will lay down a small branch, and then give you the signal to pick it up. This exchange will mean you come in peace," she said and smiled.

After she responded to her auntie's call in their native language, we slowly proceeded forward and stood right underneath the gate entrance. I was so humbled to be standing here, observing this beautiful tradition. I have such an appreciation for their culture and traditions. The warrior's Haka was so expressive, and each movement held the strength and courage of his ancestors. I was already on the verge of crying happy tears, but it was too early for that just yet. The warrior laid down the small branch of leaves and gestured for me to pick it up.

An elder woman proceeded to make a series of four calls, called karanga, that welcomed me to the land, and their Sky Mother and Father, followed by karanga for the winds of four corners and the guardians of the natural phenomena around us. The second call was to acknowledge all of my ancestors that had passed and had made this journey with me to guide me safely to their ancestral home. This call would unite my ancestors with their ancestors that had also passed, connecting us all through spirit.

As she made the first two calls, Tina responded, holding my arm as we walked slowly towards the ancestral house. There was a group of about fifteen local performers of all ages standing outside singing their welcoming songs, before we proceeded to enter the marae. This sacred space, was a place of worship, where religious and cultural activities continue to take place just as they always have. The third call was made to welcome me into the physical connection I would have while visiting their homeland. This call also allowed me to enter the marae and prepare for the next step of the ceremony.

Before we entered, we were told to remove our shoes and then go inside. I was overwhelmed by how incredibly beautiful this sacred place was. Tina ushered us to stand on the right side, across from about ten more local people that were waiting inside.

An elder man came forward; he was their main speaker and chief (Rangatira) that would be performing the formal speeches and traditional prayer. We continued to stand as he acknowledged their land, ancestors, natural phenomena, and their Māori king. Then Tina introduced me and asked me to step forward to greet everyone, and to speak of my ancestors and culture. I proceeded to greet them in my Yurok language, and then explained my words after.

> Aye kweé ne-toó mer
> Skueyeń wé-chmey
> Wokhlew kee mek 'en-es
> Nek' n-ew Donell
> Spokane mé Womechok

"Hello relatives, and good evening. Thank you for coming. My name is Donell Barlow and I am from Spokane."

I could see their eyes light up, and I assumed it was the first time they had heard my language.

"I am enrolled Ottawa from my father's side. My ancestors were best known for their trading, as they traversed in canoes along the rivers of Northeastern United States and Canada. Many tribes in that area benefited from this trade economy, with the French, English and the Dutch. This competitive livelihood eventually led to intertribal ware fare among them and forced the Ottawa along with the Hurons and the Potawatomies to move towards the western side of Lake Michigan. My ancestors continued to travel great distances heading south towards the Ohio River, and then onto trans-Mississippi west. Due to the continued intertribal ware fare of the fur trade, and the movement of American pioneers dispersed the Ottawa through Kansas, Michigan, and my Otter clan in particular resides in Oklahoma. My mother's side is Yurok. We were never moved from our ancestral lands in Northern California, and we still reside there today. We were great fisherman along the Klamath River, and the river provided our most essential traditional food, the salmon. The Yurok were known as skilled basket weavers, and my grandmother was well known for her skills by our people."

I proceeded to explain the Yurok basket hat I was wearing and its flying geese design. I also explained the other regalia I was able to bring for this ceremony. I then gave a brief explanation of the work I do with Native American youth at home, about how I teach communities to use food as medicine and the importance of getting back to our traditional foods and the ways of our ancestors.

Tina also asked me to speak about Standing Rock and my experiences there. She wanted to give the tribal members a chance to hear what was happening from an insider's perspective. The information they could access about Standing Rock was limited, and the people were eager to learn more.

"I traveled to Standing Rock two days after the dog attacks had occurred on the water protectors," I told my listeners. "A restraining order had been in effect against the Army Corp of Engineers upon my arrival. When I pulled into camp, a crazy storm was brewing and it was time to seek shelter. My mission and the service I wanted to provide was cooking in the main kitchen at Oceti Sakowin camp, to feed the protectors."

I didn't expect to get emotional during my introduction, but then I got into the connection to spirit and to our ancestors that was undeniable when you set foot at Standing Rock.

I continued, "The sense of community was a beautiful thing to witness. There was plenty of food and donations of clothes, blankets, and other necessities to go around. At camp, we were living like our ancestors did, and everyone used whatever skills they had to pitch in."

Then, as my eyes really began to water, I looked around the room to see these completely engaged beautiful humans just waiting to hear more. I took a breath to gather myself and said, "I had never seen so many tribes come together. It was a historical moment in history for Native American people. I felt fortunate to hear so many different languages be spoken at camp. It was a beautiful thing to witness, everyone gathered in prayer for one cause: to save our water. I felt incredibly blessed to be there, and I will hold this special time dear to my heart. "

I thanked them for allowing me to be in their ancestral home and taking the time to welcome me to their land. After the formal introductions were done, they formed a line so I could greet them in Hongi, their traditional way of greeting the breath of life. One by one, I took a moment to touch forehead-to-forehead, or nose-to-nose, and take a breath. I had been looking forward to this moment. Hongi is such an incredible tradition to greet another human. To take the time to breathe with one another is rare in my everyday culture back at home. I felt honored to be there, they felt like family now, and my heart space was filled with gratitude.

Then we all took our seats again, and the elder woman stepped forward to explain the carvings and the meaning behind them. She was the storyteller of the group and was passing on their ancestral history through speaking her native language. And even though my ears could not understand her words, my heart felt the impact. The Māori people truly understand the importance of passing down their oral history, and I felt honored to be among them. To experience their tradition of storytelling, as if they were my shared ancestors, was a unique and special gift.

The group of dancers and singers stood up and went back to the front of the marae and performed a series of traditional dances. The Poi dance was used back in the day for warriors to improve dexterity of their wrists. The Poi are soft, handheld white balls attached to string. These balls can be singular or in pairs and can vary in length. Today, women mostly do this sacred dance, and the movements are singular.

The Poi dance was followed by the Waiata ā ringa, which is an action song. The dancers used their entire bodies, including their hands, to tell story, and the words that were being used in the song. It reminded me of some Polynesian dances I had seen during my travels in Hawaii.

Then it was time to gather and move into the kitchen for a traditional dinner (Kai Hakari) that was prepared especially for this gathering. It took me about fifteen minutes to make it that way, I had gotten myself into some conversations with a few people in the marae.

I couldn't believe that when I walked in everyone was gathered waiting for me to eat first. This felt very unusual to me, and it felt strange being the first one to be served.

I explained to Tina, "In my culture, the elders always eat first. And a prayer plate is made, with very small portions of each dish. This plate is then prayed over by an elder, before anyone is served."

She replied, "Yes, elders do eat first, but you are our honored guest, and they will be served after you."

As we walked down this incredible buffet of traditional foods, she explained what each dish was, and some of how it was prepared. I was so thrilled to be eating their ancestral foods, and said, "I will try a bit of everything, I am open to it all."

I filled my plate with several dishes that combined mussels and other foods, and one in particular with pūhā, which is sow thistle or milk thistle. Kūmara is their sweet potato and a common starch used in boiled dishes. I loved their boiled pork dish with cabbage, and to my surprise there was fry bread. I wasn't expecting to see a traditional food from home, and it wasn't part of our real first foods. But let's be real, fry bread is a comfort food nonetheless, and I was happy to add it to my colorful plate of goodness.

A lovely older gentleman asked if he could get me a beverage. I really wasn't used to being waited on, but this was their house and their rules, and so I obliged him and chose tea. He seemed happy to be so hospitable and had it waiting at the table.

I sat down next to Tina, and across from the two lovely women I had met before entering the whare. Which served as a large dwelling place for this community to gather when eating these traditional foods. They were mother and daughter, and both had a strong but soft female presence about them. Tina wanted us to connect because the daughter was facing her own version of Standing Rock in New Zealand. She explained to us, "A corporate hotel chain has plans to bulldoze and build on top of sacred ancestral grounds." She and several others had been fighting this battle for some time, and the bulldozers were set to come in January.

"I'm so sorry to hear this," I replied to her. "Corporate greed has no understanding of our connection to our Mother and ancestors." I then shared with her some of the inhumane acts that were bestowed upon the water protectors at Standing Rock. I tried to offer any support she might need, and told her, "There is hope, sister. The power of prayer is undeniable."

I told her during my stay in New Zealand I would make some time to visit the sacred space that was being threatened and join in her cause. I thoroughly enjoyed everyone's company, and the meal was exactly what I needed after a long day of travel. The love that goes into the food is an essential part of why it tastes and feels so good. And I was honored to be sharing this meal with these beautiful people that welcomed me into their home.

I wanted to take this time to present a special gift I had brought for Tina, because she had organized this ceremony for me and she was such a beautiful soul. Before I had left for this trip, I decided I wanted to give her one of my Yurok necklaces. The one I picked had a diamond-shaped abalone shell at the bottom, with long white dentalia shells and red beads up the sides. I could see how honored she was to receive this special treasure. She smiled and said, "Oh, wow, I love it, and it looks like yours. I'm going to wear it right now."

We continued enjoying our lovely meal, sharing stories of culture and traditional ways of our people.

I couldn't help but notice a striking elder woman that was sitting at the table across from mine. I had seen her during my ceremony, and she was so captivating, that I knew I wanted to meet her. She had the kindest eyes, and the deep-set wrinkles on her face spoke wisdom and told a story. Her hair was shorter, completely white and still very thick. She was one of those elders where it was impossible to tell her age because she is a timeless beauty.

I had brought some special gifts from my tribe and prayer bundles from home to give to the group for their service. And I was thrilled to share the stories and meanings behind them. I said to Tina, "I have brought two tobacco baskets to give to the elder woman and the elder man of the group."

She pointed at the woman I was so mesmerized by and said, "Over there—that is her. And over by the kitchen—that man is the elder man of our group."

Tina also mentioned that both elders happened to have the last name Barlow. This was incredible to me—that I had travelled all the way to New Zealand to meet other Barlows. Message received, Creator, I thought, knowing at that moment, that it was confirmed that I was exactly where I was supposed to be.

I picked up the baskets and walked over to the elder woman and said, "I have something special, that I brought just for you."

She smiled and said, "Oh, really, for me, dear?"

I looked at her with her with pure joy in my heart; I was so thrilled to be giving this special gift from home.

"This is a tobacco basket, made by my grandmother. She was a great basket weaver of the Yurok people. We used these baskets to carry our tobacco, which we used for offerings, prayers, and ceremony. It's made of willow, spruce root, and bear grass, and adorned with the friendship design."

I placed it in her sweet, strong, aged hands. She gave me the recognition in her eyes, and I knew she understood how special the gift was.

She replied, "Thank you so much, my dear. I will treasure this always."

We both smiled, knowing this exchange of culture was so special. "I know you will," I said. We hugged, and I asked, "Can I get a picture with you, Grandmother Barlow?"

She replied "Of course, my dear."

I told her I, too, was a Barlow, and she lit up once again. I could feel her love through every gesture we shared. And even though she wasn't my grandmother, she certainly embodied the medicine of the one I grew up with.

I then walked over to the elder man. He was a very colorful fellow in his mannerism and the energy he put out. He had dark short hair, and those same kind eyes. I said, "I have something for you. It's a tobacco basket, woven by my grandmother. She was a well-known basket weaver of her time, and this is made of willow, spruce root, and fern."

I explained the meaning behind the basket as I handed it to him. He smiled and hugged me right away, and said, "Thank you, my dear. This is very special."

I then told him I was a Barlow. He was pleasantly surprised and replied, "There are several more Barlow's here you must meet."

He ushered them over, and three other women came across the room to greet me. I hugged each one, as we were so delighted at this rare coincidence upon us. The last woman I hugged grabbed my hand and placed something in it. I opened my hand to find a long rectangular green stone necklace.

This stone comes from the south of New Zealand, and the locals call it Pounamu. Māori refer to the Pounamu as the god stone, for its importance and significance. And it is said and believed that the Pounamu has spiritual powers to evoke strength and prosperity. Gifting this stone is an expression of love and kinship that offers protection, growth, and harmony.

I felt so honored to be given such a special gift, and I was so grateful to have this experience. This felt like family, and I hadn't been around this many Barlow's since I can even remember. The bloodlines didn't matter here, that entire room was filled with my new relatives (ne-toó mer).

After we took several family photos, I wanted to present the prayer bundles I traveled with from home to the rest of the group. I let them know I was very nervous bringing them over, and I wasn't sure that customs was going to let them through.

"It was the first time I had to declare prayer," I said, and we all found humor in that statement.

"These prayer bundles were made special for you. They came from my homeland. A Spokane Indian woman gathered these sacred plants, ground them down, and packaged them for this trip. There is sage, cedar, or sweet grass in each individual bundle. We use these plants as our offerings for prayer, in ceremonies and medicines."

I could see that everyone's faces were so thrilled that I was able to bring these sacred prayers from my homeland. I explained that our heart space must be in a good place when gathering these plants. As I passed the bundles around, everyone was quick to smell the bundles. I will never forget the expressions on their faces, smiling and enjoying this exchange of culture. It was a gift for me to have the opportunity to give my special treasures to the Māori people. I had no doubt that they would hold these treasures dear to their hearts, just as I do.

Before the evening ended, the group did a special performance in honor of Tina and her dedication to her work. She is such a strong leader of her people, she is passing on the traditions of her culture to the future generations. I felt blessed to witness this dance, acknowledging her passion for this work. She was so pleasantly surprised, and this was a special moment to end the evening.

I made my rounds before leaving and took my time, saying goodbye and thanking each one of them for being a part of my ceremony. I made an effort to find Tina before I left, feeling that I had to share a few more words and express my gratitude. We hugged one last time, and she said, "You are welcome back anytime. This is your home now, too."

Those words lit up my spirit. I could feel a vibration of energy run from my toes, up through my spine, and all the way to the crown of my head. Perhaps, it was energy from our ancestors, coming together to guide me as I was about to embark on this new chapter in my life.

"Thank you, sister. You have done more than you could ever imagine," I replied.

I walked back outside and everyone waving goodbye. I said, "Chu," which is Yurok for goodbye. They all smiled and said "chu" back to me.

A new healing had occurred this day. This was one of those rare moments in time that I would never forget. I knew this was exactly how I needed to start this trip. I had guides from all directions now to watch over me. And for the next two months of my life, I could live with a freedom I had never had. This time was to not to be ever taken for granted. And that Creator had cleared my path for me to be here, right now, for reasons I would come to later understand.

I hopped into the car and took a moment to process the precious time I spent during this gathering. My wonderful host in Auckland, Morri, was kind enough to drive me here, and I was thrilled they allowed me to bring a guest, so he could have this experience as well.

Morri was fourth-generation local but had never gotten to experience a welcoming ceremony. His family roots were of originally of English and Irish descent. Being extremely tall man, with a head of thick grey hair, it was not hard to spot him in a crowd. Morrie had a very sweet demeanor about him, and his hospitality was beyond anything I could have ever expected.

He mentioned during the car ride over, "Even though my family has resided here for quite some time, I still at times don't feel like I belong here."

As we began to drive back home, I could see he had thoroughly enjoyed the evening's events. I asked him, "Okay, now do you feel more connected to this land, after having this experience?"

He replied, "Well, yes, in some ways, because I felt very welcomed by the locals tonight."

I was very happy to hear this news, and grateful to be sharing this experience with him. The rest of the way home, we shared our stories of certain individuals we met throughout that evening. Once we pulled up to the house, Morri took a moment before leaving the car and said, "Thank you Donell, for bringing me with you, and allowing me to be a part of this experience."

I replied, "It was my pleasure. Thank you for allowing me into your homeland and taking me there."

I turned in early that evening, still adjusting from my travel and the day's events. I couldn't have imaged a better way to spend my first day. I crawled into bed and closed my eyes, feeling so blessed. I knew that even in the dream world, I couldn't possibly dream anything more magical than my first day in New Zealand.

I woke up early, still adjusting to the twenty-one-hour difference in the time and lay in bed journaling my experience from the night before. Plus, I was on holiday and really had nowhere to be.

The weather in Auckland was not quite summer yet, but definitely warmer than the winter I had left back in Washington state. The weather here was unpredictable—after all, it is an island, and can rain one minute, and blast you with sun the next.

Morri had mentioned I should go check out this fabulous park down the way called Western Springs Lakeside Park. It had a variety of bird species, with lots of trails that surrounded the lake. It sounded like a great idea to me, and so I planned on heading that way in the afternoon.

Morri made me a lovely cup of tea, while I put together a yogurt parfait for my first breakfast in New Zealand. We sat down at the table for breakfast and reflected on last night's ceremony a little further. It was fun getting to know Morri during my stay here, and I was happy to keep him company. His wife was away back in the states dealing with some family matters. And with Christmas arriving tomorrow, it was nice that we had each other. I was used to spending the holiday with just my dad anyhow. Morri was more than a decade younger than Dad, but the connection was familiar, and that was comforting while being so far away from home.

After we finished breakfast, Morri said, "There is something I want to show you."

I followed him down the hall into his office that sat at the front of the house, with large windows that allowed the natural light to come in. He wanted to share some of the photos he had taken of the ceremony the night before.

"These are incredible, and how I love the picture of the elder woman. I am now referring to as Grandma Barlow." I was thrilled to see how he captured her essence in these pictures, just as I had seen her with my eyes the day before.

"Isn't she just so beautiful, Morri?" I said, as we scrolled through the several portraits he had shot. I went on to say how the connection I felt with her the night before made me miss my grandmothers. The love a grandchild receives from her elders is special and unique, and that time that you spend together is limited and precious.

"At home I try and take any opportunity I can get to receive what I call elder medicine," I told him as we continued to look through all the pictures.

Morri and I shared a few stories of our grandmothers, reflecting back in that time and what our world was like growing up. I found his life experiences so interesting. We came from two very different worlds, and the sharing of stories is what life is all about, the understanding of what shapes us to be who we are.

The weather had cleared up, and the sun was shining bright. I figured this would be an ideal time to head down to the park and get some fresh air. And Morri had a lot of work to do for his clients. He is incredibly computer savvy and creates websites, offers technical support, and solves anything computer related.

I filled my backpack with a few essentials. I didn't want to be uncomfortable in case the weather had any surprises in store this afternoon.

"I will be back in a few hours," I said as I headed out the door.

Morri replied, "Have a lovely time, dear, and make sure you have your key, in case I'm not here when you return."

I began walking down through the neighborhoods, admiring my new environment and surroundings. I stumbled upon the most magnificent tree that had bloomed these bright red flowers that were so different from anything I had ever seen before. The flowers were made up of a mass of thin red stamens with yellow pollen tips that shot out from the base, creating a dome-like shape. Morrie had mentioned that this flower is called the pohutukawa and is celebrated as the Christmas tree of New Zealand, because it only blooms this time of year.

The creation story tells of a young warrior named Tāwhaki, who wanted to avenge the death of his father. His perilous journey through out the heavens was unsuccessful, and he fell to this earth. His blood was spilled and now can be seen among the crimson flowers of the pohutukawa.

I continued on, along down the road, taking a moment to give recognition to the sheer beauty of the trees, honoring so many I had never seen before. Their bark is bright green in spots with layers of browns, and other colors, so completely different from anything at home in the Northwest. Orange and white butterflies continued to grace me with their presence, reminding me of the transformation it took within myself for me to be here right now.

With nowhere to be, and no concept in time for once in my life, I felt like a kid again, in that my perception of what I saw before me was all magic.

These trees, these plants, and even the air were new and foreign to me. I thought to myself, there is so much we take for granted in a day, and no doubt I am guilty of that as well. However, on days like these, I can just be in the moment and feel the magic in a simple walk.

Within about ten minutes, I arrived at one of the entrances to Western Springs Lakeside park. The park was breathtaking. It was clear that this sacred space was well maintained and cared for. I chose a path and begin making my way around the lake. The park was filled with so many bird species, and the number of geese and ducks was quite overwhelming at times. It did feel somewhat familiar to home, when I take my morning walks along the river. However, these geese were used to being fed. Before I knew it, I had a gang of them on my heels, giving me the shakedown for some food.

I made my way around to the other side of the lake to escape the madness of the geese and find some much needed solitude. I stumbled upon a trail that seemed to go off into some kind of wilderness and away from the water. I could hear many varieties of birdcalls, calling my attention, asking me to come investigate further. At home, I love to observe the animals. They are our creature teachers and guides. Our ancestors learned our medicines and important life lessons by taking the time to be still and observe their ways. I found a small clearing with a log, as if it was just waiting for me to take notice and stay awhile. This was to be my first sacred space of the trip to decompress, pray, and be still.

The birds continued to call each other and fly from tree to tree. I could hear a variety of sounds traveling around me, but nothing close enough to observe with my eyes. So, I thought, why not close them, and just feel their presence? You are safe here, I told myself, and this is a part of why you choose to come all this way.

I closed my eyes, taking the time to find my breath, one that would calm my mind so I could focus. The breath is a giver of life, not to be taken for granted, and when used with intention, the possibilities are endless.

I imagined a simpler time when my ancestors lived off the land and our days were spent in harmony with nature. Everyone was family, and the sense of community was undeniable. What would it feel like to live that way, to have the freedom to live off the land? No concept of time or day, no worries of First World problems or careless matters. How would it feel to live that way of life I imagined, to have that understanding of my place in this world? These ideas and thoughts circled around in my head, and it made me think of my own family. A few happy tears trickled down my face as I felt a sense of hope for good things to come. I opened my eyes to remove some tobacco from my pocket, placing it on the earth to make an offering to the Creator. Closing my eyes once again to begin my prayer, I thanked the Creator for this day, and every day before this. Without the bad days, I wouldn't be here, and as a result, I wouldn't appreciate the good ones as much. I trusted the path he had chosen for me and asked for continued patience and guidance.

This moment felt right, and I was ready to gather myself and head back into the park to enjoy whatever else it had to offer. This time around, I choose to watch the people and families, and how they interacted with one another. The loving gestures and unique mannerisms that ranged from one to the next. Observing the little ones feeding the ducks, while the parents supervised—some with more caution than others. One little girl was feeding the ducks quite large pieces of bread. Her father continued to say, "Small bits, honey, small bits."

She wasn't grasping the concept, or really didn't care. I giggled to myself watching their dynamic, and how special a father-daughter relationship is. I imagined what those days were like with my father, and how patient he had always been with me. I know we shared many moments like these, for he had always been my greatest role model and was always there when I needed him.

As new families continued to pass by, I tried to see part of myself or someone I loved within each dynamic. I imagined what it would be like to have a family of my own someday. To be a mother, and a wife, and how magical it would feel. Definitely a bit scary, seeing as I had reached a point of complete freedom for the first time, with no one left to depend on me. Having a family of my own would be a dramatic change that would entail major adjustments to my schedule. Was it something I was ready for? I honestly didn't know, but I couldn't help but come back to reflect upon the words a wise man once told me: "The whole purpose of life is to love and be loved."

And if that held true, perhaps a having a family would make an incredible addition to my life. I suppose it starts with meeting the right man, and from my experience that seemed like a daunting task. Let's be real, I did have hopes of meeting a Māori in New Zealand that could perhaps sweep me off my feet. I believe in love at first sight, soul mates, and all that mumbo jumbo shit. The reason is because I have to. My spirit needs this understanding to know that there is someone out there who completes me. This doesn't mean it has to be perfect, we shouldn't always get along or have the same interests. I imagine a man that accepts me for me, including the scars from my past. I see him being an amazing father and devoted husband, just as my father had always been.

These were the thoughts that crossed my mind while families continued to walk by, and I couldn't help but hope that perhaps I would know that feeling someday. To have a family that is my own, to look into my child's eyes and see parts of myself. To experience that kind of love for another human, a life you created. These were life moments I had not known I would ever want, until the last few years. Without my continued healing, I don't know that I would have come to feel the same way.

Perhaps that's part of why I had to experience those struggles, to have a better understanding of what I really wanted in life. To make the conscious choice to spend my life with someone, and together create another life inside of me. That feeling of knowing everything happens for a reason has its benefits, but it brings suffering.

I closed my eyes again and chose to lay down awhile and reflect on what had brought me to this moment. How did I get to this complete freedom, and a chance to take the chosen path that Creator had made? Each breath cycle took me deeper into the past, and back to a time when my life was completely different. I kept myself constantly busy and had a schedule for every detailed event. I myself was very different and was living a life that had joy but wasn't feeding my spirit. I had made commitments to particular people that I chose to live out. And I would have just kept living the day to day if that upheaval of life hadn't been chosen for me.

As those years played back in my mind, they took me in so deep that I fell asleep. My subconscious has always known the way, revealed what's ahead of me and my true spirit desires. I began to retrace my Medicine tracks and the process in which they led me to this point. Medicine tracks are intuitive steps one takes to find a new path towards self-healing. They can lead you to particular people and places that offer great joy. However, with in these same experiences can end with suffering and turmoil. This form of medicine is challenging and requires patience. This process is meant to ensure the growth that needs to occur, in order to achieve a new profound healing from within.

When I wake up, I'm back at the beginning, four years ago, when life was completely different—back to the moment when everything changed.

CHAPTER 2
Butterfly Medicine

M Y MARRIAGE THUS FAR had experienced many ups and downs, some years full of joy and adventure and others consumed by arguments, lack of trust, and little affection. Thirteen years is a long time to invest in one person you met at the age of twenty. But back then, everything felt perfect, and this person gave me constant butterflies. He would stay up late into the evening to talk with me about the universe and the meaning of life. He understood me better than anyone I had ever met. He became my best friend, and later on, my soul mate.

I married James at the age of twenty-five, in the hope that we would be together for the rest of our lives. We were in love, and it was very real—not forced, as some may experience. This love was genuine, and we both set intentions to continue to help each other grow and offer support as we grew old together.

Our marriage was never perfect, as none of them can claim to be. We both had our faults, and some were harder to recognize than others. I'm aware that I am someone who needs to be right in an argument, even when I might be wrong. Every part of my day was planned, and at times I ran a tight ship. James was more of a free spirit and liked to take his time going about his day. We were very different people, but that was the beauty in it. We created a balance between us, and one offered what the other needed. At least, I came to believe that was our dynamic. We helped each other and stuck it out through the hardest of times, and I believed that was enough to keep the love and the marriage together.

James had suffered from depression and anxiety throughout our time together, but I never left his side. For him, it came in the form of alcohol abuse that took years to get under control. With a lot of moral support from friends and family, over time, he was able to kick the habit. He had been sober for six years now, but by this point, dealing with his chaotic emotions and heavy energy had taken a toll on me. I felt a strong need to connect with spirit, and to find new ways of bringing light and joy into my life. I found some new outlets in taking the training to become a yoga teacher, and I went back to school to become a holistic health coach. I felt if I fed my spirit with these new passions, the change would be good for us both. I knew he felt my resentment for the scars he had created in the past, and that I was responsible to do some healing of my own. I showed my frustration and hurt at times in the form of anger, which became an unhealthy expression for us both. I wanted to become a better partner, to show more affection, and leave behind any baggage from who we both were before.

It was June and a beautiful sunny day in my hometown of Spokane, Washington. I was packing my things, getting ready to head out to a Forrest Yoga Retreat for the weekend located in Tacoma. This was to be one of those events that created more space for healing, so I could come home with a more peaceful heart.

I was intrigued with Forrest Yoga, after learning how Ana Forrest incorporates Native American practices into her yoga retreats and teachings. I read her book and was moved by her storytelling. This woman is warrior, to say the least, and overcame numerous adversities throughout her life. She was able to find her healing through yoga and channeling spirit.

I found it strange that this particular morning James chose to leave for work early, without saying goodbye. This was not like him, and he knew I was leaving today for the weekend. How could he have possibly forgot to send me off? This hurt my feelings; I didn't know what to make of it. We weren't fighting at the time, but he had seemed to be distancing himself a bit lately.

I head out the door to greet one of my yoga buddies, Beth, who came to swoop me up from the house for our road trip. We met through a mutual friend, and both being part of the yoga community, we just clicked. Beth is a beautiful human inside and out. She has that fit yoga physique along with a kindred spirit inside her. She embodies the animal totem of the deer, being so graceful with her practice and showing compassion for others. This retreat was our time to get to know each other better, and I had been looking forward to spending this time with her.

The drive would take roughly five hours, depending on traffic in Seattle, so we all had plenty of time to get acquainted along the way.

I had tweaked my neck a few months back, and during this trip I was still recovering. I climbed into the passenger seat and adjusted my neck pillow against the window for support. This injury occurred due to what I called "a series of unfortunate events," and those physical activities got the better of me. In the last few months, I had needed to adjust my life due to the pain and restrictions, but I wasn't going to let that stop me from participating with what my body allowed. The incident occurred during my own recent yoga teacher training, and I was able to modify most positions.

I allowed Beth to talk the majority of the trip. I didn't mind just listening, and I was still feeling uneasy about James not saying goodbye. It bothered me enough to keep more to myself than I usually would, and Beth and I didn't know each other well enough yet for me to express my concerns. I hoped this retreat would lighten the load, and I would realize everything was okay by the time I got back home.

Once we arrived at our destination, and began to drive through the college campus, I was feeling lighter already. We checked into our dorm rooms, dropped off our things, and began exploring the campus grounds. I was impressed by the space and looked forward to my time spent here. That evening, we were all asked to join together in the gymnasium for introductions and to receive a basic syllabus for the weekend. Of course, as expected, there were a few group exercises and icebreakers to start off, followed Ana's introducing the staff.

Before we were excused for the evening, Ana asked two of her spiritual advisors, Alex and Chenoa Turtle, to lead a few songs and end our day in prayer. I was aware of their work and had been looking forward to a healing session I booked with them during the retreat. I was hoping to connect with my family that had passed, some of whom had crossed over when I was younger. I imagined that through this medicine, I might be able find another type of healing in my life. At this point, I had never experienced healing practices from a Native American medicine man. My spirit was calling me back to do this type of medicine, the medicine of my ancestors. I felt it in my gut. I had been experiencing strange dreams and I knew that this weekend was going to change my life in some type of spiritual way. The evening orientation concluded with a song and a prayer, and I went to bed that night feeling a little lighter than when I arrived.

Day one began with a light breakfast, as I struggle to eat early in the day anyhow. My body prefers the first meal to be around brunch time, after I work out, or I can get really nauseous.

Beth and I headed to the first class of the day. It was quite a large group; looking around the room I saw close to one hundred participants. The majority, of course, were female, which is typical of yoga classes, but also reflected Ana's continued work with empowering feminine energy. I noticed there were Kleenex boxes throughout the room, and Ana referred to them as "props." Her words and her practice allow you to release your suffering and to help find healing. The body is known to show us messages through our physical pain, telling us that our spirit is suffering.

The time had come to get the full Ana experience in her classroom and to be guided by her energy and the intention she had set for us today. I was a bit nervous and intimidated by what I had heard; from what I understand, she a very strong alpha female. Ana entered the room and she had a commanding presence. Her energy was so powerful it filled the entire room. She embodied the attributes of badger medicine, a mix of courage and aggressive behavior, along with being a conduit of energy and very grounded. Her strength came from facing hardship and utilizing her aggression, which I suppose had protected her along the journey. Her long wavy hair sat just below her lower back. She was crazy fit to say the least and exuded natural beauty. Anna was comfortable in her skin and walked with her authentic self, and within her badger medicine, she also became a healer and someone I greatly admire.

Before we begin class, Ana asked us to write our names down on our mat, and if we had any injuries. I wanted to let the leaders know my neck was compromised, so this was a good answer to my concerns.

Ana began guiding us through a seated Prana Yama breathing technique called "Bhramari," or bee breaths. This practice allows you to quiet the mind and helps with anxiety so you can focus better.

Ana instructed us, saying, "Sit up straight, close your eyes, and place your index fingers in your ears by the cartilage. Take a deep breath in, and when you breathe out move your fingers in and out of your ears. Continue doing this while making the sound of a humming bee."

I found this technique quite energizing and had tried it a handful of times during my teacher training. The room was filled with buzzing bees. We came together like a hive, and Ana was our queen. She continued to guide us through more rounds of this technique, going deeper into our pain bodies and meditation. My eyes had remained closed the entire time, so I was a bit startled when I heard a voice whisper in my ear.

"Let go of the pain that is holding you back. It's not about your neck."

I was caught by surprise, and I couldn't have imagined that Ana had just whispered this truth into my ear. It had to be her, or if not, was I now hearing voices in my head? I was caught between feeling spooked by what she had said, but also a sense of heightened clarity. What did she mean by that choice of words? Was I carrying an emotional pain alongside me that was visible to someone of her stature? And did she plan on elaborating later on, to better explain why she felt she needed to express such advice? She walked to the front of the classroom and asked us all then to open up our eyes and come back into our bodies.

I turned to Beth and asked, "Did Ana talk to you at all?"

She looked surprised and quickly answered, "No. Whoa, what did she say to you?"

I explained what I heard but wasn't exactly sure how to take it or what it meant. She was just as perplexed as I was. We let it rest for now and got back to focusing on the class—which continued to be brutal, because we weren't accustomed to Forrest technique and the use of placing bolsters under your gut for lengths of time. Shit, I was relieved I hadn't eaten much, or I would have had to excuse myself from class. I struggled with several uncomfortable poses that left my guts feeling not at well—not to mention that what Ana had said that morning continued to bother me and took me out of the game mentally and energetically. I wanted answers. Her words struck such a strange chord in me, and I didn't know how to handle it.

The rest of the day was filled with a variety of seminars focusing on emotional and physical well-being. This retreat really allowed us as practitioners to choose our own adventure and learn specifics about topics we gravitated toward. The meals also exceeded my expectations, offering organic local quality foods and catering to food allergies. Every bit of the cost was worth the investment, and I hoped I would leave with some new understandings and perhaps some healing.

I couldn't wait to share with James what Ana had said to me in class and ask his take on what she meant. Because James was my best friend and my go-to discussion partner for everything, I thought he could offer some valuable insight.

That evening, we finally connected, and it seemed I had caught him at an awkward time. The energy I received on my end of the phone connection felt strange, and my gut told me something wasn't right. I begin to wonder, Is he at home making bad choices? James had continued to be strong during his six years of sobriety, so I wasn't sure where this uneasy feeling was coming from. As we continue to engage, I couldn't help the feelings of pain and insecurity from the past that were all coming back. I knew something wasn't right; my gut never lies.

His first words after hearing my voice were, "I'm going out with my friends tonight, so I can't talk long." He said it with a lot of conviction in this tone. I was not expecting this response, and these words held power that was hurtful. I figured by now, he would be happy to hear from me, instead of continuing to avoid me.

I choose not to get into my story about Ana. This wasn't the time, and he made it clear he was far from interested in listening. I focused on getting more answers to understand his weird behavior. However, he couldn't get off the phone soon enough and cut the conversation short, so instead I just let him know, that I missed him and that I cared.

'Have fun babe, but be safe," were some of my last words to him.

I knew without a doubt that night that something had happened or was going to happen that wasn't good. I even asked him to please call or text me when he got home, no matter how late.

That night I didn't sleep for even a moment, tossing and turning in that dorm room bed. I stared at my phone and out the window, just waiting to hear some response from James. Every fiber of my being knew foul play was in effect, and that he was doing something self-destructive. It wasn't until seven a.m. the next morning that he finally chose to connect and called me on the phone. His voice was distant, and his tone was the coldest I have ever felt. Something clearly had happened.

I asked him right away, "What's wrong? Is everything okay with you?"

He replied, "I want you to enjoy your retreat. We will talk when you get home."

I was frantic, and I felt like I couldn't breathe. I responded, "I can't enjoy this place if I don't know what's going on."

He was clearly avoiding some bad news and was too scared to share it with me. This back and forth continued on for a while, until I eventually pleaded with him to communicate. He took a deep breath, and few seconds of silence to collect himself. Then came the words, "I am not happy, and I don't want to be with you anymore."

Hearing those words from my best friend, the man I loved, held so much power, a power so strong that it traveled through the phone into my room to crush my heart and my spirit, leaving me with no power of my own. I felt paralyzed with pain and shock, and fearful of what he was going to say next.

"I don't understand. Where is this coming from? Surely we can work and discuss this when I get home." It was the only response I could muster within the moment.

He said, "No, you are a Type A personality, and you will always be that way. This doesn't work for me anymore. You are not kind, and some of my family and friends think so, too."

At this point, his words had already taken my power away, and now they were digging deeper to strip away any light left within my body. As I looked around the room, I could visualize the light that was once inside me circulating in the room to dissipate into thin air. I was left with just a shell still in human form but missing the most important parts that make us human.

I immediately broke into tears and was so overcome with emotion that I didn't know how to handle it. I pleaded with him to wait to make any harsh decisions and to give us the chance to talk about this when I returned home. I told him I was incredibly sorry he felt this way, and I wasn't aware of how I had made him feel. I asked him if he could allow me to show him better, and that I would do whatever it took. But he made it clear in his conviction that his mind was already made up, and there was nothing I could do.

This had to be coming from something else, to make such a big decision without even mentioning it before. I had to ask him a few times, "Is there someone else?"

Each time he responded, "No, I want to be alone. I have never had time to myself before."

I knew it was true. Since the age of nineteen, he had never been single. He had jumped from one relationship to the next, almost always ending with infidelity on his part. But why did he feel the need to experience this now? It made no sense, how all of a sudden, he felt so compelled to end our marriage and the life we built together, with no notice or effort to fix it. In our thirteen years together, we faced so many hardships and worked as a team to stay together and do the work that was necessary. Maybe this was what they referred to as "a midlife crisis," since he was a few months away from turning forty.

When we hung up the phone, I felt incredibly lost and had no idea what to do with this shell of human I had become. I began to play back and believe the things he had said. Perhaps I am the monster he says I am, and not a kind person, I thought. Perhaps I don't show him enough love or support. I thought to myself, over and over again, What's wrong with me? Am I not a lovable person? Do his family and friends really feel this way, too? And if so, maybe he is right, and he deserves his freedom, and later on, someone better than me.

What I was sure of was that I wasn't going to do any more classes and would offer minimal participation the rest of the weekend. I couldn't think straight, my stomach was in knots, and the last thing I wanted to do was be social. I had nothing to offer, as I felt completely empty, and I didn't want to burden those around me with my heavy energy. Going out for a morning run seemed like the best option for my emotional instability, and a chance to seek peace from the outside world. I made my way down to the water, a good distance away from campus. I pondered about how this felt like the worst timing ever to be gone, and I wished I was home talking it out with James.

The only thing I looked forward to that day was my afternoon session with Chenoa and Alex. Maybe the session would provide some clarity and offers some healing. I walked into the tent for my session with the intention of channeling my family. However, the recent shit storm that just blew in had changed all that.

Alex greeted me with a smile. His presence felt like bear medicine—very comforting while holding great strength and instinctive healing power. Alex was a medicine man of Navajo and Cheyenne descent, and the bear can offer guidance through the natural world. His wife Chenoa was Lummi and S'Klallam nations, a ceremonial leader and medicine carrier. She holds the cougar medicine within her divine feminine strength and is a spiritual warrior. The cougar has found balance between the mind, body, and spirit and can be a messenger between the human world and divine beings. Chenoa was an ageless beauty, a mother goddess, and I felt very grateful for her energy and the balance that she brought to this session.

As soon as I began to introduce myself, Alex stopped me and said, "So, tell me about this curse you have on you."

I was taken aback. How could he have known about this curse that I hadn't thought about since I was a young adolescent? I barely knew my grandfather, and only met him a handful of times when I was little. For whatever reason, he was never really a part of my life, so I chose to believe my grandmother as I went on to explain to Alex, "Well, my grandmother used to tell me that my grandfather put a curse on all the women of my family to get cancer and die. And so far, that holds to be true."

"Yes, that is it. We need to do some special medicine on you, my dear," he replied.

With this on top of what just happened with James, I felt overwhelmed with emotion. I proceeded to completely break down, and began sobbing with tears running down my cheeks, with no end in sight. I told them about what happened with James, and that I felt broken and completely lost. I honestly didn't see this coming and had no idea how to fix it. They gave me some time to collect myself, and once I had calmed down, Alex turned to me and asked,

"Are you familiar with the sucking method, used in traditional healing?"

"Yes, I have read a few books about it. And I want you to do whatever medicine needs to be done," I replied. I had complete confidence that the Creator chose this time for me to receive any medicine he found necessary.

He said, "Okay, but I don't do it on just anyone anymore. They can get freaked out and don't understand the medicine."

I assured Alex that I understood this healing method and was prepared for whatever came with afterward. Alex then filled his pipe with special tobacco for our prayers and offerings to be used in this session and offered to the Creator. I closed my eyes and sat down in a chair and prepared myself to be able to receive this kind of medicine. Alex came over and blew the tobacco smoke over my face, around my head, and eventually over my entire body. The smell of the tobacco was comforting. I understood its healing powers and how sacred it was to my ancestors. Alex began to speak in his Native tongue, asking Creator for his assistance and sending prayers up to the Sky World. Chenoa was saying prayers for me in English and kneeling down on the ground by my side.

I became overwhelmed within the moment, and the sheer power of their medicine. I began to cry again—not from a place of pain, but from a place of healing. At this point in my life, I had never received Native American traditional medicine, and to be given this session on a day like today was a gift in itself. Alex went over to his ceremonial treasures and picked up a special straw made of natural materials to be used in the next step. He walked behind me and placed the straw on the back of my neck, even though I never mentioned anything about my pain there. Then he gently pressed my head forward, while Chenoa cradled me from the front as if I was her child. They had me in a vulnerable position, but I felt completely safe in their care.

Then I began to feel strange sensations running through my body, similar to energy but nothing I had ever experienced. I could feel the presence of my grandmother, mother, and sister surrounding me in their protection, helping Alex remove this curse. I knew in that moment I was exactly where I need to be and doing the work that was required for me to heal.

Alex then pulled away from me and began to cough so hard that he struggled to take a breath. He grabbed a tissue and spit out a strange black bug that had come through the straw during our session. I didn't recognize the insect and was shocked that he had pulled it from within me. I had read in books about this sucking method, and that a healer can extract various objects from the body, such as a chunk of metal, a feather, or even types of insects, as in my case.

Alex himself even seemed surprised about what he had pulled, but we all felt relieved that the medicine had worked. He turned to Chenoa and said, "Burn this bug immediately. We must dispose of it properly."

Chenoa tried to light the tissue that held the insect on fire. She made several attempts, but it just wouldn't catch fire. The three of us looked at each other in a state of confusion, with a growing understanding of how strong this curse had really been. Eventually she did get the tissue to light, and she disposed of the insect properly so we could move forward with our session.

We then dove into some of the details of my marriage, and what James had said to me over the phone. Alex was unsure about was ahead of me but said a few prayers to bring comfort and begin the healing process. I had no doubt in my mind that the timing of this session was a divine intervention, and this strong medicine was to give me inner strength and connection to Creator. I also knew Alex and Chenoa were placed on my path to guide me on my journey and to lead me to my medicine tracks that revealed the new path that was waiting for me.

I left my healing session with so much to process, and I couldn't help but think that I wanted to share this experience with James. I wanted to tell him what happened with Alex, and how he knew things, and the magic that had occurred. But I didn't hear from him till much later in the day. By then I was less enthusiastic and back to the feeling the pit in my stomach and the ache of a broken heart.

I continued to avoid all the other activities of the retreat. My head was spinning, my spirit was heavy, and I just wanted to be alone. Instead I walked around the track of the campus, listening to music and observing my surroundings. Music truly has the healing properties to let us escape from our reality, if only for a moment. Being outside in the sunshine with my jams gave me a sense of comfort. But honestly, I was still so eager to be home. I wanted to be with James more than anything else. I wanted to be there to fight for our marriage, and to fight for all that we had been through all these years. If I were home, we would be holding each other by now, and I could be loving on him in the way he needed and deserved.

Earlier that day, right after I hung up the phone with James, I had phoned a few of my close girlfriends. I needed their support and wanted to find out their thoughts about his erratic behavior. Lindsey is one of my oldest and truest friends, and we have known each other since we were kids. She has been there for me through the most difficult of times and has always been a good listener. She embodies the crow medicine of being authentic, having a strong spiritual strength, and being a messenger. I thought she might have some valuable insight to what was really going on. On the phone, she told me his behavior seemed strange and not like him at all, and my other friends felt the same. All of us felt perplexed about where this had come from, and I knew I had to be home to get any answers.

Eagerly waiting for the longest day of my life to be over, I was ready for bed early, praying I would wake up from this nightmare. I pondered that thought countless times through the day. Maybe this was somehow a crazy long dream, or I would wake up out of a coma and this nightmare would finally come to an end. I truly believed that James loved me, and this was all a mistake. I didn't sleep again that night, tossing and turning while starring out that window waiting for the sun to rise again. I played out possible scenarios in my mind of what would come from of all this and wondered whether my marriage was really over.

The sun couldn't have come early enough, and I was more than ready to hit the road headed to home. It seemed like an eternity waiting for Beth to get up, get ready, and pack to leave.

The drive back was painful as I sat in silence most of the way, gazing out the window, wondering what I would come home to. The continuous road construction added another hour and half to the commute, leaving me more anxious the longer it took. Finally, around six p.m., we pulled up to the house, Beth gave me a hug and wished me luck. I grabbed my bags, took a deep breath, and walked up the stairs to my impending doom. James was there to greet me at the door. I walked into the living room and couldn't believe my eyes.

Our two dogs were barking and feeling anxious, aware that something was wrong but also happy to see me. Jackson is our twelve-year-old Boston terrier who is crazy but loveable, and Apollo is a Rottweiler who just turned nine. He loves to play and doesn't know his own strength.

But what I saw before me was boxes, packed boxes in our living room, full of all James's art supplies and belongings. It was clear he had been packing while I was away and had planned this before I left.

James turned to me and said, "I'm staying at my mom's house tonight. I think it's best."

I couldn't believe what I was hearing, and I pleaded with him. "What, are you really leaving me? Like, right now?

He responded with no hesitation. "Yes, there is no going back from here. It's over between us."

I couldn't believe these words were coming from my husband and that he was showing so little emotion while doing it. I didn't understand after all these years how he could just pack up and leave me like this, with no notice or chance to work it out. I begged him to sit down and discuss this some more, but I could tell he didn't want to and felt uncomfortable around me. He kept repeating, "I just need to be alone for once. I have never had this time to myself, and I'm not happy."

I responded, "Is this a midlife crisis? We can go to counseling, we can work this out."

I couldn't help but sob, imagining that when he looked at me now, all he saw was my shell. That he felt repulsed with who I had become, and believed he deserved a new start to life and something different. In the hope that I had one last chance to change his mind, I pulled him in close and kissed him as passionately as I could. Our cheeks were soaked by my tears, and I looked deep into his eyes as if it was the first time I said I love you. This was my last desperate attempt to try and connect with him in some way, to make him feel the love we once had.

"Do you feel this? Are you still in love with me at all?" I asked.

Once again, he didn't hesitate to respond. "No," he replied, but he said it with pain in his voice, showing some emotion for the first time, as tears began to grace his cheeks.

I realized in that moment that his mind was made up and there was nothing I could do to save us. My mind began to race, reflecting on how intertwined our lives were. We shared countless friends, and my hair clients got tattoos from him and vice-versa. And I myself was covered in his tattoo work. I had become his walking billboard and best advertisement. I was proud when I was asked, quite frequently, who had done them, and I was happy to say that my husband had. However, now these tattoos would represent regret and painful memories of our life together.

We loved how blessed we were to do work that we loved and that we could help each other out with sharing clients. We had a great thing going, and for the most part a beautiful life together. This was just one of those slumps that married people go through from time to time. But he had made it clear he was done riding this ride with me, and he was moving on.

Sharing the same friend circle with James was complicated. They were like another family for me. I thought about the upcoming birthday bash I had been planning for our friend Nikki, and how awkward it would feel for both of us to be there. Nikki had come up in my thoughts a few times during our conversation, and my gut told me to ask, "Have you told anyone about this. Did you tell Nikki?

She was one of my dearest friends, but I also understood they had strong friendship. I had been okay with that, because I trusted them.

He responded, "Yes, I shared with her some things about our marriage."

I became immediately furious, feeling that he had deceived me and crossed a line that is forbidden.

"Why would you do that?" I asked. "She is one of my best friends. That's crossing a line."

He responded, "It's getting late, and my mom is expecting me."

It was obvious he wanted to leave. I could tell he was lying, and there was so much he was hiding and not ready to share. He was acting like a rabbit living in fear of telling the truth, whether it was because he was a coward or afraid of what would come of it. We hugged goodbye, and then he walked out the door, closing it behind him.

As he left, the room went dark, and out of nowhere a crazy storm blew in just as he was leaving. That storm became a direct reflection of how I was feeling inside my soul and within my heart. The heavy rain came first as if it was mirroring my tears, filling the streets with water so fast and deep, causing an almost instant flash flood. The storm's intensity continued to build alongside the pain within my heart space that grew heavier. My unsettled spirit reached out to the thunder gods and cried for help. They answered with a great powerful sound like several large round drums had been placed over the sky, beating down one at a time and sometimes in unison to alert that that they were angry and to seek shelter. The drum circle in the sky sent down beams of light that took no prisoners. These powerful surges of energy struck down some trees nearby, causing havoc wherever they touched the earth. I pondered running out into the middle of the street, to be standing in inches of water and to be so lucky to get struck. The pain I was feeling consumed by would then be gone and I could be united with my family again.

However, I came to my senses quickly, as I still had my father, and he counted so much on me. My responsibilities outweighed the consequences, and that was never meant to be my path. This indeed was no ordinary storm; this storm was created in direct reflection of my pain. Somehow energies beyond my understanding knew what I was feeling and chose to show me how connected I had become.

Hearing my dogs barking in fear, I came back inside to console them. The storm, as well as my behavior, had startled them both, and they understood that I was not okay. I began to pace around the room and was struggling to breathe, beginning to process that my marriage was over, and that James had left no hope for reconciliation.

When I finally chose to listen to my gut, it all began to make sense, and I knew the answers I was seeking. I went back to the beginning of my six-year friendship with Nikki, and how I had noticed when she and James met, I felt energy between them that made me uneasy. During the first six months of our friendship, I experienced a disturbing dream involving them both. James told me in this dream that he was leaving me for Nikki and was very cold about it, with no remorse. I woke up the next morning and shared my nightmare. James wasn't very responsive and just said "huh," which was even more unsettling. But several years went by and they seemed to have more of brother and sister relationship—or at least that's what she wanted me to believe. I admit, I felt uneasy and a bit suspicious at times, but in time, I came to trust them both with and without me.

Then I remembered around a month ago, I had encouraged James to attend this rap concert with Nikki. I knew it really wasn't my kind of thing, and they would both really enjoy it. James rarely went out, and I wanted him to see one of his old-time favorite artists with someone who appreciated it as much as him. I had no reason to worry at this point. These two humans both really loved me, and I loved and trusted them.

Plus, Nikki and I had recently been on two trips together, and I felt closer to her than ever. Less than a few months prior, we spent a week together in Arizona discovering new raw food dishes and their healing benefits. That weekend, we became so joined at the hip that the other participants believed we were a couple. Then, a few weeks later, we attended a yoga retreat in Montana and even bunked down to share a bed. During our five years of working together at the salon, our friendship had really grown into more of a sisterhood. At times, we had become so inseparable that a few of my other friends had become a little jealous. We had one of those rare and special friendships that I believed would last our lifetime. She had attributes that I admired and had taught me how to be more affectionate with friends and family. She had grown up with this dynamic, one that I admired and was a bit jealous of, and always had lots of family around her.

Her fox medicine made her very energetic and outgoing, which seemed to attract people around her, including myself. She was spontaneous with her actions and more eccentric than most. Within these qualities, we developed a strong friendship, and I felt she was perhaps my best friend. I shared some of most vulnerable moments about my marriage with her, and how hard some of the struggles had been with James in the past. She literally knew everything, and I trusted her with all I had shared.

However, things how been different between us for the last month or so. She wasn't returning any of my texts. I didn't understand why she seemed to be avoiding me all of a sudden, when we had just spent all that extra time together. I had run into Nikki at yoga class right before I left for the Forrest retreat and she acted extremely strange and a bit distant. I asked her if she wanted to have coffee, and she replied, "I have to water my plants, and then head to work."

She made it clear by her body language that she didn't want to spend time with me, and I felt like I had upset her somehow. She couldn't get out of that studio fast enough, and I didn't understand what I had done to upset her. When I got home that day, I mentioned this interaction to James, and he really didn't have much to say. I found this odd at the time but brushed it off and figured it would work itself out.

As I began to reflect on all these memories, I became even more unsettled and continued to pace around my living room. The pieces of my divorce puzzle started to take shape. My gut had always known the truth, which I wasn't ready to know, or at all ready to accept. My dreams tried to warm me six years ago that this was going to be my reality, and I chose not to listen.

Shortly after I had come to these conclusions, some of my girl squad arrived at the house. We began playing detective and were trying to process a whole other type of betrayal. Grace, Rose, and Lindsey arrived in full sisterhood ready to embrace me with support and love. I'm so incredibly grateful for these women: over the years they have become my family. I don't know who I would have turned to without their friendship. The girls took a seat and wanted to hear every word, every detail, and what I thought might be going on. After I finished sharing all the details, I could see in Rose's face she wanted to tell me something but was feeling hesitant about it. She could see I was broken and seeking answers, so she said, "Donnie, I have a weird feeling that James is into Nikki. When I got tattooed last week, he kept talking about the concert and how amazing Nikki was. It was the same way he usually talks about you."

She went on to explain that she told Grace what had happened, but they both couldn't conceive that they would do such a thing.

I thought again about those two recent trips I had just gotten back from with Nikki, and how I had shared so much with her about my relationship with James.

During this time, I was trying to work even harder our friendship because I had chosen to leave her salon. It wasn't personal, I just wanted to be closer to home. The last five years working at the salon together had been so special, and I loved coming to work every day.

I valued her friendship, and I was having a hard time accepting the fact that she was the other woman. But foxes are also good at deceiving and being opportunistic, known for sneaking into homes without being caught. Perhaps everything I had shared with her was a trick, to get closer to what she really wanted, my husband. After discussing all of this with the girls, we came to the conclusion that there was foul play, and that James was indeed romantically involved with Nikki somehow.

That week, I hardly ate and barely even drank water. I lost eight pounds in seven days, my sleep was minimal, and getting through the day was my only goal. I became the empty shell that I had envisioned that morning when James said it was over. Consumed with heavy energy, all I could do was grieve. I was so anxious to speak to James. I needed to ask him some hard questions and be prepared for the answers.

He chose not to call me until three days later. I knew my window was small and I needed to act fast, so I asked him once again, but in a more direct tone. "Is there someone else?"

He once again replied, "No."

I said, "I am curious to why all of my friends have reached out over the last few days to check on me, but I have heard nothing from Nikki."

"She is staying out of it. She doesn't know what to say," he replied.

I could feel a sense of rage taking over my emotions and I shouted, "What the *fuck*, why would she feel that way? She is supposed to be my friend."

He got real quiet, and I demanded that he answer. "Are you cheating on me with Nikki?"

He gasped, and said, "Well, yes—no, I mean, she isn't the reason I'm leaving you."

I can't fucking believe he expects me to believe any of that horseshit, I think. He must think I'm a total idiot. And his response just made my anger grow. Every part of me was screaming to access my inner badger and rip him a new one.

My worst nightmare was officially confirmed, and I felt another type of betrayal that consumed me even deeper.

The pain overwhelmed my body; I collapsed to my knees and felt paralyzed by the truth. Whatever light I was holding onto had gone into the darkness and taken me along with it. I was being suffocated by a truth I could not accept, for the pain was too great. And the fact that my subconscious had warned me about this impending doom years ago made me angry within myself. My last words to James were, "Do you remember, I had a dream about this six years ago?"

He responded in a soft whisper. "Yes."

We hung up the phone. He was right: what's done is done, and we were really over. I should have known something wasn't right before. The last month, he was always on his phone and she wasn't responding to my texts. There was some distance they had created between them and me. I knew my marriage wasn't perfect, but I did truly believe in my heart that he was my soul mate, and she was my friend. I honestly never imagined my life without James. Everything was different now, and I had been betrayed by two people I thought loved me.

I took a week off work, having no concept of time. I still wasn't taking care of myself. When I did return to the salon, my struggle was obvious from my dramatic weight loss and the fact that I wasn't sleeping. I already had a smaller frame, so the weight loss was a significant change to my build. Being five foot six inches tall and only weighing in at one hundred and fifteen pounds looked dramatic. My clients are family to me, and some of them I have seen my entire seventeen years of doing hair. As they arrived for their appointments, it was impossible to pretend that I was at all normal or even at all okay. I had reached the point where I had no more tears left, crying for days on end until the river ran dry. My eyes had become so swollen it became embarrassing, and the puffiness drew even more attention from those around me.

Word spreads fast in my town. With all the mutual friends and shared clients between James, Nikki, and I, it didn't take long to get around. Feelings of anger and betrayal had sunk in and secured space within my heart space. At first, it was hard for me to feel this hatred toward Nikki. I struggled to say harsh words about her character that were unkind.

By nature, I'm not a violent or combative person, and I chose to keep distance from them both. Regardless of the pain I was feeling, I already knew at that time that I wanted to handle this upheaval of life with grace. I wasn't going to let them get the better of me or make me out to be a horrible person. Don't get me wrong— of course I wanted to choke her out, tell her off, and make her feel my pain. I wanted them both to suffer as they had cut me so deeply. But I also yearned for some peace, and I quickly understood that if I continued to be fueled by anger, it would only destroy me.

My dreams have always been a place for healing. Since I was a young girl, my family used the dream world to visit and communicate with me. Being able to access my dreams, and then becoming lucid in this reality, was a true gift.

The Iroquois used the dream world as a major component of their spirituality. For example, they would find a deer to hunt and ask it for its blessing to feed their families while in the dream state. Then they would wake up the next day to find this very deer in the spot they had dreamt of. The wars between the tribes and colonizers were also strategized in the dream world. The Iroquois used the morning time to discuss these dreams among their people and look for hidden messages or visions.

This gift of mine came from my ancestors, and it's a gift we can all tap into if we put in the work. The first dreams I experienced after the divorce was incredibly painful. I would be around Nikki and want more than anything to rip her apart and tell her how she had hurt me. With every inch of my being I would make desperate attempts to come at her with rage. But every time, I would stop, held back by some unseen energy field. I would try to scream as loud as I could, with only a whisper making it out of my mouth. This energy field would not allow my body to hurt her, and I became even more frustrated with each attempt. No matter how hard I tried, somehow, she was protected from my wrath. I felt defeated now even in my dream world, the one place I had gone to seek some justice.

At that point, Nikki still had never reached out—not one word or one gesture. She completely wrote me off, as if our friendship never was, and she had done nothing wrong. About ten days after the truth had been revealed, I did run into her at the market. She darted off as fast as she could, just like the cunning and deceptive fox she had become, and it didn't surprise me in the least. The two of them basically went underground and into hiding, not just from me, but also from anyone who knew what they had done. For months, they tried to hide their dark secret from the outside world, claiming they had done nothing wrong.

The next few months I saw James a handful of times as we began the divorce process and the sale of our house. He thought he was being kind by offering me the house and the dogs, which was all the responsibility. I didn't want anything to do with that house now. It was no longer a sacred space for me. We spent nine years together making that house a labor of love, and every nook and cranny had stored shared memories. We agreed to sell the house as soon as possible and get it ready while the summer market was still good. I had moved out after a few weeks and had been staying with close friends. While I was waiting to secure a place of my own, I felt so blessed to have such amazing humans to lean on. I knew I needed a fresh start, my very own sacred space to make new memories and begin my healing.

As the weeks went by, my interactions with James got stranger; they went from heartfelt hugs with rolling tears to little or no emotion. He was distancing himself emotionally and trying to find a way for him and Nikki to be victims in what had happened. One such instance occurred at the park, and it got me crazy heated and feeling so disgusted by his behavior. This was about a month after he had left me, and he had already moved in to her place. He came at me with anger for how she was being treated by our peers and friend circle.

"Tell our friends to back off from their hateful words of contempt," he said. "She is a good person and it's not her fault."

I couldn't believe in the midst of this scandal, he saw her as the victim in this. Who in the hell was this man I thought I knew?

"I don't control our friends or what they do," I told him. "You have to understand that you both hurt them, too. And trust that I have made it easier on the both of you. The backlash could have been far greater."

My response agitated him and drove him to become even more hurtful. Then he took it one step further and chose to kick me while I was down with these words that I will never forget.

"I was never in love with you, I just convinced myself I was. And now when I'm with Nikki, I know what true love is."

Those words held more power than he realized, coming from the man who I believed was my best friend and the love of my life. I had no response; he cut me so deeply in that moment that part of me died inside. This wound that I felt within my soul could possibly never heal, as I never imagined he would be so cruel. I hoped it was said out of anger, and that he didn't really mean it. But what was said was said. I left the park that day holding even more pain than when I arrived. And I didn't understand how he could be so cold, after what he had already done. Maybe I never really knew this man the way I thought I did, and this was his true self.

I hoped by speaking to his mother I could get some insight on to what he was experiencing and why he was behaving this way. A few weeks after he left me, I was able to make contact with Lori, his mother. She and I had become very close during my relationship with James, and she had become a mother figure to me. I wasn't sure what he had told her. I assumed it was something like what he shared with me back at the retreat: that I was unkind and not a loving person, and that he was unhappy.

Over the last thirteen years, Lori and I had formed a mother-daughter bond, and I had a strong attachment to our relationship. I had cut her hair my entire career, even while still in beauty school. We spent months together planning and making décor for our wedding. I was so grateful to have her in my life, and I knew Creator had put her in that role for me all these years.

We spoke briefly about the divorce, with no mention of Nikki or what really went down. Our conversation ended in tears, and she said to me, "I love you and I will miss you. Perhaps in time we can be in each other's lives again. "

When we hung up the phone, I understood that this was his mother and it didn't matter who was at fault. I dearly loved all of his family. We had spent several vacations together and countless holidays. But with these kind of circumstances, there was no way to be in each other's lives. They would stand by James and support him, as family should. After all, this was always his family. I was just an outsider who had gotten to experience their dynamic for a period of time. It was time to let go, at least for now, and move on.

Staying with good friends during this time of transition was good medicine for me and what I needed at the time. I found my new sacred space while staying with my girlfriend Grace, when a loft had just become available. Grace is a total babe; she carried the hummingbird medicine, with a petite build and always traveling long distances. She could easily adapt to new environments and made the best with what she had. Grace was adorned with a unique look and fashion sense that seemed to attract many admirers.

Her place was located in an old brick building in the middle of downtown that had been converted in lofts in last few years. The trains that pass by can be annoying, but it also adds some character and flair. The location is only a ten-minute walk to the river, and within walking distance of my favorite shops downtown. When we inquired with the landlord, she mentioned a couple with a new baby had just put their notice in and that I could come see the place that week and decide if it was a good fit.

I told her over the phone, "I will take the space regardless."

I knew that this was meant to be my new home, and I had no doubt in my mind that it revealed itself for me at this time. Living in a loft would be a whole new world, different than I had ever experienced. I wanted to embrace this change of environment, and it would feel completely different from my life with James. There was a huge sense of relief to know where I would be starting over. I just had to wait three weeks to move in and for that reality to come to life. Little did I know that this was the beginning of dramatic change for me, and I needed my strength.

I made time to visit my father, to talk about the details of what had happened. He still lived in my childhood home, the dream house that he and my mother had designed together. It was a fairly spacious, light grey, three-story structure adorned with large windows for natural light and high ceilings that added a dramatic effect. The house was full with furniture, but never with people. After I moved out, my father was the only one living there for the last thirteen years. I knew he had to be lonely in that big house all by himself, but I never imagined he would want to leave.

When I told my father the news about the divorce, I didn't receive the response I had anticipated. However, he wasn't the same man that had raised me. His behavior and even his personality after his second open-heart surgery were indeed different. His memory was fading, and as a result, he began experiencing regular anxiety attacks. I am a daddy's girl, and it didn't take long to see his face with the tears that came on like waterworks.

"It's over, Dad," I told him. "James left me for Nikki, and we are getting a divorce."

"I'm so sorry to hear that, Donell. I went through a divorce, too. But I have to tell you, I was jealous of all the time you spent with James."

I was taken aback by his words. This was not at all the reaction I needed or expected. How could he possibly be jealous of my marriage? In a fucked up way, he seemed kind of happy about this outcome.

"Dad, you had no reason to be jealous. James was my husband, and I had to nurture that relationship. You are my dad, and I will always do my best to make time for you," I replied.

This behavior wasn't like my father. He was very independent and had raised me to be the same. Dad was of average build, around five foot ten inches tall, with dark grey, short, thinning hair. He wore rimmed glasses and always a smile. For my whole life, he had sported a classic mustache that at times could rival Tom Selleck, back in his prime. My dad had always possessed the medicine of the buffalo, using his inner strength to help others facing their adversities. His success in life was a result of his long consistent drive and dedication to sharing his gifts. The stability of the buffalo allowed me to never have to worry about food on the table or a roof over my head.

After he retired, some things began to change. He preferred sweatpants and tennis shoes as his regular attire. No more suits, and even slacks were a struggle at times. He said if his sweatpants had a back pocket, they were now considered "fancy" and should be treated as such. This man typically didn't like change and had a way of holding onto things way past their expiration date.

After my mother passed, my father chose to admit himself into the hospital for a while, to process what had happened. During those two months, my grandparents cared me for. At seven years old, I didn't understand why he would leave me at a time like that, when I needed his presence more than ever. My little heart became angry with him for leaving, and with my mother for leaving me as well.

I never got to say goodbye to her. Toward the end, things got so bad that I was constantly sent off to stay with friends. My last memory of her was forgetting who I was; I suppose the morphine was to blame. The pancreatic cancer had taken its course, and she was suffering and waiting for the peace to come. I remember being so angry with God for taking her from me, when I had prayed so hard for her to stay here and to get well. But the reality was that my prayers weren't enough, and this felt like punishment of the cruelest kind.

My parents raised me in a Baptist church, followed by a Christian church, and then, after my mother passed, on to an Episcopalian church. I didn't really feel connected to the church the way they did, or to organized religion in general. The routine of when to pray and when to kneel felt robotic and not at all natural for me. My father and sister would use guilt and the fear of God to try and sway me, but those tactics just pushed me farther away. And I thought if there was a God, why did he take my family from me? What did I do wrong for him to keep punishing me like this? Clearly, he didn't care.

Jason was my older brother: my parents adopted him as a baby, eight years before I was born. Jason was Navajo, with kind brown eyes, a full head of beautiful hair, and a happy disposition. He loved to play baseball, and during one of his games he passed out suddenly on the field. He was rushed to the hospital, and the tests revealed he had terminal brain cancer. My parents had no indication that this was coming, and the diagnosis shocked my entire family. That weekend, my ten-year-old brother Jason passed away. I was only two years old at the time and don't recall much. But as I grew up, I missed having an older brother and wished we had more time together.

In my teenage years, I chose to rebel and my father had to deal with my poor choices and erratic behavior. We argued a lot during that time, and when I was especially upset, I expressed to him, "Why did he take her instead of you?"

And he always would respond, "I don't know, Donell. I ask myself that all the time."

Those word I expressed were incredibly unkind, but I was angry and that's what surfaced when we fought.

My father was more prepared than most single dads would be to deal with a rebellious teenage daughter. At Crosswalk, a shelter for teens in our town, he worked with homeless youth and teens abusing drugs and alcohol. In addition to being a counselor specializing in grief and loss, his experience and education kept him grounded. My dad was constantly busy with meetings and committee engagements and had to be out of town often. So, it was fairly easy to be reckless with my choices, throwing parties at home and causing collateral damage.

He pushed me into public speaking, sent me to charm school, military camp, and forced me to go to a Catholic church, all in an effort to keep me focused and staying on track for my future. Then shit really hit the fan, with more upheaval of life, and there was nothing he could have done to stop my self-sabotage.

At the time I was seventeen, I woke up around three a.m. feeling absolutely awful. With great urgency, I leaped out of my bed and ran down the hallway to my bathroom, and with immediate force began to empty my entire system. It was like a scene from a horror movie. I was sick in every way imaginable and could barely function. It felt like some demon spawn had taken over my body and was now trying to make its way out. This came with no warning, and I felt panicked that I couldn't control any of my bodily functions. What the hell is wrong with me? I thought. My body had never experienced sensations like this before, and my anxiety was heightened as I continued to purge everything left inside of me for the next few hours. This was not a stomach bug, or any type of common flu. I understood already that this was something more serious. I tried to backtrack over my day, examining the choices I had made. Being a somewhat sexually active teenager, I started to wonder if I was pregnant. It would explain why how I felt was like nothing I had ever experienced. Or perhaps maybe God was punishing me for the path of self-destruction I had been walking. Regardless, relying on God to ease any kind of pain for me seemed pointless.

I wasn't aware of my strong connection to my gut instincts at this age or that I held any power within myself. Most of what I had been feeling was anger, fear, self-doubt, and grief, and the more I could escape from these emotions the better. It was a break to feel nothing and what I believed to moving forward was to numb the pain by altering my state of mind with substance abuse.

What I knew that night was that something clearly wasn't right, and once my body gave me any sense of relief, I attempted to pass out on the bathroom floor.

About three hours later, I crawled back to my bedroom and was finally able to lie down. But no matter how hard I tried, even with feelings of pure exhaustion, I barely slept. I felt unsettled, not just with my body, but also from something else deep inside me. What in the hell was my body trying to tell me? I wondered, but there was a huge part of me that was too scared to know the answer. I pondered not going to school that day and just staying home to rest. But by morning, my guts had calmed down, and I decided to make the effort to go. I figured maybe doing my regular routine would get my mind right, or at least keep me distracted.

The day went normally until about eleven a.m., when I was pulled out of my English class and sent down to the principal's office. I was frightened, unsure about what this could be about. My stomach began to turn again, and I was beginning to sweat. My mind was on overdrive as I tried to prepare myself for whatever news they were about to lay on me. Am I in trouble? What did I do? Was coming to school today was a big mistake? Should have I just stayed at home today, after all?

I entered the room of the vice principal's office and saw my dad sitting there, with his pastor by his side. He looked broken and fragile; I could tell by the energy in the room he had bad news.

His eyes are telling me to prepare myself for pain, and he said, "Laura passed away in her sleep last night, Donell."

The room begins to spin. I can't breathe, and the tears come as I collapse to my knees. I was right, I am being punished, and God has once again taken my mother away. My grief is already matching my anger, and I need answers.

"What happened? How is this possible?" I shouted. "I thought she was getting better!"

"Her prescription medications interacted and caused her to have a heart attack in her sleep," he replied.

This made no sense to me as an angry teenager. How could the doctor and the pharmacist fuck up so badly that it actually killed my sister? Laura had been battling breast cancer for some time now. She was diagnosed during her pregnancy and had to receive chemotherapy and a double mastectomy. She never complained about how hard her struggle was and still continued to take care of her other two kids, along with everyone else. She delivered a healthy baby boy, and I spent the summer helping her care for him. She taught me how to cook some of her classic dishes, and we shared many heart to heart talks. She seemed to be getting stronger and I was under the impression that she would recover.

Laura was the strongest woman I knew, and she was a fighter. She had always been my butterfly medicine, and after my mother passed, she, at seventeen, became my mother. She knew I needed her to fill that female role, and she was a natural at motherhood. She embodied grace and balance in all things and took me under her wing when I needed her most. Over the years, because of our dynamic, people just assumed that she was indeed my mother.

My rebellious behavior had made its debut around the time she was diagnosed. It was no coincidence that I felt the need to escape when my second mother became ill. She knew I was into mischief I shouldn't be, and that I was making our father worry about my poor choices. I carried that guilt with me, even though it didn't stop me from continuing down my destructive path. But she never stopped being patient, offering support, and doing whatever she could to help ease my pain.

Laura loved to write handwritten cards, and during this time she had sent me one that really hit me hard.

> Donell,
>
> Congrats on getting your driver's license—drive safely please! You've been on my mind so much lately. I want you and Dad to be able to talk like two adults. Dad loves you so much—you are his whole life and you need to appreciate him and respect his wishes. If you fight with him—someday you will really regret it. The whole family loves you and wants to be proud of all of your actions. You are a smart girl and can be a leader if you want to be. I'm going through chemo again. The doctors found cancer on my rib. Remember how it bothered me when I was over at your house? This time they will give me double doses and I will be in the hospital. I'm a strong person and will make it through. I need your love and prayers. You know how to pray, Donell, remember how we prayed together. You don't have to treat me any different or say anything special, just be my friend and my sister and love me and pray for me. Dad is stressed out, so please cheer him up and be supportive. I have great faith in you as a person, and I expect great

things from you as a grown up. I love you so much and wish I could give you a big hug right now. I will see you at Christmas time. God bless you, sweetie.

Love you, sis,

Laura

To say our relationship was special was an understatement, and when she died, part of me died with her. While I began to process this news, my dad and the pastor just sat in silence and allowed me to weep. I felt this cruel trick being played all over again, as if someone found it amusing, as if God found some delight in causing me pain and taking away my butterfly. It was ironic that she had been seventeen when I came into this world, and now, as I was seventeen, she had left me behind.

Later that evening, I was informed of the exact time of her death. I felt chills run through my entire body, realizing it was the exact time that I had become deathly ill. Somehow, my spirit knew she was crossing over and was sending me a clear message I needed to receive. Laura understood she was leaving this world, and I guess that was her way of saying goodbye.

I didn't understand at the time that her butterfly medicine is one of great transformation, and its purpose is to set everything aside to embrace an entire new way of being. Butterflies are known to be spiritual messengers and are here to teach us how to handle dramatic changes with grace, to help us use them as an opportunity for spiritual growth. Laura had accepted this transcendence into an unknown reality, but I was far from realizing her medicine was a gift that was meant to be short lived. Just like the lifecycle of a butterfly that only lasts a week or two, her life was cut short. But the impact that it made on my spirit could not be measured, and when I was able to accept that, her medicine would return.

Back then, being stricken with grief and losing another mother reopened wounds from my past, and I didn't handle it well. The cut ran so deep that I lost who I was for a while. I wanted to escape my reality through any means necessary. I stopped doing the things that kept me close to my culture and to my spirit. I cut my hair in mourning and stopped fancy dancing—the dance that resembles the butterfly, where dancers are dressed in colorful decorated shawls with heavy fringe to create the illusion of butterfly wings. The footwork is fast paced, and the regalia shines the brightest when a dancer turns with her shawl opened up as if it was a butterfly spreading its wings. This dance had always been a big part of my life and my favorite expression of my culture, but in my anger and grief, I turned away from it.

I stopped praying or having any hope or belief in a God that loved me. This so-called man in the sky for some reason had chosen to punish me, and I had no interest in honoring him. Instead, I choose the path that I felt would bring me the least pain. Drugs and alcohol became my allies to minimize the suffering. I didn't care that was hurting my father; my anger fueled my choices and my poor behavior. I couldn't see past the pain, so numbing it was what I chose to do. It took a few hard years for me to wake up to my self-destruction. During this time, my dad never gave up on me and stayed patient with my path. He kept the lines of communication open and continued to support me when I allowed it.

Needless to say, Dad and I had lost a lot together, and he was my rock through every step of the way. When I told him the news about the divorce, I expected him to be more empathetic. I came to him for some guidance and wisdom, or perhaps just comfort. I shared the details of what happened with Nikki, as he had to come to know her well. He loved all the girls at the salon, and she greeted him with a hug at every visit. Normally, my dad was a great listener, but that day, he continued to change the conversation to his past divorce, which had taken place before my mother's time. It was strange to feel that he had a sense of relief that I was getting divorced now, that he imagined I would have more free time to spend with him.

I wasn't used to my dad being so needy. He was always pushing me out of my comfort zone, and in front of a crowd.

"This is good for you, Donell, and will help you grow," he would say, and I would just roll my eyes and do it anyway.

I told him I would be moving out and getting my own place in about three weeks, that I needed a fresh start. His eyes lit up, I could see the wheels turning,

"Maybe I will finally move to The Ridge," he said.

I couldn't believe what I was hearing. I had tried so hard the last few years to get him into this retirement community. My dad was so emotionally tied to that house, the dream house he and my mother had created together—not to mention that my mother had chosen to pass away in their bedroom, instead of at the hospital. Now, suddenly, when my life was in complete chaos, he wanted me to move him, too. I felt mixed emotions about how he had come to this conclusion so quickly. This had to be the worst timing. My plate was beyond full, and I had no family here to help me.

"Dad can you please wait until after I'm done moving and get settled in?" I pleaded.

He responded with a lot of conviction in his tone. "Well, I'm going to start the process right now. I want a change too!" he exclaimed.

I didn't have the energy for this conversation and I chose to let it go for now. I gave him huge hug and told him, "I love you, Dad. I will call you later."

The next few weeks, I met with James a handful of times to get our affairs in order. He was so eager to the papers filed and was more than enthusiastic about his new life with Nikki. We had agreed to meet at a park with our dogs one afternoon to discuss the details. As I pulled up, I could see him waiting for me. He had lost significant weight and was looking younger than ever. His new haircut was obviously done by Nikki, and the sight of it made me cringe.

By this point, he had separated himself completely from me emotionally and withdrew from hugging or any physical contact. I could still see the guilt in his eyes and feelings of shame for what he had done, but it was overshadowed by his new over-proclaimed happiness with my best girlfriend.

"I feel so good, like a weight is off my shoulders. And I have never felt a love like this before. This is true love," he said.

Once again, I became that dead horse he kept beating, with no concept of the impact his words had on my spirit.

"Did you ever think that maybe it's just because it's new? We felt this way in the beginning to," I responded.

"I made myself believe that I was in love with you" he replied.

My tears began to run, but this time they were fueled by anger. "Then why did you stay with me all these years, if you never loved me? I tried to leave you when your drinking got out of control, and you begged me to stay," I shouted.

He looked away and down at the grass, and answered, "Because I was too scared to be alone."

That was it, no more words needed to be said. I was already broken, and I couldn't handle any further rejection. He had taken it yet another step further and now wasn't even validating the love we had all those years. This was all too much, and it was more than I could bear. This wasn't the man I married, or my best friend, but a stranger.

Before parting ways, he mentioned once more, "Could we get together soon to sign the papers?"

I replied in disgust, "You will get them soon enough."

No hugs were given that day, or any day after that for a very long time.

CHAPTER 3
Birthday Medicine

S EVERAL WEEKS LATER, the papers were signed and filed, and I was in the midst of my big move. I didn't want to take anything that reminded me of my life with James or that held our memories. I gathered my clothes, along with a few personal family treasures, and left everything else behind. These were just things—things that represented the life we had built together, that I now had no choice but to let go of. Otherwise, I would succumb to the weight these items held in my heart space. The more I could leave behind, the less it would haunt me later.

James had maintained the house while it was up for sale, but basically was living with Nikki the entire time. He didn't take much either and chose to have a garage sale for the majority of our shared items. I, of course, wasn't present, and wondered that day if the reality of what had happened ever occurred to him, if selling our belongings wrapped in memories to neighbors and strangers sparked any kind of remorse or sadness within him. Or maybe it was just another task at hand to move on, and to move forward into this new life he seemed so eager to live. For me, this time was devastating. I still loved my home and all the labors of love I had put into it over the past nine years. I would miss my plants, and nurturing my garden, and laying in my hammock on a perfect summer day, reading a good book. Within the walls of our home, I had found comfort, refuge, and peace of mind, and having to leave felt unfair. But staying would be even more painful, and in order to heal, I had to move on.

When I walked into my new home for the first time, I knew it going to become a sacred space to begin my healing. The small loft had an industrial feel, with brick exposed walls and a hardwood floor. The entry hall opened up into a large living space with an open kitchen. One wall was dedicated to natural light, with windows spanning the entire length. The floor plan was open throughout the space, but still offered privacy for the bedroom. Walking through my living quarters, I began to envision how I would make it my own, and where to best showcase my special treasures. This felt like the first day of healing for me. I could finally call somewhere home. No more bouncing between friends and sleeping on couches. It occurred to me that, in fact, I was looking forward to living by myself and rediscovering who I really was.

"You are safe here—only new memories to make from here on out," I told myself. "Things can calm down a bit now, and you can just breathe and take it in."

That feeling of relief ended quickly when I got a call from my dad shortly after. I could feel the excitement in his voice.

"I signed on an apartment at The Ridge, Donell," he told me. "And I'm set to move in two weeks."

I sighed with discontent, feeling irritated. I had just settled in and hadn't even gotten a moment to collect myself.

"Dad, really? I just moved and I'm still finishing up. Can you wait a month so I can get settled?" I replied.

"No, Donell, I'm ready to move now!" he responded.

I knew the responsibility of helping him move would all fall on me, because I had no other siblings or family around. Deep down, I was happy for my dad, but his timing was leaving me with resentment. I felt like he was being incredibly selfish and making this change in my life about him. But his mind was made up, and the papers were signed. I knew how hard it was to secure a residence there, and I understood we had to act fast and get the ball rolling.

I had to take off even more days from work to prepare my dad for the big move. We hired professional movers for the heavy stuff, but the rest was up to me. I arranged an estate sale for what he couldn't fit into his new place and arranged for everything that wasn't sold to go in consignment. I felt prepared for the big day and was looking forward to getting it over with so I could go back to some me time.

Around six a.m. on the day of the move, I got a frantic call from my dad. I could tell he having a hard day. He said, "Donell, I changed my mind. I don't want to do this today."

I felt crazy pissed, having had to reorganize my life around his move, to learn that now he was bailing. I had to force myself to not yell and be calm. I knew this was coming from fear. He must have come to realize he was finally letting go of the home he and my mother had built together. It should have been their sacred space to live out their final days and grow old together.

"Dad, we can't cancel. The movers are booked for the next month. This was your choice, and I took time off work to help you. This is happening today," I told him. "I will be there soon."

He didn't like my response, but he understood what had to be done. When I arrived he was acting manic, and I had seen this behavior before, during his anxiety attacks. As I mentioned, this man doesn't like change, and is a creature of habit. He holds onto things of the past for as long as possible, whether they work or not. He even kept my mother's mail for an entire decade after she had passed.

This wasn't the first time I knew my father was changing. Several signs told me his memory was quickly fading. During the last year, he continued to forget times and dates that we would schedule to meet. He would forget parts of conversations and people I had introduced him to countless times. I had a good reason to worry that this was the beginning of a difficult truth to come, but for now, I could only deal with one thing at time.

I came upstairs to his bedroom and gave him the task of organizing his clothes in piles of what to keep and what to donate.

He told me, "I just can't, Donell. I told you, I don't feel well, and I'm not ready to do this."

I was very aware of how scared he was feeling, and how this change he had wanted so badly had become too overwhelming for us both. But I knew this was in his best interest, and I had no other options to give him.

"Dad, I know you are scared to move now, but I'm so happy in my new space. If I can do it, so can you. "

He allowed himself to smile for a moment, and I could see a little more calm in his demeanor. He replied, "Okay, I will try."

He walked over to his closet and began to go through his clothes, separating them into piles. Little by little, we attacked each room, and we eventually called it a day.

Dad's move was more exhausting than my own, and I felt so relieved to have professional movers' assistance. My ex-brother-in-law Clark, who had been Laura's husband, came up to help that weekend, as he remained close to my dad, even after Laura passed. I was grateful for his help, and my father loved the extra company.

It took some time for my dad to get settled in to his new apartment at The Ridge. He continued to question if he had made the right decision. But he was a social man, at least, and I hoped he would make some new friends. The facility offered a lot of activities, and my dad loved staying busy.

It became too obvious after the move that Dad was struggling, and his behaviors were becoming even stranger. We decided it was time to take some tests to see if our concerns would be confirmed. I knew by the time we finally went in, we had put this test off for far too long. I suppose both of us were in denial, knowing what was ahead.

As we reviewed the results with the doctor, she told us, "With his level of education, he should have been able to answer the questions correctly."

My dad had received his master's degree in education at the University of Idaho and had a doctoral degree from Penn State. In 2006, less than five years ago, he was elected as a state legislator in Washington. He was always reading a book, or several books, throughout my entire childhood. To say he was well educated was being modest. My dad never stopped learning.

The full results of the tests came back, and my dad was diagnosed with dementia. The doctors weren't sure how long he had suffered from it, but they needed to treat it now. They prescribed some medication to slow down the process, but eventually his memory would completely fade. This was unsettling news, and our worst fears were now confirmed. I wanted so badly to call James and tell him the news and hear some support. He had always been my go to, and a good listener. But things were dramatically different now, and I realized I was alone in this. My father's well-being was my responsibility now, and I had to dig deep to find my strength.

As I could have expected, our roles began to shift dramatically, and neither my father nor I were prepared for that battle. He was now taking several medications, and the dementia meds were just another to add to the pile. I tried to educate him on natural medicine and diet alternatives, but he was convinced that I couldn't possibly know something his doctors didn't. He was old school and believed that the doctors always knew best.

My dad was losing not just his memory, but also his freedoms. In the simplest of ways, he was losing everyday tasks that we all take for granted. No more driving for this guy, or walks alone too far from the facility. I would have to provide transportation or get other resources to assist me. A nurse would administer his pills daily, eliminating the risk of him forgetting or taking too many. The more freedoms he lost, the more depression sunk in for him. I found it incredibly hard to watch this process.

For a while, he took Buddhist meditation classes, which pleasantly surprised me. For being such a devoted Catholic most of his life, I had never imagined he would be open to experiencing other forms of spirituality. When he mentioned he quit going, I felt disappointed for him. I had hoped it would give him some peace.

"Dad, I thought you liked these classes."

He looked down with a sense of defeat and replied, "In class, I couldn't remember what I experienced or how to explain it. I felt embarrassed during group discussions, feeling at a loss for words."

It broke my heart to hear this: he was having to let go of another thing that made him feel so good. He stopped reading books completely, and no longer read the morning newspaper, which had been a daily ritual. I realized while watching my father change that as the mind goes, the body will soon follow. His balance was highly affected, which made most of his past physical activities too difficult to manage. I had to monitor his steps, watching him carefully as he walked up and down stairs and curbs everywhere we went. I wondered if this was what being a parent feels like and viewed my dad through a different perspective.

A few months back, I put his house on the market in addition to my own. I used the same realtor, figured it would make things a little easier on me. The stress from selling both of our houses was overwhelming to say the least, and my dad chose to make it even more difficult. Suddenly, he didn't trust me or my intentions with his estate. He called me constantly, every day over the phone saying, "Why is this taking so long? It should be sold by now. I want you to find someone else, Donell."

Meanwhile, I was busy at work trying to make up lost income, and still dealing with all the drama of the divorce. I felt extremely annoyed and taken for granted, with no thanks for helping me move, or for the other million things I did for him. I want to scream at the top of my lungs or run away and never look back. I love my dad, but he was driving me batshit crazy, and I was trying so hard to just deal. I had to calm myself before returning to the call.

I assured him, "Dad it's only been two months. Give it some time. The realtor is selling my house as well. Don't worry."

He wasn't thrilled with my answer but decided to let it go for a week or so.

My reassurances to him didn't last long, and soon his calls became constant. If I didn't answer, he panicked even more. I was at work most of the time, and I knew he was being difficult. There were a few times I answered the phone already annoyed and was short with him. Later, I regretted my behavior and vowed to only answer his calls when I was calm. He wasn't trying to drive me crazy, he just needed my attention. And I understood even then that at some point those calls would stop, and I would miss hearing his voice.

This time was a lesson in patience, and it took me a great deal of time to realize that I needed and asked for this lesson. My experience so far has taught me that the deepest level of learning is through these kinds of hard lessons. He didn't realize that he was still playing the role of my teacher. Even through his dementia, he had gifts to share with me and ways to mold me into being a better human.

The next few months of that summer passed quickly. I was still trying to adjust from the divorce, to find my new normal or some kind of routine. One day would roll into the next, and I was very much still filled with grief. But the initial blow was over, and I was ready to start creating my new path.

I never imagined I would be single again, and the dating scene was so incredibly different from back in my day. I began dating James when I was twenty years old. We had cell phones, but still had real conversations over the phone. Texting hadn't taken over the lines of communication yet, and we certainly didn't have emojis. There weren't dating services online like we have now, and it was a whole new concept, completely foreign to me.

I really wasn't in a place in my healing to be looking for someone special, but I thought it could be a nice distraction. I most certainly didn't trust men, or even some women, at that point.

But I longed for that human connection again, I wanted to be held and cared for, to feel like I was wanted. James had said so many hurtful things during our divorce that shattered my ego. I usually felt fairly good about myself, but at this point my self-esteem had taken a big blow. I was in need of some new male distractions; I wanted to feel someone else's touch and know they wanted to feel mine.

My girlfriends were not prepared for me join the single life either. They were all in committed relationships, and they continuously gave me a hard time about dating apps of any kind.

Lindsey was one friend that liked to mother me. "You never know who is on the other end, babe. Could be a serial killer for all you know," she would say anytime I mentioned interacting online. I would typically respond, "Babe, you don't understand, this is how people date now. I know it seems weird, but this is the new normal."

She would roll her eyes and sigh. I knew her intentions were good, but it was impossible for her to understand where I was coming from.

My girlfriend Rose was a little more playful with the idea, but she voiced her concerns as well. She was one those friends that likes to bring the laughter medicine.

"We are releasing you into the wild, Donnie," she would say. We would always have a good laugh about it, and it always lightened the mood.

And I still wasn't really dating, I just was chatting with a few men at a safe distance. I didn't have time or care to pour time into anyone else, other than my dad, anyhow.

My birthday was coming up, and I thought it might be nice to get out of town and create new memories. The first holidays without your loved ones always seem to be the most difficult, and the road would be a good time to clear my thoughts.

I didn't really have a plan, but I knew I could stay with my niece Jewels for the weekend. She and her boyfriend had a really cute loft space up in west Seattle. I loved that neighborhood, and you could actually find parking. Jewels and I were raised like sisters, being only six years apart in age. Laura had taken on the mother role for me, and when Jewels came along a sisterhood bond was formed. I really don't get to spend that much time with her anymore, so I was looking forward to catching up.

I hit the road by nine-thirty a.m., to arrive around two-thirty that afternoon. I was planning on avoiding Seattle rush hour traffic. I had to get someone to watch my little pooch Jackson James and I had split up the dogs when I made my move. It just was easier that way, and it meant we didn't have to see each other anymore. Jackson was smaller and didn't have to have a yard, and Apollo needed a yard and was more accustomed to James anyhow. I missed my other pooch, but so is life, and I just had to let go.

The drive was good for me. I got to listen to music and let my mind wander. Details of the divorce circled around in my head, things that were said and daydreams about what I would say if I ran into Nikki. I wanted to be somewhat prepared if that were to happen. I used that drive to process some of the dramatic change that occurred the last few months.

I was so happy to get away for a bit. I had really wished I could escape for a good long while. But Dad still really needed me, and I was fortunate enough to have at least this time to myself.

The four-and-a-half-hour drive went by in a flash, with my mind so consumed I lost track of time. I picked up Jewels from her waitressing job downtown and drove us over to the west side to her place.

Jewels and I don't look a whole lot alike, but we do have my mother's deep-set almond-brown eyes and strong check bones. Her curly dark auburn hair comes from her father's side. She is built more like my sister with a few curves, but a smaller frame. I have a tattoo on my chest to honor my sister's life, a woman's face with angelic-looking hair, and it seems to embody motherhood. Laura's name is written underneath, along with two floating butterflies that represent us both—that we are forever joined together. With the small age difference between me and Jewels, people find it strange when we say I'm her aunt. We always get a good laugh afterward.

"It's so good to see. I have missed you," I told her.

Jewels smiled and hugged me. "I have missed you, too, and I'm so sorry for what has happened," she said.

I dove a little more into the details, telling her about what had happened. But I was here for healing and change, and I wanted to spend my energy in good spirits and connecting again with her.

We took the elevator up to the roof, to enjoy the view and nice weather. This building was modern and had really great underground art featured on every floor. There was an exercise room located on the bottom floor, and a private yoga studio. But those Seattle views from the rooftop could not be beat, and it was the perfect place for us to catch up. We had to wait for Tim to get home, then we could head out for a nice dinner in the city.

Jewels and Tim were both vegans and knew the best places in town for that particular cuisine. I had been a vegetarian for the last ten years and was vegan for six years of that time. But I had recently decided to incorporate bone broth and eggs back into my diet again. I was slowly transitioning into eating quality meat from time to time.

My dad had raised me on processed food. He was busy single parent and never cared or liked to cook. By my teens, I was having multiple digestive issues and needed to see a gastroenterologist. After seeing a few specialists, I still wasn't feeling better. The doctors never asked me about diet or any food allergies. Fed up with the system, I decided to start eliminating processed foods my diet and go from there. It wasn't an easy journey, but I was able find a healthier diet that fit my needs. Our bodies' needs can change as we age, with stress and current environment also being factors. I did my own research and, through trial and error, found a way to heal my gut through diet.

At the time, I was unaware that this struggle with food would lead me to a new path of using food as medicine. I became incredibly passionate about helping friends and clients with their nutrition concerns. I chose to attend The Institute of Integrative Nutrition and received my holistic health coach certification. My graduation was a few months before the divorce began. I wasn't in a place emotionally at that time to take clients, but I wanted to be more open with my diet again. This led me to allow some meat into my diet, and to see how I felt.

The three of us made it out for a fabulous dinner but kept the evening short, for tomorrow was my thirty-fourth birthday and we wanted to make the most of it.

Tim mentioned, "I would love to take you for a run around Lincoln Park for your birthday in the morning, if you're up for it."

"Yes, of course," I replied. I couldn't think of a better way to start my birthday. The night ended early. I was beat from the travel, and from life in general. I was anxious and looking forward to the morning.

We both woke up early, and Jewels stayed in bed for a little extra sleep.

"Are you ready for this run?" Tim asked. "I will go as long as you wish, and we can come back whenever you want."

Tim was an ultramarathon runner. He was around five foot eleven, and he had that classic long and lean runner's build. He had medium short brown hair, and the plugs in his ears gave a little edge to his look.

"I'm up for the challenge," I told him. "I just might surprise you."

I knew his background in running, but I was seasoned runner myself. I had completed a marathon a few years prior and was actively competing in local races in town. We were sizing each other up, in a friendly but somewhat competitive way.

And we were off, heading down Fauntleroy Avenue to our destination, Lincoln Park. We found a pace we were both comfortable with, and he led me through some neighborhoods and somewhat busy intersections. It only took about twenty minutes to get there, and I was so impressed with this secret gem of a park that I had never seen.

The park was filled with countless paths to choose from, and magnificent trees that stretched across the view. I was able to feel like I was out of the city and in nature, with fresh air to breathe and the rich smell of earth.

Running had always been a place of healing for me. With each step, I could get lost in my thoughts. No matter how upset I was, running grounded me through each breath. I could let go, even for just a moment, and running had become my best outlet for stress relief and centering.

After we made it through the park, we went down some trails that led to the water. The park is connected to the edge of Puget Sound and has the most spectacular path to follow along the water. I couldn't believe how beautiful this place was, and I felt so blessed to start my morning medicine in that way.

We had reached around seven miles at that point, and Tim asked, "Are you ready to head back, Donell?"

"I think so. Thank you for bringing me here," I replied with a warm smile. I wanted to go dancing that evening, so I figured I would save the rest of my energy for later.

Jewels and Tim were excited to take me to Plum Bistro in Capitol Hill. They had planned it special for my birthday. It was their favorite vegan restaurant, and they knew I would love it.

That evening, we sat down to an incredible feast. The food was beautiful, with so much attention to detail in every dish. There is such a thing as food porn, and the dishes before me that night fit the description. The presentation alone made my mouth water, and boy, did those dishes deliver on flavor.

After dinner, we walked our full bellies around the streets of Capitol Hill. There was no agenda, and it was a beautiful and warm summer night. Tim ran into some buddies outside a music venue, so we stood for a while as he was visiting with them. Suddenly, a dance flash mob came together right in front of us. I realized Jewels and I had seen them practicing in the park, earlier that day. We looked at each other and giggled and continued watching their routine.

I noticed an extremely handsome man across from us, watching them, too. He had a buzz haircut, dark brown eyes, and a nice build. We kept catching eyes and exchanging smiles from across the way. This playful game lasted about fifteen minutes, and then Tim walked over and asked if we were ready to go.

"I'm kinda checking out that guy over there," I replied, blushing like a schoolgirl.

"Well, go talk to him and say hello" Tim said.

My eyes popped open. "No way, I can't! I don't approach men, I'm too shy."

Tim gave me a look like he had an idea. "Okay," he said. "Well, I'm going over there to talk to him, then."

I almost tried to stop him, but I wasn't going to make an introduction. He crossed the street and I could see them chatting. After a few minutes, they walked right toward me.

"Oh my God, I am feeling so nervous," I said to Jewels.

She smiled and giggled a little.

I looked at the man again and our eyes locked, but I could barely keep looking at him. I was blushing ear to ear.

He smiled and me and said, "Hello, my name is Mies. I am visiting from Switzerland on holiday. This is my first trip to America."

He had the sexiest accent that instantly melted me into the sidewalk.

"Hello, my name is Donell," I responded.

"What are you out doing tonight?" he asked.

"I have no plans, but it is my birthday. We were going to have a few drinks. You and your friend are welcome to join us."

It was obvious from the way our pheromones were interacting that there was an unbelievably strong attraction between us.

"Let's go to the Unicorn," Jewels suggested. "It's just down the way."

We all agreed, and our group of three became five. Once we got to the entrance, Jewels and Tim entered first. Mies got stopped by the doorman, who said, "I can't accept your ID. I need to see your passport."

Mies responded, "I don't have it on me. I wasn't expecting to need it."

He looked at me and said, "You are welcome to come hang with us on the houseboat we are staying at."

I couldn't believe I was considering it. "Okay," I told him. "I will find Jewels, talk to her, and be right out."

It took me a minute to find her in the crowded bar. I saw her and said, "The doorman won't let them in without his passport. And I want to hang with my new friend."

She was very hesitant about all this, but I am her Aunt after all.

"So, you're going with them? What about your car?" Jewels said.

"I will let you two drive it home. Don't worry, I will be okay."

She sighed and I could see she had worry in her face. Perhaps these two men were serial killers, or something.

"Well, text me when you get there, and send your address."

I gave her a hug and responded, "Yes, of course. I know this seems crazy, but it feels right."

I came back out of the bar and was instantly greeted by Mies. I looked into his intense green eyes. He smiled, and we started walking to their car. I thought to myself, "You are crazy, girl. You don't know these men at all." But there was energy here I couldn't deny, and after all, it was my birthday.

The friend, David, hopped in the front seat, and Mies and I took the back to ourselves. David was also from Switzerland, but of Thai descent. He was very charming and spoke English much better than Mies.

David started telling me of their recent adventures in the States. Meanwhile, Mies and I were getting cozy in the back, holding hands and snuggling a bit, while somewhat listening.

Around eleven p.m., we arrived at a parking lot and headed down to the dock. The houseboats were incredible, each one so unique and charming. I had never really spent time on a houseboat and felt quite lucky to be there. We walked all the way down to the end, and before me was the most spectacular houseboat. It looked like a vacation home straight out of a magazine.

The boys told me to take a seat outside, and they would grab us some drinks. I glanced around, admiring the peaceful lake before me under the stars.

We spent maybe an hour outside hanging out and just getting to know each other. David could feel the energy between Mies and I was getting hot and heavy.

"Well, I'm off to bed, guys. Enjoy your evening," David said.

Mies and I looked at each other like the other was magic.

"Would you like to follow me into the bedroom?" he asked.

He reached out and grabbed my hand. I answered him using my eyes, and we walked into the house.

There was a smaller room off to the right, and he said, "Make yourself comfortable. I have to use the restroom and will be right back."

I sat on the bed, once again questioning my choices, hardly believing I was really going through with this. I told myself, "But this is your birthday, and this man tonight is your gift."

As soon as he entered the room, we were like two wild animals, full of passion and crazy desire. The clothes didn't last long; we wanted to feel each other's skin, smell, and taste. Mies was an incredible lover. I don't know if it's a European thing or what, but no complaints from this girl. There were a few times our language barrier got tricky, but the energy between us said enough. I will say it was a long and special night, just the kind of medicine I was in need of.

It felt good to be wanted, loved on, and desired. I didn't want the incredible feeling to end, because there was also some healing taking place as well.

The next morning, we woke up slowly together, and he said, "Let me make you some breakfast."

A crazy sexy Swiss man wants to make me breakfast? This has to be a dream, I thought to myself.

I sent a quick text to Jewels: "I'm safe having breakfast and will be back soon." I had forgotten to text night before, and I'm sure she was worried.

We got dressed and entered the kitchen. But to my surprise and complete embarrassment, I saw an older middle-aged couple sitting down to breakfast.

My face turned red, and I could barely look at the woman. She said, "Hello, my name is Diane. I guess, welcome to my home."

It was incredibly awkward; I had no idea there was other people there. And perhaps they could hear the late night I had shared with Mies. I gathered myself and tried to act like this wasn't weird.

"Hello, my name is Donell. You have a lovely home."

She gave me a half smile, and then returned to her breakfast. This woman must think I'm a total slut, I thought. This behavior wasn't like me at all. We shared a few more words. She said the boys were good friends of her sons, and so they were accommodating them while they were in Seattle. She was a nice lady and I began to feel somewhat okay. It was just a very strange way to be introduced.

Mies asked me if I would like to paddle board that afternoon. I couldn't believe how much more magical the last twenty-four hours could get. I told him I would love to, but I had to get my car and my things back at Jewels' house. On the car ride over, we still just couldn't keep our hands off each other. I couldn't remember the last time I felt this, feeling butterflies about someone.

"I will grab my things and head back to the boathouse in an hour," I said, leaving the car. We kissed goodbye.

Jewels and Tim were home and anxiously waiting to hear my story. I gave them the "long story short" version.

"I'm heading back to the boathouse, to go stand-up paddling, now," I said.

They were surprised but also happy for me to have found some new joy in my life.

"Well, be careful, and stay in contact," Jewels said as I hugged them both goodbye.

"Thank you for everything, guys, and don't worry about this one." I winked and headed out the door with my things.

I arrived back at the houseboat and changed into my swimsuit. Mies walked me over to the dock, handed me a paddle and we carefully sat onto the same board. The sun was shining bright, and it was a hot day in Seattle, which is something to really celebrate. He began paddling us away from the dock and out onto the lake.

I took a breath and looked around, observing kayakers and boat enthusiasts enjoying their time on the water. My attention turned to Mies, watching his strokes and the way his muscles moved. This beautiful creature is so romantically paddling me around the lake, I thought. How could I be so lucky?

I had planned on heading back to Spokane that night. I had clients in two days and wanted some downtime, but I wasn't ready to part from Mies, and he wanted me to stay. The only option for us was to get a room together and go from there.

Long story short, I didn't come home for another day and we stayed a second night in the hotel room. My girlfriends back home were freaking out, wondering if I had lost my mind and wasn't coming back. All in good jokes, but they had a right to worry. I wasn't acting like myself—but it felt good, and I didn't care.

I had become addicted to Mies's touch and we had limited time. I figured this was it and wanted to make the most of the time we had, while we could.

Mies mentioned, "I have a few more travel destinations, but I will be coming back through San Francisco, and have a week to spend there. We should get together again."

"I would love to," I said, "But I don't know that it's possible."

After this conversation and several hard make out sessions, we finally said goodbye. We exchanged all information we could use to keep in touch.

I drove back really late from my rendezvous with Mies. I hadn't slept a whole lot last few days, and it was finally catching up with me. I never drink coffee but had to stop about two hours into my drive to pick some up. The shitty grin that I left with stayed on my face for at least a week. And when I got back to the salon, my squad wanted to know all the details.

I most definitely gave them a scare, but they were happy for me that I was smiling again. The joke of the salon was that I was moving to this Swiss Alps; my friends are so funny that way.

Mies and I stayed in touch for the next six weeks while he traveled around the United States. He kept asking if I would meet up with him on his way out. I hadn't planned on how I could afford another trip so soon. But I remembered I had credit from a flight I had cancelled with James to go to Hawaii that Thanksgiving. Why not use it to see my Swiss German lover? Plus, one of my besties, Lidz, lived there, and I could spend time with her too.

After discussing it with a few close friends, I decided to go and Lidz was going to be happy to see me too.

I arrived in San Francisco around three p.m. Mies said that he and David would be picking me up from there. They were running late, and I had a bit of panic because I hadn't heard from Mies earlier that day. After about thirty minutes, I saw them pull up to the terminal. Mies jumped out of the car.

"I'm so sorry we are late, Sweaty. The traffic was really bad." Mies calling me "Sweaty" had become of term of endearment and a running joke between us. The language barrier, especially when sending texts, was quite entertaining. He had meant to call me Sweetie, but texted Sweaty, and we thought it was hilarious.

I gave him a hug and a passionate kiss. "It's okay. I'm just to glad to see you again."

During the time we spent together, I knew he couldn't have completely understood everything I was saying, but we would just laugh and move on. It was also really good to see David. He was such an interesting guy, and we also needed him at times to be our interpreter. The three of us spent a few days together, then a few more friends from Switzerland came to join the boys.

Everyone was really friendly, but I have to say, at times it was strange. When they all chose to speak German, their first language, I had no idea what they were saying. I didn't mind. They were all good people, and it was fun having a larger group.

The next five days we had to spend together in the city flew by. We spent a good deal of time exploring Haight and Ashbury, such an eccentric part of the city. I purchased a dope hat from Goorin Bros. and a few gifts for my girl squad back home. What I loved most about the area was the quality and quantity of street art. I have a huge appreciation for underground art, and some of what I saw that week blew my mind. Of course, what I spent most of attention on was Mies. Our playfulness was so natural, and I had forgotten what that feeling was like.

Mies was so completely different from James, in so many ways, and it was such a needed change. Every meal we sat down together, he offered to share his food, and I loved that. He even joined me for a workout in the hotel exercise room, which to me was very romantic.

I could rarely get James to go the gym with me. He didn't care much for daily physical exercise, at least not in a gym setting. I could get him to go on some hikes with the dogs and occasionally a summer bike rides. But those activities were short lived. He never understood what those physical activities as a couple meant to me.

Mies knew briefly what had happened with my divorce and what happened with James, but there was no reason to go into detail. He mentioned he had been single for about six months, and that was enough to know. Needless to say, we couldn't always understand each other; so long, deep conversations were limited.

What both of us did realize was that our time together was limited and special. I had no expectations of what this amazing experience could lead to. Neither one of us was healed from our past and had no plans on seeing where this could go. We talked a bit about me visiting him overseas, but I had so much responsibility at home. And I knew I couldn't afford a European vacation any time soon.

Soon, it was time for him to leave and head back home, but before he headed to the airport, he and the boys dropped me off at Lidz's place, up by Golden Gate Park. I looked deep into those green eyes for the last time; the magic between us had never left since we met.

"I will miss you, Sweaty. Stay in touch," he said.

"I will miss you, handsome," I replied and kissed him one last time. I grabbed my bags and began to walk away down the street. Then, I chose to turn around for just a moment, to see him watching me go.

The rest of my trip was reserved for one of my oldest and craziest friendships. I was so excited to spend quality time with Lidz. We went through a lot together as kids, and still remained close. She was one of the friends that knew me when I was rebelling, partying and getting into trouble. Some of it I regret, but a lot the reckless adventures we had together were fun. She carried the dragonfly medicine, always carefree, with a strong imagination and a lightness about her. No matter how much time we had spent apart, when we saw each other, it was like family and that never changed.

I texted Lidz that I had arrived, and she came down to greet me. It was so good to see her face; it had been a couple of years since we got to spend some time together.

Lidz always had an interesting look about her. She was never one to blend in or follow certain trends. This visit, she was wearing tight black jeans with a little sag, an oversized tee-shirt, and stylish sneakers. She didn't wear makeup and preferred to keep her long wavy light brown strands on the natural side.

We walked up the stairs to her apartment so I could set down my things and we could catch up. Lidz was not only a good friend of mine, but also a good friend of James's. She was the one who could best understand us both, and I wanted some of her insight on what had happened. She was surprised at what had taken place, but she had high hopes for me and my new path.

It was time to have some fun—enough of this drama. We wanted to live it up while I was in town.

"There is a dope afternoon music party at the El Rio today, if you're interested," she said.

I had no plans and was up for anything. "Yeah babe, I'm totally down. Whatever you think is fun. And you know I love good dance music," I replied.

"Girl, you know I got you covered. Let's change and head down to The Mission" she said.

No matter what we did, we always had fun, and as adults now at least we made smarter choices. The venue was super sick; we walked out to the back patio where everyone was dancing. I loved me some good house music, and it was bumping hard that summer day. As time passed, the place got more packed, and we just danced our asses off, like we used to as kids. It felt like old times, but even better, because I was in a better place with spirit and had more understanding.

The morning before I left, I was able to go on a run to Golden Gate Park. I had anticipated this run and was looking forward to it. It happened to only be less than a mile away from Lidz's place, and I took that as a sign it was meant to be. Golden Gate Park had to be one of the most vast and unique parks I had ever had the pleasure to run through. I saw small waterfalls, prehistoric plant life, and then I came across some buffalo.

Say what! I had to stop and get a closer look. There was actually a buffalo reserve in the middle of the park—unbelievable! There were so many sporting events and races going on at the same time, too. I had no idea this park was so huge; I could spend days running here.

Running for the past fourteen years had been medicine for me. The repetitive motion took me into a meditative place, and for a long time I believed it was my only medicine tracks. The state allowed me the space to gather my thoughts, find clarity, and tackle most situations with a more peaceful heart. For the first time in a long time, I could reflect on some joy in my life. I had been able to connect with another human being in a way I never imagined I could have with anyone else but James. I felt wanted and desired, which couldn't have come at a better time. Mies was my birthday medicine, and I was so lucky to have that gift extend into this other trip. I couldn't help but smile and think to myself, so this is what healing

feels like. This passionate whirlwind romance had been the perfect salve for my pain, and in reality, I understood it was meant to be short lived.

CHAPTER 4
Music Medicine

M Y BLISSFUL STATE FROM VACATION was quickly replaced with anxiety. My current reality of being back home and having to sell my house as well as my father's, felt like a burden that I wasn't at all prepared for. I'm having a hell of time communicating with James. Even though I knew he wanted it to be over, he was also somewhat checked out. I feared that if we went into winter, I would be stuck with an extra house payment I couldn't afford. I was the only one on the lease when we had originally signed, and I didn't want to get screwed. A few people came to look, but we weren't getting any offers.

Then, low and behold, one of my dearest friends, Ronnie, got engaged, and she and her finance Calvin were looking to buy. The timing couldn't have been more perfect, and I was crossing my fingers it would all work out.

Ronnie is a unique beauty; she has charisma that fills a room. Of course, she is beautiful, from her green eyes to her full lips. And it would be impossible not to mention her large breasts—us girls mention them on the regular. Ronnie's light shines bright through her songbird medicine. She can capture an audience with just one note.

One afternoon at the salon, she mentions, "Babe, I am interested in buying your house. I'm going to talk it over with Calvin and see if he's down." I can't believe it. This would be a big weight of my shoulders.

"Really? That would be amazing. Let me know," I replied.

I pondered over my mixed emotions. While I was happy to let go of the house, it could be strange to have it go to one of my best friends. But if she wants it, she can have it, I thought. I would rather see someone nurture my home. And maybe it would be incredible to still be able to see my plants grow. I had put so much love into that house over the last nine years, and perhaps this would be very healing.

Calvin agreed on the purchase, and we started the paperwork. After the inspection several minor things had to be done. But I will give credit to James: he got everything done that he could, and soon the house was ready for a final inspection.

By that time, the only communication James and I had was business. There was no point in hashing out our affairs. He was still living with Nikki and appeared to be happier then I was comfortable with. Not that I didn't want him to be happy, just not with her.

Ronnie and Calvin moved into my old house shortly after, making it their own and giving the space a new look. The couple threw a housewarming party about a month later, and I offered to help because I had always enjoyed entertaining guests.

However, I wasn't at all prepared for how it would make feel. When I got to the house, Ronnie was finishing up appetizers and asked me to answer the door when guests arrived.

I heard a knock and went to open the door, as I was accustomed to, and saw a couple that was surprised to see me as well. They weren't sure they had the right house, because we didn't recognize each other. They were coworkers of Calvin's, I assumed, and I said, "Hello, this is the right house. I used to live here, but I'm just helping out. Please come in."

More guests continued to arrive, and I still felt the need to explain the situation. By the end of the night, it had become a running joke. Ronnie's guests thought we were making it up and playing a prank.

"No really," I told them. "I'm a ghost, and I'm haunting this house." We kept it lighthearted. No real talk about the divorce, this is a party.

But I did find myself throughout the night taking a step back and trying to process how I felt being back in this house. Entertaining guests, like I did so many times when James and I were married. But this isn't my house anymore, I told myself, and new memories were being made.

I stayed until about ten p.m. I had started to feel emotional about the situation and chose to excuse myself so I didn't show it. When I got home that night, I cried.

It was painful to for me to feel that energy while in my old place. And trust, I was grateful that the burden of the house payment was gone, but it was that night that it really felt like it wasn't my home anymore. There was some closure that occurred, but it came with lots of salty tears.

Dad received a potential offer on his house, so we had to scramble to make sure it would pass any inspections that would follow. He was anxious to close the deal, even though it was painful for him to let it go. But he needed the income from the house to pay for help his expenses at the Ridge. It was unbelievable what it cost for him to live there, but that's where he wanted to be. At least he was still in his neighborhood and could go on short walks without getting lost.

I got a voice message from Dad. "Hey, it's me, your dad," it began. He always said that, even though it was obvious and made me giggle. "I was wondering what day we can go to coffee this week and catch up. Give me a call back. Love you, goodbye."

I picked him up later that week. Of course, I had to remind him every day when it was, and I always had him write it down. By this time, we were in fall weather in Spokane. It might be the most beautiful time of year here, with the leaves full of warm rich tones. Most people don't realize we are the second largest city in Washington next to Seattle. Growing up here, I became accustomed to not dealing with heavy traffic, and experiencing all four seasons, even though I could do without winter. We are a friendly city and manage to keep the cost of living more reasonable than most. I don't plan on living out my days here, but this place will always be special to me and close to my heart.

Dad was waiting for me just inside the door of the Ridge. I could see he was dressed in slacks and a sweater I got him last Christmas.

"Wow, Dad, you look really nice today," I said.

He got into the car, smiled, and responded, "Thanks, I felt dressing up a little."

It was a good sign when Dad was looking nice; it meant his mind was in a good place. I noticed the days he didn't care to shower and stayed in sweatpants; on those days, he was feeling low or anxious

We headed to his favorite Starbucks, where he knew the staff and liked to be social. He ordered a drip coffee with room for cream and a blueberry scone. I ordered chai tea and planned to nibble on his scone a bit. We found a comfortable place to sit down and catch up.

"I used to drive myself here almost every morning to read the paper and have coffee," he said. He has said this to me countless times before, but he doesn't know that.

"Yes, you did, Dad. You seem to like it here," I replied.

"So, tell me about what's going on in your life. How was your trip to San Francisco?" he asked.

"It was great, Dad. I got to spend time with Lidz and see the Golden Gate Bridge. I even got to run in the park by the buffalo."

I left out the part of Mies. He still is my father, after all.

"You remember Lidz, Dad, and all the trouble we used to get into?"

He nodded, and I could see the wheels turning and processing the past. My dad still remembered some of my friends from childhood, but really struggled remembering anyone else after that.

"Buffalo? Wow, that's really neat. You're really lucky to be traveling like this, Donell," he said and took a bite of his scone.

"I am very lucky, Dad. I know you miss traveling like you used to," I replied as I took a nibble of the scone as well.

"Yeah, I do miss traveling. But I can't be away for too long, and it makes me anxious," he said, looking away, and, I assume, reflecting on why things were different now.

"Well, you could still take short trips to Seattle, to visit your brother. Right, Dad?" I asked, with hope in my tone.

"I suppose I could, as long as I feel okay and for up it," he said.

Sometimes we just liked to sit there and observe our surroundings. My dad's personality was, in some ways, very different from before. He was never really into little ones. He loved his grandkids, but they didn't live in town. And he wasn't one of those grandparents that would have offered to babysit anyhow. I saw light in his eyes, as he watched children now, and he would want to interact with them or get their attention. I loved seeing this side of my dad. He had always been a gentle and kind man, but this was different and special to witness. We wrapped up our weekly coffee date, and I drove him back to the Ridge.

"Love you, Dad. I will talk to you later," I said as he got out of the car,

"Love you, too. Talk to you later," he replied and walked back inside the building.

The offer on his house went through, the inspection was passed, and he signed the papers. I felt a sense of relief, but I loved that house, too. It was my home from the ages of seven to twenty. No one else had lived there but us, and that was a hard thing to process. The time had come to say goodbye to my childhood home, the place where my mother had left this earth. My hope was that a new family would bring some life into the house and love it as much as we did.

That year I had to learn to let go of the old life that defined me. An incredible amount of change had occurred, but by then I had to come understand that change is inevitable. You can choose to walk with it or be dragged screaming.

I felt the same way about the holidays now, and I was really not looking forward to it all. Those first holidays without the family you are used to bring suffering, not joy.

I thought about James's mom, Lori, his sister, Denise, and his step- father Frank. I loved how much effort Lori put into the holidays. She loved Christmas and went over the top with decorations and festivities. I enjoyed their warm company, and it felt like family. And, certainly, it was nice having a place to go with my dad.

The holidays for us after Laura passed were lonely, and we missed the rest of our unit. But we did always have each other, and we could get through anything together.

I always struggled with finding good gifts for my father. He was actually quite hard to please in that department. I wanted this Christmas gift to be extra special. He had gone through so much change himself, and I could tell this time of year would be difficult for him as well.

One evening, I saw a clip in my news feed on Facebook, and it was called "Alive Inside." It showed a man with dementia so severe he could barely communicate. It seemed that he had lost his light and checked out. The video explained how dementia or Alzheimer's did not affect the part of the brain that recognized music memory.

A social worker named Dan Cohen took it upon himself to get iPod Shuffles for dementia patients and loaded them with their favorite music. A nurse put headphones onto the man's head. Big band swing music began to play, and his eyes immediately lit up. He started being aware of his surroundings. Then he began moving to the music, fully engaged in what he was hearing.

When asked if he like music, he responded, "I love music, I love the sounds." It was very unusual for this man to ever talk or answer questions, and clearly hearing his music had made some incredible changes. If even for a moment, it was a beautiful thing to witness.

I proceeded to watch the entire video on you tube; I was able to see several others come alive as well. Their memories would start to come back as the music played. I couldn't help but cry happy tears, and I knew it would be the perfect gift for Dad.

I grew up listening to his jams as a kid, so I was very aware of what he liked. After the iPod shuffle arrived, I loaded it with artists like Huey Lewis and the News, Frankie Valli, and the Four Seasons. I added the Commodores and some Native American flute music. I couldn't wait to give this to Dad and see him light up with memories of the past.

This time of year was incredibly busy for me. I had taken a break from my yoga teacher training after the split with James. Not only was I not in the right mindset, but every time I tried to practice, I couldn't do so without crying. I had to set up a time to explain to my teachers what had happened. They were completely understanding and allowed me to finish later in the year.

Depending on the practice, yoga can stir up many emotions. Connecting your breath to your movement can release pain stored in the body. The breath can then assist you with opening up energy centers, or chakras.

The human body is said to have seven chakras starting at the base of the spine that connect all the way up to the crown of the head. Each one of these chakras runs on its own vibration, through the intention and breath and movement that can be activated and aligned.

Native American people associate the chakras with our creature teachers, or animal guides. We understood the animals are our teachers, and that we can learn a great deal from observing them in their natural habitat.

The eagle represents the crown chakra, for his ability to see the whole picture. The mountain lion represents the third eye, for his wisdom and openness to learning the lessons of our ancestors. The throat chakra can be an individual's personal power animal, one that teaches you to honor your gifts with courage, while staying humble. Wolf is our heart chakra, for his ability to love and nurture this community. Bear represents our solar plexus, for his strength in standing alone, and his understanding of forgiveness. Badger is our second chakra, and he teaches us the power in the vulnerability of life and it sacredness. Mole is our root chakra, and he understands the alchemy of the earth and honors our Mother planet.

Yoga is great for physical exercise, but its true intention is to connect with whatever fills your heart space and to utilize the breath with an understanding of the mind-body connection.

I finished up my two-hundred-hour yoga teacher training that fall, and it wasn't easy to do my practice at first. But after several classes, I was able to find healing within my practice again. The tears that came during that time were healing tears.

I had never expected I would become a yoga teacher, but I figured it would be a good complement to my health coaching practice. And I was proud of myself for what I had accomplished during such a difficult time in my life.

Christmas came too soon, and even though I wanted to be alone, I had to spend time with Dad. Don't get me wrong—I wanted to spend time with him, but I preferred to be alone while feeling emotional, and the company of my pooch Jackson was really all the comfort I needed. My friends of course always gave the invite, but I knew it was best to keep it low key, and I didn't want to be a burden on them in some way.

Christmas Eve morning, I took my time to roll out of bed. It had snowed overnight, and the city was blanketed in fresh powdering goodness. I loved to walk Jackson down by the river; it was morning medicine for both of us. With no one out on the roads, we got to set our path while creating fresh footsteps, one after the next. The stillness the winter brings was undeniably peaceful. I had nowhere to be for a while, and I could take my time and enjoy making new holiday memories.

I found a good place to get closer to the river. I wanted to smudge and pray to the Creator, asking him for strength and letting him know I was listening, I took out my cedar stick and lit one end, starting with the smoke at my feet, and up to my head. I fanned the smoke over my face, and then turned around, taking the smudge down my back and finishing with the back of my heels.

I closed my eyes and said, "Creator, please give me the strength to get through these holidays, and to be patient with my dad. I do trust in your lessons, but my heart is hurting, and I need some comfort."

The steady stream of tears came as I watched the cedar stick slowly burn out. I grabbed Jackson and we headed back up on the trail to finish our walk. We were about fifteen minutes away from home, and Jackson's paws were frozen. He wasn't moving well, and I could tell he had reached his stopping point. He was an old boy, but still possessed so much energy that I seemed to forget, at times. It was similar to my father: I was so used to him being a strong and capable man that I had to remind myself that things were different now.

I was fortunate that Jackson only weighed twenty-eight pounds, and I picked him up out of the snow.

"Okay, boy, I get it. We will be home soon," I told him.

I carried my sweet boy half a mile in that powdery goodness, leaving only my medicine tracks behind. I didn't mind that he needed me, because I understood how much I needed him, too.

One of the few traditions Dad and I shared during the holidays was going to a Christmas Eve movie; he always looked forward to it. I tended to let him pick the movie because I wanted him to have some interest in it. Around twelve-thirty, I arrived back at The Ridge, and Dad came out, once again in dressy casual attire.

I always made the effort to tell him, "You look really nice today, Dad."

He smiled, liking to hear these words. "Thanks, I picked it out myself," he says.

The movie wasn't the real event. It was about spending time together. And I wasn't entirely sure if he fully understood what we watched. It happened to be a very serious murder mystery, but when I asked him about it, I could see he had not fully processed the plot.

After the movie, we headed into the food court to exchange gifts and have a snack.

"I think you are really going to like this gift," I said, as I passed it to him over the table.

"Oh, boy! What could this be?" he responded, removing the tissue paper. He wasn't sure what was, and my dad wasn't a big fan of technology. He was from a different era and liked to keep things simple.

"This is an iPod Shuffle, Dad, and it's filled with some of your favorite music," I said as I put the headphones on his head.

"You know my favorite music, Donell?" he asked.

"Of course I do. I grew up listening to it all the time on our road trips," I replied.

I pressed play and skipped forward to the Four Seasons song "Sherry."

He said, "Wow, this is cool."

I was thrilled and responded, "Dad, go ahead and sing along, if you wish." He started moving around, opening and closing his eyes. The chorus played again, and Dad chimed in.

"Sherry, Sherry baby. Sherry, Sherry baby."

I could see in his face that he was thrilled when he realized he knew the words. We sat there and listened to several songs, each one bringing new light into the room.

It made me so incredibly happy to observe my father reconnecting again with memories of his past. This music was his medicine and made more of an impact on him than anything else we had tried up to his point.

It's said that the first man a girl trusts is her father, which holds true in my case. However, the walls I had built around my heart were nowhere near ready to be torn down. I really didn't trust men at this point, and my father had set a high standard for the qualities I was looking for in a man. Dating was very foreign and unusual to me, since I had been out of the game so long. I went on a few coffee dates that didn't amount to much. I tried a few dating websites, just to see if it was possible to meet someone great that way, but I realized online dating is a huge time sucker, and I couldn't stay on any of them very long.

At first, I tried to meet guys that were totally the opposite of James, gym junkie with big muscles who cared about everything they ate. It didn't take long for me to realize that this type wasn't good a fit for me either.

I needed someone with balance, to help keep me grounded. I had been a fitness junkie myself, and I didn't want to date someone whose entire life was consumed with fitness. I wanted a partner that took care of his mind and spirit as well as his flesh. If we couldn't hold deep conversations about the universe, there was really no point. Perhaps I was being too picky, but I wasn't healed anyhow and was in no rush to be in a relationship.

My girl squad liked to give me a hard time about it, making countless remarks and addressing their personal opinions. I knew it was out of love and concern, but they couldn't possibly understand my perspective. Sure, I gave them a right to have some worry, but I'm a big girl and I can handle myself. I had to learn to keep some things to myself, out of a fear of judgment or unnecessary projection.

Plus, my dad needed me and I only had so much time to nurture anything else. Perhaps the timing wasn't right for either of us. It felt like the old days, when I was just a kid and he was raising me all alone.

I was more than ready for the new year to come, and for all the first holidays without James to be over. We hadn't spoken for several months now, but then I received some past due bills from the house that he hadn't paid, and collections came after me instead. I was infuriated with him and texted him to call me. When we actually had words that day, he denied the past bills and was on the defensive.

I had had enough and lost my shit. For the first time, I screamed at him. "You're a liar, and I'm disgusted by your behavior. I don't believe anything you say, and I hope karma comes for the both of you for what you did to me."

I was crying, full of rage and shaking uncontrollably. I went on to say, "She is a fucking bitch, and I can't believe you told our neighbor I was the one that cheated."

I was surprised that he didn't fight back or hang up. He waited for me to pause and then replied, "I hope that made you feel better." It wasn't in a condescending way. He actually understood he deserved the backlash I had just given, and it calmed me down.

"I do feel better. I needed to get that off my chest," I said.

He agreed to pay the bills that had come, and we hung up the phone.

The new year did bring some new joy into my life. I was anticipating a new position I had been offered to teach yoga and spin, after I completed my training as a yoga teacher. I was beyond terrified to do my first class, because I hadn't gotten to practice teaching much during my certification, even though I was fairly comfortable speaking in front of a crowd, thanks to my father's lessons growing up.

"This will be good for you, Donell," he would always say, while I responded by dramatically rolling my eyes and crossing my arms.

But this was something totally different. What if I messed up? Or the students questioned my teaching ability? They would have to know that I was a newbie, and I didn't want to look foolish.

I had spent most of the holiday season practicing my classes. I would make a timed playlist for exactly an hour. Then I would plan the class from start to finish, pairing each pose with the movement and body alignment needed to complete the flow. I felt overwhelmed. How could I possibly do this for entire hour? I had so many doubts about my abilities as a teacher running through my head. I wasn't accustomed to anxiety, but as the big day approached, I thought my heart was going to jump out from my chest.

The grand opening of the gym had arrived, and free classes were offered that first week to get clients excited about the new year and our concept as a boutique gym. I had agreed to teach three classes a week, one of them being spin on Saturday mornings. I was already so busy at the salon, and not sure what I was thinking, but it was too late to go back now. I arrived to the gym early to greet new clients and add to the buzz everyone was feeling about the new space. I checked the computer to see that my class was a full twenty students. There were even people on the waitlist. I thought, "Oh shit, here we go."

I greeted the students as they were coming in and smudged the room with sage, to bless the space and to give them a sense of calmness. I had to excuse myself for a moment. The anxiety was setting in, and I needed to gather my thoughts in the back broom closet. I closed my eyes and told myself to take a breath and let those nerves go. "What's the worst that can happen?" I asked myself. "So what if you suck? You will only get better with practice."

I walked into the studio and told everyone, "It's time to begin. Please lay on your mats, and slowly come down onto your backs."

I chose to begin class with Native American flute music. I find it very grounding and it used to help me with the insomnia I had during my teen years.

I then instructed them, "As you close your eyes, begin to calm your mind and find your breath. Let go of today's worries, or what you have planned after class. Right now is all we have. Just focus on connecting your breath to your movements."

I paused for a moment then said, "Inhale to the count of four, and exhale to the count of four." As I instructed them how to find their center, I realized how essential it was for me to follow my own words.

Once I felt the tone had been set, I instructed them to raise their arms up over head, pulling their fingertips away from their toes. "Open your heart space," I told them. "And lengthen your spine."

Things were going smoothly so far. I was still feeling nervous about going into the flow, but I had to keep going. I was the teacher.

The class wasn't perfect, but I was proud of what I had accomplished in my first class. Every teacher has their first day, and at least that part was over. For the first several months of teaching, I had to practice each flow and what my cues for the movements were. But it didn't take too long to begin to feel comfortable with sharing my practice, and I began to realize the impact I could have on my students. Never in a million years did I think I would become a yoga teacher, or that my students would in turn become my teachers.

Teaching spin was quite different from teaching yoga. It was loud, and the energy was intense and bold. It was, by far, the hardest form of exercise I had ever endured. Trying to instruct others' movements while doing your own at the same level of intensity was exhausting. But I loved every minute of it. And we had a great time. I stumbled upon a large foam finger and would make everyone stand and sit on its cue. The students found it quite entertaining, and this was just another fun element I added to the class. We had black lights and party lights that could be set on cues to our playlists. This wasn't your typical spin class, this was a party on wheels, and this form of exercise was fun to experience and teach. I even came up with a few themed classes, just to add a little more to the mix. I wore a leotard thong for our eighties theme class, which seemed to go over well. I loved my students and my fellow teachers, and the gym became another family for me.

Anything I could do to stay busy worked for me. If I was stressed or emotional, I always turned to exercise first. I felt strong and limber; I was invincible and I never stopped moving. Exercise became my main strategy to silence the pain and coming to a point of complete physical exhaustion made my feelings easy to ignore.

I started going out a lot to experience the nightlife, something I rarely did as a married woman and had barely experienced even before that. Ronnie talked me in to a girl's night out at the casino nightclub in Airway Heights, just outside of town. No matter what we did, Ronnie was always down for a good time. She was a known and talented singer in town, a songbird and a social butterfly. I lost track of her at times that evening. She liked to meet new people and seemed to see familiar faces wherever we went. I only went out to bars or clubs because I loved to dance. It was the only reason I went out at night, other than to listen to good music.

That evening, I was approached by a man named Dave. He was about five foot eleven, with a shaved head and brown eyes, and I found him quite handsome. Earlier in the night, we had caught each other's attention a few times, and he took the opportunity to come ask me to dance. I really enjoyed his company, and I wasn't used to men ever wanting to dance—from my experience, that is. There was a magnetic connection between us, and I was happy with the distraction. At the end of the evening we exchanged numbers, and he asked, "Can I please see you tomorrow?"

I was pleasantly surprised and replied, "Well, yes, if you would really like to, I suppose."

I gave him a hug and kiss on the cheek goodbye and waited to hear from him the next day. We made plans for him to come over that afternoon, to get to know one another a bit more.

Dave was very shy at first. I wasn't sure if he was feeling uncomfortable or this was his usual behavior. He mentioned that he served in the Air Force and was divorced with two young daughters. I had never dated anyone from the military, or with children, so I wasn't quite sure how things would work out. When he said, "I don't get along with my babies' mother," I had some concern. I didn't need that kind of drama in my life. But the connection we shared was special, and it felt good to be kissed in a way that felt familiar.

After several weeks passed, I would say I was in a bit of a "situationship." It wasn't a relationship, even though he continued to ask for a commitment. I just wasn't ready, and I had seen a few red flags during that time that told me to be cautious. On several occasions, we had made plans, and he would be hours late or not show up at all. I didn't understand his behavior, especially when he told me how much he cared for me and wanted a commitment. So why would he be so flaky and blow me off last minute? I still hadn't met his girls, and I was okay with that. But I did wonder if the negative things he said about his ex were true, and whether he was not the father to his girls I had hoped he was. I chose to ignore that feeling in my gut for a few months, due to the fact that the sex was amazing. Unfortunately, at the time, this feeling of lust and being loved on was overriding my critical thinking. I had shared with Ronnie some of Dave's strange behavior and would call her when I was upset that he was being flaky.

She would respond, "Babe, you're being foolish. He doesn't deserve you."

I knew she was right, but I hadn't had these feelings for anyone since James. After a few months of dating, as his flakiness continued to progress, I came to the conclusion this wasn't healthy for me. I came to find out that he had a drinking problem, and it was to blame for his odd behavior. I assumed it had been a catalyst in his divorce as well.

I told him, "I cannot be a part of this. I have already endured this struggle with my ex."

He begged me change my mind and said, "I will change, and I will stop drinking."

I explained that these were just words, and I had heard them too many times before, with James. My eyes welled up and I tried to stay composed.

"I just can't go through that again. I'm sorry, but this has to end now," I told him.

There were a lot of lessons that came out of the romance I had shared with Dave. I realized that I was attracting the same type of man, and I needed to figure out how that was. I knew I needed someone where alcohol wasn't an issue, someone who could put me first. I didn't want to have to fix something about my future partner. Was it too much to ask that they had done the work themselves?

I would like to say that this was the last time I saw or spoke to Dave. But we had a few more rendezvous when I was being weak and craving his touch. I couldn't discuss it with my friends. They really didn't like Dave by that point and knew he wasn't good for me.

We had seen each other only a handful of times over the next few months, but there was little communication. I went on a few dates, trying to move on and move forward. I finally had to put my foot down and tell him to let me be. He made several attempts to reach out, but I had finally come to a place where I understood what I wanted and what I deserved. Dave was both a lesson and a gift, and I was ready for that chapter to finally close. It was time for me to put my energy into other passions in my life, and to finally say goodbye to that toxic situationship.

I left that drama behind me and focused on my fitness classes. I was getting a following of regular students at the gym and I couldn't have been more thrilled. I had also completed my first half marathon in 1:42:46, and had done quite well in my races prior, placing in my age bracket and feeling very strong. One of my other favorite activities is obstacle racing. I had completed the Tough Mudder, an eleven-mile military obstacle race, in the top five percent two years before and qualified for the World's Toughest Mudder but wasn't able to make the trip.

The Dirty Dash was coming up that week in Spokane, and I had planned to run it with a group of girlfriends. We had the perfect setup, with close access to Riverside State Park only fifteen minutes out of downtown. The girls liked to wear matching shirts and then go to lunch and grab a few drinks after. Our shirts this year read "RUCK FUNNING," which was quite hilarious, and the announcer ushered us to the front to start the race that morning.

We set off in the mud, and it was time to go. We began trekking through the mud and heading down a trail to our first set of obstacles. We came upon a rope course, which was easy, and then crawled under and through a few more obstacles. I had always been a competitive person, and I like to run fast. The girls knew at some point I would be running solo, and they liked to do it for fun. So at mile two, I waved them goodbye, planning on finishing the rest of the course at a fast pace. I was feeling great, with my runner's high kicking in as I passed mile five. The obstacles were far easier than the ones at the Tough Mudder. I had reached the last obstacle, a rope you climbed to the top of an inflatable slide, and at the bottom was a large pool of muddy water that came up to your knees.

I made my way down the slide and was standing with my legs locked in the water. At that very moment, a woman came crashing behind me, and I stopped her movement with her foot crashing into the back of my calf muscle. I immediately knew I was fairly injured, but I had to finish. I struggled to get out of the pool to cross the finish line. I'm wasn't sure what to think, but I knew it wasn't good. I had to wait for the other girls to finish before I could leave or do anything about my injury. Having a high pain tolerance can be both a blessing and a curse, and for now, I choose to ignore it. The girls finished about thirty minutes later, and I mentioned my mishap, but I could still walk for now.

After the race, we headed to have our celebratory lunch and drinks in our muddy clothes. I didn't want to ruin our plans, and I also didn't have my car available at the time. Approximately two hours after the injury occurred, I was finally home. I took a much-needed shower and rested for the remainder of my evening. Going to bed that night, I prayed and hoped that this was nothing serious and that I would feel much better in the morning.

Around seven-thirty a.m., I opened my eyes. I took a deep breath, feeling nervous to take my first steps out of bed. I slowly removed the covers, placed my feet on the floor, and took a few steps. I immediately collapsed to floor in agonizing pain, tears streaming down my face. I knew then that my injury was serious.

My poor dog Jackson needed to be taken outside to go to the bathroom, but I felt paralyzed with pain at the moment. I had to take a few deep breaths before I could gather myself and stand up again. I slowly hobbled onto my opposite leg and took the elevator, avoiding the stairs, and took Jackson outside. Thoughts raced through my head. How am I going to teach classes like this? Or even stand all day at the salon, for that matter? Feeling an overwhelming sense of hopelessness for a moment, I realized I had no one to help me with my day, or with Jackson either. I needed to figure out how bad this was, and to devise some sort of plan.

The pain and the ability to walk was not getting any better after a few days, and my stubbornness finally wore off. I made an appointment to go to the doctor and learned that I had torn my calf muscle, and there was not much that can be done. But if I stayed off of it and limited my movement, it would heal in time. I had to find subs for all my classes, and I got a compression sleeve for my left leg for while I was standing at work. I wasn't used to not being active, and I began to realize how much I depended on exercise for my emotional wellbeing. For now, I couldn't use exercise as my crutch to deal with my emotional baggage, and, of course, that's when I had to face James and Nikki for the first time.

I knew it would eventually happen, and that I would run into Nikki and James in public at some point. I just didn't want to be alone. During countless nights of not sleeping, I had planned what I would say to the both of them when we came face to face. I would hold my space and look them both in the eyes and I would express, "How could you both do me this way? I loved you both. I hope that karma comes around, because you will never understand how deeply you hurt me."

And perhaps they would say, "Sorry we hurt you. We didn't mean for this to happen."

Do people even really believe it themselves when they say those words? And would it make me feel any better about what happened? I thought to myself.

As I pulled into my favorite grocery store, I saw James parking his Jeep, with Nikki in the passenger side and my Rottie, Apollo, in the back. I missed my big boy. His tongue was sticking out, panting in excitement and looking so happy to be on an afternoon drive. I never got to see him after the divorce; this was the first time I had seen Apollo in almost a year.

I felt overcome with an assortment of emotions stirring up from deep inside me. Was I ready to see them face to face? And did I really need those groceries badly enough to face these two monsters? For a moment I thought about leaving, and just removing myself from this possible confrontation. But it occurred to me that this was bound to happen at some point. And perhaps I just need to get it over with, and so I devised a plan.

I thought it would be best to get in the store first, so they could see I was there. And perhaps they might leave, and I would know then that I had held my ground.

I anxiously waited up front by the deli, pacing around, knowing they would be strolling by any minute. My stomach was in knots, my heart was beating fast, and I felt anger as I imagined seeing them together. My hands began shaking as if I had just had a shot of adrenaline. I was on pins and needles, with my mind racing through countless scenarios in a matter of minutes, to see how the first confrontation of the three of us would play out. I noticed that James came in by himself. He was still looking slim and sporting her stupid haircut. He beamed to the back of the store where the alcohol was located, the furthest section from me. I thought, "What the hell, where is she? Obviously, they know I'm here. Is she just not coming in?"

After about five minutes passed, I saw Nikki, looking straight ahead and moving as if she was on the same mission as James. Her hair was in a messy bun, looking rather greasy, I might add. But she liked that for some reason, and I didn't ever get that. It was obvious they didn't want to face me and were hiding in shame, I assumed.

I proceeded down each aisle carefully, like a stealth wild animal on high alert for any possibility that lurked around the corner. I dialed my girlfriend Grace. I needed support and wasn't sure what I was capable of.

When Grace answered the phone, I blurted out, "Babe, OMG, Nikki and James are here at the market, and I'm freaking out and don't know what to do."

She gasped and replied, "Oh no! I'm so sorry, babe, I wish I was there with you."

I told her they were avoiding me, and I was feeling so sick from being in such close quarters. Grace understood my dilemma and offered support

"Babe, just do you and never mind them. If they can't face you, then let them hide in shame. Call me when you're done and let me know how it goes."

I felt some relief after our short conversation and made my way over to the produce section. At this point, I had walked by them at a distance, but they remained with their backs turned, mesmerized by refrigerated alcohol. I kept thinking they would turn around, but they didn't, and it was obvious this was a waiting game—one where they were waiting for me to leave. I began to get angrier, and bad thoughts of revenge circled around in my head. I glanced down at some large grapefruits and oranges, and imagined picking one up, and launching it directly at the back of their heads. Maybe then I would have their attention, and they would have to face me. Perhaps a full-on food war would commence, between us and any other produce within range, followed by a screaming match.

I would shout, "How could you steal my husband? You fucking bitch!"

The other shoppers would stop dead in their tracks to watch the drama unfold. James would jump in and try and stop us from fighting, and then we would be asked to leave and kicked out of my favorite market.

I took a few minutes sorting out the pros and cons of these possible aggressive acts of fruit violence. I wished I had the balls to react that way, to not care about embarrassing myself or about what the possible repercussions could be. But what was I fighting for anyway? James chose her, and I couldn't let them get the better of me.

I needed to walk away with grace, and to know that I held my ground and was ready to face them if they had the guts to face me. It was time to check out and remove myself from this heavy energy. The checkout gal knew James and me quite well from being regular customers. She could tell something was going on, and mentioned, "Isn't that your husband back there? I saw him come in. And that other chick that's with him now was waiting outside in the parking lot for a while before she came in."

I said, "Yep, that's my ex-best friend that he left me for. Now they are hiding together back there, so they don't have to face me."

She gave me a look and I knew she understood the foul play here.

I walked out of the market and made my way a little closer to their car. I wanted to see Apollo, but I didn't want him to see me. I was afraid he might try to get out to greet me. And not being able to pet him would be sad for both of us. The first confrontation was over, and I suppose it was a good thing. It could have gone far worse than it had. No words were said, but I felt a great deal of heartache seeing them together as a couple, as if I had never been part of their lives and the relationships we had built meant nothing to them. He remained the bunny, being scared of any possible confrontation, and she the fox in hiding from the deceit and mess she had created.

When I'm feeling emotional, I tend to dream even harder, and about a week following that incident, I had a really vivid one. I was around the age of twelve, when I had long black thick hair and a heavy fringe. It was a normal afternoon and I was relaxing in my childhood bedroom, watching TV. Some distracting thought popped up in mind and told me to get up and walk over to the mirror. The mirror itself was very heavy, framed in wood and hanging above an old dresser made of oak. I took a moment to really look into this mirror. I saw myself, but it was not my reflection. It was another me.

She stepped out of the mirror and said, "I thought I would mirror you, so it's easier for you to understand what I'm saying."

This made sense, I suppose, of coming to a deeper understanding of one's self as told to me by my other self.

In this space, it felt like time didn't exist and I was in some parallel universe that would only last for a special window, then would be lost. My other self guided me to another mirror and said in a profound way, "If you look hard enough, with your heart and not your sight, you will see Creator in here."

I wasn't expecting a moment like this ever, and I wanted so badly to understand her message clearly. I looked deep into that mirror, as if it was the window to my soul and held the understanding of everything that is. What I remember seeing in the mirror was the earth, our Mother's soil, plant life, the rock ancestors and the living things within our ecosystem that provide life. There was a desert landscape with the richest red dirt, a variety of succulents, and, off in the distance, magnificently formed rocks that appeared as mountains. I became overwhelmed with the intensity of the vibration of energy, providing a passage for the light within my spirit to be fed and nourished. I remember the air smelled almost slightly sweet but mixed with the plant medicine that grew there. With each continued breath, I felt some healing, while connecting to my ancestors and my family who had passed. The life force in this space was igniting all my senses and taking me back home.

She gave me some time to feel this connection, and then told me it was time to leave and guided me back to the original mirror. She explained her experience of the afterlife thus far, and the countless options of alternate realties in the afterworld. She allowed me to ask one question only, before it was time for us to part ways and me to wake up. I spoke from my heart and had only one real concern about the afterlife and my part in it. I asked, "When I cross over, will I get to be with my mother and sister again?"

She replied, "I don't know. It all depends."

I woke up that morning feeling perplexed about what my subconscious had created. What did this message from myself mean? And unfortunately, upon awakening, the details of the dream began to fade fast, and I was losing the dialogue of what she had said about the afterlife. This train of thought, leaving as quickly as it came, saddened me. I was hoping to hold onto the words she had shared during our moment in time. And how could I find my family in the afterlife, if, as she said, it all depends? I wasn't sure to what to make of this dream, but I hoped it would circle back around and offer more guidance.

During this time, I was also constantly dreaming about Nikki, still struggling, not just with the loss of my husband, but the loss of a trusted girlfriend that I had thought loved me.

The series of dreams about Nikki began with me trying to hurt her and yell at her with restricted movement, as if she had a force field around her. I became incredibly frustrated that I couldn't confront her, not even in the dream world. Those dreams eventually turned to violent outcomes. I would see her somewhere out in public and attack her, as if I was a predator and she was my prey. I did whatever I could to verbally and physically break her, and it felt really good for a while. Sometimes, I would wake up drenched in tears, feeling the pain of expressing my hurt and the deep wound of betrayal that haunted my subconscious. For a while, it felt good to let out my aggressions and to release the buildup of emotions that left me broken at times.

It took me about a year to realize that, if I was going to ever heal, I needed to find some peace. I understood that Nikki and I would never our have face-to-face closure, nor would she ever one day say she was sorry. The dream world was my only chance at finding forgiveness and some healing from what had happened between us.

Once I began to process that it was time to try and forgive, my dreams began to shift in another direction. I remember being at some kind of open market and seeing her off in the distance. She saw me and came right over to hug me. I didn't understand why she was behaving this way. I didn't really hug her back but allowed her to wrap her arms around me. The second dream was in the city on a busy street full of people. We saw each other again, and this time, I approached her. A deep sadness came over me. I saw for a moment the best friend she once was. I told her how she had hurt me, and I didn't understand how she could do me this way. She looked as if she understood, and felt ashamed of how things had come about, but said nothing. I then choose to give her a hug, and said, "I'm working on my healing, and I need to forgive you in order to move forward."

I woke up shortly afterwards, my cheeks covered in salty tears. But this time, it felt different. These were healing tears, and I found some peace in forgiving her in my dreams at last. I knew then what I had to do to fully heal. I had to make some effort in this reality. That morning, I decided to collect my thoughts and write them down. No time like the present, I thought, and I wanted to move forward. I was ready to send this text:

> I don't hate you, but I don't love you. I am at a point in my life where I'm ready for some closure. I am going to try and forgive you, so I can find some peace in my heart. I don't expect a response, I just needed to take this first step towards healing.

I took a really big deep breath and hit send. This was the first and only attempt at any communication from either of us. I felt some weight had been lifted off my shoulders. And I honestly hoped that she wouldn't respond, because I had no idea how to handle whatever she had to say. If she said she was sorry, I wouldn't have believed her, but even a glimpse of her showing she had once cared for me would have been appreciated. Sending that message freed me of some of the emotional baggage I had been carrying over the last year. It felt right with spirit, and that was the best I could hope for at that time.

The next day, I had an adjustment with my chiropractor, Kathy. She wanted to check on my injured calf, and I wanted to share the news of my new healing. Kathy meant the world to me. We met two years back at the gym doing regular workouts together. When the divorce went down, she really stepped in to nurture my broken heart, and she felt like a mother figure. Over the course of a few years, we had already become incredibly close. I looked up to her as a mother, a doctor, and, overall, a well-balanced human being. She became my turtle medicine through her continued nurturing ways and her patient disposition. Kathy had the blondest and curliest short hair, and her active lifestyle made it impossible to guess her age. She was naturally intuitive, and I preferred to come to her when seeking advice about anything I might be struggling with.

I lay down on the table and, as she began to access my body, I relayed the message I sent to Nikki. I could see in her expression she was pleased.

"Wow, that's great that you were able to do that. And I'm really proud of you. Did she respond at all?" Kathy asked.

She turned me onto my side to adjust my spine, and I replied, "It felt really good, and I'm okay with never hearing back from her again. I did this for me and my healing process."

After she finished up the last adjustments, she said, "Yes, dear, that was for you. Please continue to take good care of yourself. Your leg still needs more time to heal. No running just yet."

I gave her the typical sigh you give your parents when you know they are right. We hugged goodbye, and I told her I would come to visit soon. I left her office feeling so incredibly grateful for that relationship. She was the fourth mother figure of my life. It's funny how Creator always seemed to find a way for the right people to find me and fill those roles.

Since my body needed more rest, and since I couldn't express my emotions through a physical form, I decided to think back to my father. I saw the magic that music had brought back to him, and the healing that occurred when he realized memories of his past. Our ailments were different, his being a continued loss of freedoms that came from his dementia, which also affected his physical abilities. I was injured for only a period of time and would not be able to access my physical outlets. That perspective opened my eyes quickly, and I got over feeling bad for myself, and my current situation. I went home that day, sat back on the couch, and elevated my leg. I spent the rest of that afternoon listening my music, being present, and allowing a space for the music medicine to work its course on me, as it did for him.

CHAPTER 5
Storytelling Medicine

A MONTH PASSED, and I was still nursing my injury, but I could go for longer walks. I was teaching yoga but doing very limited movements and being very careful. I remembered I had already signed up for the Lulu half-marathon in Vancouver, Canada, in August with some girlfriends. I knew I couldn't do the run, but I still wanted to go and see the city. I was able to walk up to four miles by that point and was eager to once again get out of town.

I had planned this trip with Alexandria and Karen, two of my girlfriends in Spokane that are physical therapists. I met the ladies at an all-women's gym, where we liked to do group workouts together. The day of the race I went on a nice walk through the park instead. I was bummed, but I made the best of it and enjoyed the rest the city had to offer. On our last day, Karen suggested we go the Capilano Suspension Bridge Park. She said, "The suspension bridge has views one hundred and ten feet above the forest floor."

We looked at the website and all agreed that it would be a fun way to end our vacation. The bus ran up there quite frequently, so we looked at the schedule and headed that direction. Upon arrival, the place was spectacular. The Douglas firs were two hundred and fifty years old, and there was vast forest as far as the eye could see. We were having a wonderful time admiring the landscape from a different view then we were accustomed to back at home.

In order to get to the treetop exhibit, there was an incredibly long suspension bridge. I observed people crossing for a moment, and realized it had a lot more movement than the ones at home. But we wanted to see the exhibit, and I figured if I took it slow, I would be okay. When I reached the halfway point, I understood I had made a bad choice. My legs weren't feeling stable, and I really had to bear down on my calf to get balanced. After we all made it across, the ladies asked me a few times, "Are you okay?"

I answered, "I hope so," knowing I had made a mistake but still wanting to see the treetop exhibit. I let them go at their pace, and I took my time going up and down a series of brutal stairs. The views were amazing, and I tried to enjoy the experience as much as I could. But I was in a great deal of pain already and had to sit at the base of the treetop while the girls finished the course. On the way back across the suspension bridge, I crossed as fast as I could and took a seat until the bus arrived.

The drive back from Vancouver was quite brutal. I was now not just feeling pain in my calf, but something was wrong with my knee, too. Alexandria had tweaked her hip during the race, and the drive home was really bothering her. We were a mess and tried to find some humor in our injuries, because it was over a six-hour drive home.

I woke up the morning after our trip feeling a hell of a lot worse than I had when we left. I couldn't walk all over again, and I feared that now I had a tear in my knee. I put off going to the doctor for a while, because that's what I do. I didn't have the money to spend, and I felt like if I just babied it and stayed off it, it would get better. But life doesn't slow down for you just because you're injured. And I still had to walk Jackson some and stay on my feet all day at the salon. I took more time off from teaching at the gym. I couldn't risk pushing my luck any further.

When November came three months later, I was finally seeing some progress, and Alexandria had become my regular physical therapist. I still wasn't able to run, but I had some movement back and was ready to try the spin bike again. I was scared, but I started slow, and was feeling strong enough to add more resistance. I fell into that zone, where you begin to sweat and those feel-good endorphins are released. I became excited and was thrilled that my injury was over and I would get my movement back and could teach again.

The next day when I went back the gym and hopped on the bike, I was still feeling okay from yesterday. This time was different, though—about halfway through, I felt a sharp pain in my knee, and I stopped the workout. I had the feeling something wasn't right and I needed to back off. When I woke up the next day and took my first steps, I once again collapsed to the floor. It felt like my entire left leg from the knee down had been ripped open. I cried harder than I had ever cried previously, and the pain was almost too much to bear. I had to use the side of my bed and dresser to prop myself up to be able to even stand. This was by far the worst of it all. I didn't know what to do at that point. I called and cancelled all my clients at the salon for the day, and it took everything in me to care for my dog. I was accustomed to the elevator and I slid my way down the hall, limping like a gimp, at the slowest pace Jackson would allow.

I had really done it this time. My body was screaming at me to stop pushing and start listening. I spent that winter with little to no progress, and nothing really seemed to help. I had been working with Alexandria on a regular basis doing physical therapy. I even tried a natural injection called prolotherapy with my trusted osteopath, Dr. Lenoue

I just loved Dr. Lenoue. He was on a whole other level of care from any other doctor I had ever met. He was younger doctor and had that "I'm an actor playing doctor on TV" image about him. Not that he wasn't professional mind you—he was just really young and didn't fit the typical doctor mold. I first met Dr. Lenoue when I saw him at the yoga studio doing his practice as a student. Then, months later, during the spring of my yoga teacher training, he came to give us a lesson in anatomy. During that class, he shared a lot of his personal story of life struggles, and it struck a chord with me. I went to see him when I became frustrated with my injuries and knew he would have a few more natural options.

He said, "We can try prolotherapy. It's a natural injection of sugar water. It will cause the tissue to reinjure, but then the fascia will lay down more smoothly and heal better."

I totally trusted Dr. Lenoue. His energy was always so positive and reassuring that I knew I was getting the best care possible. The injection went into several hot spots around my knee and down the inside of my leg towards the shin. I didn't feel much pain initially, and he mentioned, "Rest as much as you can. The next few days, it will be really swollen."

After I left his office, I had to work some, and I surely regretted that choice. My left leg became so swollen and stiff that I had to walk like a pirate with a peg leg. I had no bend in my knee whatsoever, and I took any moment I could in between clients to sit down. I only stood when I had to at work and would ice and elevate any opportunity I had.

I prayed to Creator to heal my body and give me my freedom of movement back. I expressed that I understood I didn't honor or listen to my body and took my movement for granted. I just wanted to move without fear and do the activities that made me grounded.

In order to keep my depression at a minimum, I had to continue to find other outlets and ways to feed my passions. Public speaking was something my father had always encouraged. He felt that it made you a stronger individual to present yourself in front of a crowd. I had been asked to speak about using food as medicine at a few public events that were coming up. The one I was most excited for was speaking before Native youth at one of their upcoming conferences. I knew this passion for sharing knowledge of my struggles with food growing up served a bigger purpose. And I did love working with clients and families through private sessions. But I still hadn't found my niche until the day I walked into that classroom and met with those students.

I arrived at the conference center thirty minutes early and found my way to the classroom I would be speaking in. I wanted to have time to display some super foods, books about holistic nutrition, and a few of my essential oils. The students had the option to choose what topics sparked their interest and could decide what classroom to attend. I was pleased to see around fifteen students enter my classroom and take a seat. From the looks on their faces, I could tell they were surprised to see all my tattoos, which captured their attention right away.

I knew it was something I needed to address right away when I introduced myself, so it wouldn't be a distraction.

"Hello, students, my name is Donell Barlow, and I am a certified holistic health coach. I am here to speak with you today about using food as medicine and answer any questions or concerns you might have about nutrition. Please feel free to raise your hand while I'm speaking and ask anything health related. As for my tattoos, yes, they are real, and yes, they hurt. Tattoo-related questions can be answered after the seminar is over. Thank you for coming to listen to me speak, and hearing what I have to share."

I became the Storyteller for these students and I wanted to begin with the history of our people and how our decline in health began when the colonizers came to our land. We were forced onto reservations and only allowed to eat what they gave us. Our traditional foods and ways of hunting were forbidden, and replaced with sugar, lard, and white flour. Our people became sick. This was not the fuel our Creator had intended to nourish our bodies. We did not just lose our foods, we lost the songs and the prayers that came with those traditional ways. I wanted the students to understand what our ancestors had endured, and that it was a privilege to have access to these foods once again. Some of their grandparents suffered this horrible fate, not to mention everything else that happened during that time.

I then began sharing my own experiences with food, and how I didn't feel well a lot of the time. I hoped by being vulnerable with my story, some of the kids would open up to ask me some questions. I was pleased when a few found the courage to express their concerns for family members suffering from diabetes. I was able to offer that history from where it started, when our diet was dramatically changed, followed by some helpful tips for cooking at home. Others were interested in my experiences with using essential oils at home, in my cooking, as well as creating custom scents for a variety of ailments. I passed them around the room and wanted them to take in the medicine, to have a better understanding of how all our modern medicine is derived from plants. The knowledge that our ancestors had with the earth was a gift, and they understood the relationship between all living things. If I could change the way they viewed food, and the type of relationship they had with it, I was sure that I could make a healthy impact.

Before class was over, I had a few questions from some of the adults that were supervising the kids from the back. One woman in particular mentioned she had little time to cook, and really wanted to eat healthier, but struggled with time management and the cost of healthy ingredients. I well understood this struggle in Indian Country and other places that don't have access to some of these resources. I advised her to support any local farmers in her area, and that I would send her some of my personal recipes that would meet her concerns. She was happy with my response, and then asked "Are you Don Barlow's daughter?"

It made me happy that she recognized either the resemblance or the genetics. I was happy to oblige her. "Why, yes, I am," I said, "And very proud of it, too."

We both smiled, and I concluded the class and thanked everyone for attending and mentioned a Part Two would be available tomorrow.

One of the boys who mentioned he was just getting into bodybuilding and was looking for more sources of protein that weren't from meat sources, came up to me after class. He was happy to share his experience, and said he planned on coming back tomorrow. I gave him a brand new bag of quinoa I had purchased for the seminar. It's not a cheap or an easily accessible item, but I thought he could use it more than myself.

"I would like to offer you this quinoa. It has more protein than any other grain, and it cooks really fast. It's easy to make for savory dishes, and also can be used for breakfast instead of oatmeal."

He was thrilled and expressed his gratitude after I handed him the gift.

I had a teenage girl, along with what seemed to be her best guy friend, waiting for my free attention. She asked me more about the oils and explaining how she suffered from anxiety and needed an easy way to calm down. I offered her the lavender bottle I had on hand.

"I want you to have this. Just rub a small amount on your wrist. Then breathe the aroma into your nose while closing your eyes. I assure you this medicine will help calm you down."

She immediately hugged me, and then asked for a picture of the two of us. Then I spoke with the women that had recognized me at the end of class. Her name was Debbie, and she shared that she had worked alongside with my Dad, bringing better education opportunities to Native students way back in the day. She said that all the women admired my father, for it was rare to see man step up to be a single parent in those days. She was pleased to see that I was following in his footsteps. We exchanged numbers so that we could connect again, and she invited me out to the Nespelem Community Center to work with the kids and other programs.

I started to believe I got more out of this seminar then the kids did. I left that day understanding where I needed to focus my gift on. The kids seemed to gravitate towards my ways of storytelling, and it felt like I was making a difference.

I couldn't wait to tell my father about the class, and how excited the students were to learn what I had to share. Plus, he loved it when anyone asked or mentioned in passing that they knew him; it always made him feel special.

Relationships and roles within them continued to change as my father's dementia progressed. I would pick him up for our weekly coffee dates, hoping he remembered the plans so I didn't have to search for him. He so loved going to his favorite Starbucks and sitting down to visit, while people-watching the other customers. As he observed them, I took those moments to observe my father. He was more playful and childlike. His eyes would light up if he received any attention from a little one around. I hadn't really seen this side of my father before. This was a different man that stood before me. A kind man, still, just different than how he raised me. He became more open to other spiritual belief systems, and I was able to share my experiences and knowledge of our Native spirituality. He started smudging with me and wanted me to evoke the Storyteller and speak about the creation stories of our people and how we perceive our connection to Creator.

His favorite story to date was a creation story told by the Iroquois, of a time long before the world was created and there was an island in the sky.

> The Sky people lived here and were happy, living a peaceful existence. However, Sky Woman had become pregnant with twins and the sun had not been created yet, so they lived in darkness. She asked her husband to "tear up the center of the island, where this particular tree was providing light." He ripped the tree out to reveal a hole that allowed the waters of the earth to been seen by Sky Woman. She peered down the hole in curiosity and fell through, falling towards the earth. Two birds rushed to her aid and caught Sky Woman, bringing her to safety. The other water animals pitched in to help Sky Woman soften this fall, providing whatever they could to protect her from any harm. There was no land for Sky Woman to walk upon, so Turtle volunteered to sacrifice himself for the greater good. Frog dove into the water and came up with mud in his mouth, placing it on the back of Turtle. Then all the animals collectively began to spread more mud onto Turtle's back, and it just continued to expand and grow. Eventually it was big enough for Sky Woman to walk upon, and she sprinkled dust in the air to create the stars, the moon, and the sun. Without the help of the animals, Sky Woman would have fallen to her death. We are grateful for our creature teachers for saving Sky Woman. Our creation of earth would not exist, and neither would the

medicines and lessons they teach us. From that, Turtle Island continued
to grow and eventually became the size of North America.

I could see some good things within his dementia that made it easier to understand, and the more patient I could be become, the better for us both.

However, when it came to my personal health, he could never know something was wrong. I had to keep my injuries a secret as much as I could. The dementia made him have anxiety and he would constantly worry about me. And it was easier for the both of us the less he knew, when it came to any bad news on my part.

I would just tell him, "I'm okay, Dad. It's healing and I'm getting better. Don't worry about me."

He always replied, "I'm your dad, Donell, and I will always worry about you."

We accepted those roles, even though it felt like most of the time I was the parent. But I had to let him give me any fatherly advice while he was still able to. It had to feel good to him to sometimes feel like he still played that protector role, and the last thing I would want to do was to take away more of the freedoms he had already lost. I could see the patterns of relationship to memory and connection to one's self for our life's purpose. As his memories continued to fade, his interest in things he once valued slipped away, too. He wasn't being very active anymore, and lost interest in the outside world. I alone became his world, and he looked so forward to any time we spent together.

The holiday was around the corner, and I was dreading yet another year of feeling that loneliness without James's extended family in my life. I always looked forward to all the trouble that Lori would take to make the holidays special. I didn't grow up with much of that, and after Laura passed, I had really none of it at all. Lori loved to decorate her entire house. In every nook and cranny, there was a sign of Christmas. We would feast like kings at brunch, followed by opening presents and playing board games. She loved family, and it was a guaranteed day that we would spend a lot of quality time together. I was blessed to have thirteen Christmases like this, even though it was painful to see it end. I understand that some people on this earth never experience a single holiday this way, and I was grateful for that special time in my life that felt like family again.

The first Christmas without his family had been the hardest, and I was hoping it would get easier each year. I hadn't seen or communicated with Lori much since the divorce. Things were too messy, and the distance was necessary. But I really missed her, and this time of year was when I thought of her the most. This Christmas came early for me, because I received a message from Lori that gave me some new light. She mentioned she had made her famous granola, which I was addicted to and looked forward to every year.

She said in her text, "I have some granola for you. I can stop by the salon and drop it off."

I replied immediately, "That would be lovely. I will be here all day."

I was feeling anxious but excited. We hadn't seen each other for over a year. I was working on a client when she came in and excused myself to greet her. We looked at each other just like we used to, and she wrapped her arms around me. I had to hold back the healing tears that wanted to surface during this long-awaited embrace.

"It's so good to see you. I wanted to drop this off to you because I know how much you like it," she said, handing me the tin full of goodness.

"I love it, Lori, and I really appreciate you making the trip to bring it to me." There was so much I wanted to say, but it wasn't the right time or place. But we both knew the love was still there, and our relationship was still special.

"I should let you get back to work. I hope you and your dad have a nice holiday," she said, getting ready to head out the door.

"Thank you, Lori. Tell the family I wish them well, and a happy holiday."

It took me a moment to come back to my current reality, and to get back to my client. This was a gift that I wasn't expecting, and I felt some healing after that day. I knew Lori could still be in my life, it would just take time and be a little different from what either of us were accustomed to.

I used the winter months to reflect on my healing and tried to find other ways to find some closure. The exchange I had had with Lori stirred up some of the past, and I went to bed processing everything that happened. Once again, going back into my dream world, looking for some possible answers or finding some peace of mind, I had another vivid dream.

I remember it was daylight, and I was inside a house I had never seen before, constructed from several natural materials. Glancing out the window, I could make out that the home was located in the middle of the woods. The pine trees were vast and abundant, with few neighbors around, if any. James was sitting next to me on a couch in a living room, and we were in the midst of a conversation. The mood was strange, and I wasn't sure what to make of it or why I was there in the first place. This was clearly James's and Nikki's home, and I felt uncomfortable being in the fox's hole.

I could tell James's heart was heavy and that he had something he wanted to share. He grabbed my hand and said, "I'm so sorry I hurt you, and I want you back."

I couldn't believe what was happening. How in the hell did he think I would take him back, after all the chaos he created? I wanted to yell, but knew time was limited somehow and chose to let him finish.

"I will do anything you ask. Please, can you find it in your heart to ever forgive me?"

He looked deep into my eyes, searching for an answer and anxiously waiting for my response. I had no plan on taking him back, but part of me wanted to hurt Nikki. When he leaned in to kiss me, I allowed him press his lips against mine, and then I kissed him back. I didn't feel butterflies or magic anymore, just his guilt and my suffering from the past. I kissed him in hopes that it would hurt her and whatever type of relationship had formed between them. I wanted their trust for one another to be broken, just like our marriage had been. And I wanted to get caught, so she could finally get a glimpse of the pain that she caused me.

Nikki walked into the room shortly after. I wasn't surprised to see her. Somehow, I knew she was in the house. We exchanged a look, one that felt intense and meant so many different things. This look recognized our past friendship and where we were now because of the choices they had made. Neither one of us spoke, but the look gave us an understanding of what roles we had played, and now she was feeling a part of the betrayal that I had.

I woke up shortly after, feeling all kinds of weird and perplexed by my actions. Why had I felt so strongly about kissing him just to hurt her? Why would my subconscious dream such a thing? I must still be holding onto a lot more anger then I wanted to own up to. My dream world had always been a source of truth. It didn't sugarcoat the hard facts of my psyche, and it revealed what I already knew but didn't want to accept. I had no romantic feelings for James anymore; this dream was about my desire to hurt Nikki. The dream medicine showed me where I was at in my healing, and clearly more work to address these emotions needed to be done.

With the Christmas holiday over came another new year, with the countdown to midnight and me with no one to kiss. It's strange how that tradition came to be, and how I relied on that kiss always coming from James. Now, being single, it meant something different, feeling left out with a sense of jealousy. Not that I wanted to kiss James—the thought of that was quite repulsive to me now. I liked to imagine someone special that understood how I liked to be kissed. A man that knew the dance steps and the art in kissing a woman, in a way she will remember and long for. There is precision timing and a steady but fluid movement of passion involved with the exchange in energy. There is an effort involved, but it shouldn't feel that way. I consider the art in making out essential, and no point in participating if the players aren't connected.

Being in the shallow end of the dating pool gave me little to no hope for love, anyhow. I had dated a few different men over the fall and winter, but it never felt right or natural. I learned more about what I wanted, and what I wouldn't settle for. I hoped to meet someone who was active, but who was also balanced with his time. Someone I could have long, deep conversations with, about the universe and our connection to spirit. And from what I had experienced thus far, those two qualities were hard to find in one man.

I had gotten glimpses of what it would be like to be with different types of men I thought embodied what I was looking for, but none felt right, and my gut knew I was still healing and not ready to nurture a relationship. A few pretended to be connected to spirit, just to get me where I was most vulnerable, all in the hope of making our way between the sheets. They have been referred to as "New Age fuck bois," preying on women by pretending to be in touch with their feminine energy. This manipulation tactic can be very successful and leaves us feeling not just an emotional scar but also a spiritual one. The contrast to that was Mr. Emotionally Unavailable, good at making plans but quick to not follow through. This one would tell me he didn't want a commitment, and I was okay with that part. But then, somehow, that meant not expressing passion when in each other's presence. This type of man left me feeling undesired, or unworthy of something more. And perhaps for me the one who played the most mind games was Mr. Narcissist. He came with some of the best qualities of charm, intelligence, and, from what I experienced, being incredibly handsome. In the beginning he showered me with compliments, made me feel special and like I was worthy, only later to become bored and distant once he got what he wanted and his ego wasn't being fed. He walked with a sense of entitlement and took no responsibility for his own actions. These men were lessons and gifts, moments of excitement and disappointment, all wrapped up into one crazy experience.

Regardless of my experiences with them, I was still carrying my own baggage. I needed to put focus on feeding my passions, and not worry about finding the one or someone to fill that spot just to keep me company. I had to find a way to be happy alone, to love myself without needing the validation from anyone else.

I had been making New Year's resolutions since I was young. I found it was a good way to keep me focused. Granted, most of the list didn't succeed in its completion, but I at least made an attempt to cross several off the list each year.

I went into 2015 with new goals and plans for a great year and hoping for some good results. These were my resolutions.

1. *Stay present and be grateful*
2. *Get back into shape like I was before my injuries*
3. *No new injuries, and listen to my body*
4. *Give back more to my community with volunteering time*
5. *Be more patient with Dad*
6. *Save and book dream trip to New Zealand*
7. *No relationships, don't settle for less*
8. *Grow my health coaching business*
9. *Stay open to all opportunities*

It didn't start off well with number three. I broke my toe and finger during that holiday week, and I started having weird issues with my lower back the following week. My body was clearly telling me something, rebelling against any movement I did. I was back to teaching yoga at the gym but doing limited movements in my yoga classes. I tried to rest as much as I could but had to stand all day at the salon. I wasn't taking Jackson on regular walks. I only had the energy to take him out to use the potty. I felt bad for the little guy, but he was really showing his age and couldn't stay out in the cold too long. I was learning to really love living alone, and Jackson was all the company I needed.

At this time, number six felt like a pipe dream, but it was still worth putting out into the Universe. Since I was a young girl, I had been fascinated with Xena the Warrior Princess and had dreamed of the day I would visit New Zealand. She was a badass, and back then, we had so few leading women being portrayed as forces to be reckoned with. The fight scenes along with the landscape had me hooked, and I knew one day I had to see this place for myself. I was familiar with the book *Eat, Pray, Love*, and I knew if I had that chance, I would choose New Zealand as my place for healing. I wanted to experience the culture, share stories of my ancestors, and be embraced with a whole new environment so different from my own. I understood this dream could not come into reality in my current situation. I didn't have the financial means or the freedom of movement to make it happen—not to mention my father could not go that long without my help and consistent communication. This resolution would have to be set to the wayside for now, but I was determined that, one day soon enough, I would follow it through.

Number four would manifest with my newfound gift of speaking with Native youth about health and wellness. I had big plans in the next year about how to put these plans into action and create something special for the kids.

For the most part, these were realistic goals, and I had every intention on following through. I am a firm believer in the saying,

> What you think you become.
> What you feel you attract.
> What you imagine you create.

I needed to find a creative way to make number eight, growing my health coaching business, take effect. I had a few clients since graduation, working with a few females on specialized eating plans and giving cooking lessons to a few families. I loved the work I was doing and how it could be catered to an individual to fit their needs.

My first few clients were some of my regular hair clients from the salon that had voiced some nutrition concerns, along with health ailments that had been plaguing them for years. After sharing detailed information about their current diet, I was able to better assist them with finding their hidden food allergies. Through a series using the processing of elimination and regular food journaling, we were able to discover the trigger foods that were to blame for the symptoms they had. Hidden food allergies can appear with a huge variety of symptoms, ranging from a variety of stomach issues, skin rashes, and frequent nasal congestion.

I grew up with gut issues, and I understood the toll it takes on your body and how that changes your relationship to food. When that relationship becomes compromised, unhealthy eating patterns arise. This results in a misunderstanding this is the new normal, and not feeling well becomes routine. Those who suffer from frequent pain after eating are not receiving the vital messages the body is sending. Our gut is made up of its own working central nervous system and is very complex when it comes to communication. We have known for centuries that to heal the body, we must first heal the gut. Hippocrates said, "Let food be thy medicine and medicine be thy food," centuries ago. I wanted to share with potential clients the benefits of using food as medicine, along with how I was able to heal my gut and learn to love food again.

When we look into the history of what all our ancestors they ate, it's a commonality that they ate in season and in harmony with our Mother. Before the colonization of this land, my ancestors didn't eat processed food, refined flours, sugar, or alcohol. They lived off the land and didn't take more than necessary to feed their families. What our Mother provided within each season was more than enough for us to live at full vitality. After the colonization began, my people were not allowed to hunt, forage, or gather their traditional foods. As a result, my ancestors lost their foods, along with their ceremonies, prayers, and songs that were intertwined with these sacred foods.

During this time period, many Indigenous people from all over the world were also being affected by colonization and the loss of traditional foods. I learned about such studies through my schooling at the Institute for Integrated Nutrition, documented by Dr. Weston Price. In the 1930s, he was a dentist by trade and began a study that documented the health of the teeth and facial bone structure in regards to specific diets and nutrition of Indigenous people. His goal was to find what type of diets are responsible for good dental health and prevention of disease. During his ten years of traveling across the globe studying different isolated groups, he found the diets of the healthiest participants were consuming four times higher in water-soluble vitamins, and ten times higher in fat-soluble vitamins A & D. These two vitamins are necessary in order to absorb minerals and utilize our protein sources. Each group had what he called "Activator X," found in organ meats, shellfish, and butter. Indigenous people understood the importance of preconceptual nutrition for both parents and made necessary preparations for healthy future conceptions. Dr. Price concluded from his studies the value of these traditional diets and the countless benefits to eating as our ancestors did.

I had knowledge I wanted to share and felt so passionate about helping others understand their own unique nutritional needs. The seminars I held with the Native youth had given me a unique opportunity to really share this information, and I planned to take that concept further. I wanted to help the kids, as well as reaching a broader audience, and make using food as medicine exciting while entertaining. Then perhaps I could grow my business.

When I did have cable, the only station I couldn't get enough of was the Food Network. All the cooking shows had their own unique market and way of putting love into the food. I loved the feeling of being in their kitchen for a special meal, as if we were preparing it together. As I mentioned before, I didn't grow up with many home-cooked meals. Cooking shows had become not just educational, but healing for the young girl who didn't get to experience that family cooking dynamic much.

I do have some fond memories of both sets of my grandparents making some traditional foods for me growing up. My grandma Vera lived in Eureka, California. She was a well-known basket weaver of the Yurok Tribe. I loved staying in her quaint seaside home during the summer months. She would always have lots of crab, shellfish, fresh berries, and my favorite fish, salmon. I remember her saving the fish heads for last and eating the eyeballs as a delicacy. She knew that I loved seaweed and would dry it out just for me in huge batches, not at all like the fancy snacks out now in the markets. Everything about her life had a purpose, and she was never in a hurry. I loved to watch her cook and observe her ways of working with different ancestral foods around her region.

My dad's parents loved to make big batches of traditional corn soup, with deer meat and fry bread. Anytime the whole family got together, they made sure that soup pot was on early. The meat would simmer all day in a rich broth, with a few fresh herbs. Then it was mixed in with heaps of the freshest, sweetest corn, a dash of salt and pepper, and it was like liquid gold to my taste buds. Though not traditional, fry bread was a staple in Native American diet after colonization. And you can find fry bread at most gatherings among Native people today. It's not healthy, but it is made with love. My grandparents had spent years perfecting their dough, and we could taste that difference. It was the fluffiest and lightest fry bread these lips had ever tasted, and I loved to top it off with a little melted butter and honey.

Thinking over these memories, it hit me. I should make my own cooking show where I would talk about nutritional benefits and plant medicine. I could educate my audience about using food as medicine and showcase local food producers. I had always known about the difference it makes when love goes into the food from the experiences I had with my grandparents. In my show, I wanted to put my own unique love language into the cuisine. My love language when cooking came in the expression of dance. Since I was a young girl, I have always had a passion for the arts of dance. I grew up fancy dancing at powwows, followed by a few dance lessons in my pre-teens. I went through a huge EDM (electronic dance music) phase in my teens and still had a special place in my heart for house music. I wanted to bring a variety of viewers into my kitchen and make them feel welcome in my space. My normal routine is to dance while my food cooks, and I hoped a little dancing segment would add some flair and interest to my message. By the end of the day, I had named it Dance Jam Kitchen, and I was beyond thrilled to see this idea play out.

My old buddy Paul, who worked as a freelance videographer, offered his services at a killer deal that was perfect to start the project. I had known Paul a bit from back in those raver EDM days, and we had several mutual friends. He was a bit shy at first. I think being behind the camera so much made him an observer type of personality. Paul was rather tall and a bit husky with a well-groomed beard. He could totally pull off the "lumbersexual" trend that seemed to be going well for single men here. I'm joking, of course, but it is an actual thing in the Northwest.

We met one afternoon to discuss the details and vision I had for the project.

"Okay, so tell me more about what you envision for this first episode, and what are you making," Paul said as soon as we sat down for a cup of tea.

"I want to keep it simple for the first one, and rather quick to make. I'm making chocolate collagen marshmallows," I replied, sipping my tea.

Paul looked puzzled, not knowing what the hell those were, and I didn't expect him to.

"They are delicious and healthy, and something simple that kids can enjoy making, too," I explained.

He looked reassured and replied, "Sounds good. Let's set a date and time for the shoot."

We agreed two weeks later on a Saturday afternoon to meet back at my place to film our first episode.

I spent those few weeks leading up to the shoot perfecting my recipe and getting my kitchen ready for the big day. I loved my open kitchen space. I had always dreamed of a kitchen like this, and it couldn't be more perfect for filming. I had a large oak island with metal shelves in the heart of my kitchen. The counters and the sinks were stainless steel, and the shelves above the counter were a light wood and totally open for viewing, so I wanted to keep it clean and simple. I tried to imagine other cooking shows and their set up. I believe less is more, and I didn't want any extra clutter to be a distraction. I rearranged what I decided to keep up and deep-cleaned every nook and cranny possible.

The big day arrived. I premade the marshmallows the night before, so we could film the end at the beginning and save some time. Feeling nervous about making my idea come to light, I slept poorly in the days leading up to the shoot. I feel pretty comfortable on camera, but this was something new, and I didn't want to look foolish. Paul walked in with his equipment to set up, and I played the song for him I wanted to dance to in the episode. I put on a special apron I had been saving for this occasion, took a glance in the mirror at my mug, and was ready to shoot.

"Start whenever you are ready," Paul said.

I took a deep breath and looked into the camera, to say my introduction.

"Welcome to Dance Jam kitchen. I'm your host, Donell Barlow, and today we will be making chocolate collagen marshmallows. I am a certified holistic health coach that grew up with a lot of gut issues. My goal here to share with you how to use food as medicine by using my simple and fun recipes."

The intro went down fairly smoothly the first time, and after that, everything got worse. We had a lot of laughs and figured we could use the material as bloopers at the end. It was important that I seemed genuine and my message was well received. My true personality needed to come through, in the hope that viewers would appreciate my effort and perspective. Going into the recipe, I began explaining the process of making this fun and easy treat. I wanted to use a local farmer with each episode and was delighted to use a local honey farm for my special recipe. I love using honey in replacement for sugar. It's better for diabetics and has countless benefits. It also helps with seasonal allergies. When you buy local honey, you get the bees in your area that pollinate the food and plant life around you. This farm was special, too. My girlfriend Rose coached boys' soccer and this honey farm belonged to a couple of her players. The kids used the money towards tuition for college, which I was more than happy to support.

"In a large pot, bring a half cup of water and three-quarters cup of honey to a simmer for ten minutes, and continue to stir frequently," I explained while standing over the stovetop. "Then in a small bowl, mix a half cup of water with three tablespoons of quality gelatin, and let it sit for ten minutes."

Everything seemed to be going smoothly and I had some downtime. This was where the dance segment came in. I looked at Paul to cue the music.

"Let's burn some calories," I said.

I did dance few moves while holding my spatula and standing over the stovetop. My knee was still bothering me that day, so I couldn't let loose and get too crazy. But I still did what I could and showed how I put love into my food.

Time for the next step. I added one and a half tablespoons of raw cacao and one teaspoon of Mexican vanilla to the pot and gave it a good stir. Before pouring the hot mixture into the bowl, I added a dash of salt and chili powder.

"Now, let's combine our collagen into the bowl. Using your electric mixer, start on low and work up to high for four full minutes."

As I mixed, I went on to explain the benefits of collagen and why I love to incorporate it into my recipes.

"Collagen can heal the leaky holes in our gut and repair the body's connective tissue. Bone broth is a good example of utilizing collagen and its healing benefits. And all of our ancestors made some variation of this sacred food," I said, while forming the peaks that added lots of air into the mixture. Just after four minutes, it was ready to be spread out in an eight-by-eight-inch pan and laid out to cool overnight. I had previously spread parchment paper in my pan, covered with two tablespoons of crushed almonds and unsweetened coconut.

"Now, you can gently pour your mixture over the top of the nuts, and let it sit overnight. Feel free to use whatever nuts or flavors you like," I said.

I reached for my finished marshmallows from the day before and began demonstrating the next step.

"The next day, when the marshmallows have set, they are ready to be cut. You can use scissors, or make fun cutout shapes," I explained, while letting Paul get a few closeup shots. It was time to close this episode and say my exit.

"Thank you for joining me on my first episode of Dance Jam Kitchen. Sending love from my kitchen to yours."

We wrapped up in two hours and were pretty happy with our first attempt at a cooking show. I had a mess to clean up, no doubt, but I was happy we choose a quick and simple recipe for the first go around.

"I should have this edited and ready to view within the next two weeks," Paul said, while carefully putting away his equipment. Meanwhile, I was busy cleaning up some of marshmallow mess I had created during the show.

"Sounds great. Thanks again. I really appreciate your help," I replied.

We wrapped up, and I couldn't wait to see the finished results. I hoped I didn't look foolish or like I was clearly an amateur. I felt vulnerable putting myself out there like this. And if even only ten people watched it, this project was still a reflection of me.

I received the rough copy from Paul around two weeks later. He said, "Let me know what you think, and if I need to change anything a bit."

I was at work when I got the text and had to wait until in between clients to take a look. My clients have always been supportive of my other passions, and I feel very lucky to be supported by them in more ways than one. I was working on one of my favorite clients at the time, Britney. She had become not just a client but, over the past eight years, a trusted friend. She embodied the crane medicine, one of intelligence, and was very independent. Britney has a very unique perspective, being a philosophy teacher, and I like to ask her opinion. We had known each other through many of life's changes. We tended to share stories during our appointments and check in on life in general. And ever since the divorce, my clients seemed to take a more personal interest in my other life affairs. I mentioned to Britney during her appointment that I had filmed my first episode of Dance Jam Kitchen.

She said, "Oh, wow, I would really like to see it, if you're willing to share it with me." After her appointment, I viewed it with her on my phone, and showed a few of the other girls at the salon. Everyone seemed to like it, but I also knew my support system that loves me would enjoy it regardless. I was proud of myself, but I also saw lots of room for improvement. There were many things I could have done better, but I choose to release it to the public anyhow and see how they took to my message. Can't please everyone, and I know I have to put myself out there if I'm going to try and make an impact with my voice and perspective on using food as medicine.

A few days following the big reveal, I had my weekly coffee date with Dad, and I was excited to show him the project. I picked him up out front the Ridge as usual, but this time he wasn't there. I waited for about ten minutes and then gave him a call, but there was no answer. Sometimes Dad would forget our meetings, and I would have to go search for him in his extremely large and ever-expanding retirement home.

I parked the car way down the street. Due to construction, there was never any parking. I felt annoyed, but this was just how it was, and Dad had a really hard time remembering a lot these days. I walked in and asked the receptionist if she had seen him, she said, "I saw him this morning, but I'm not sure where he is. Did you call him?" she asked.

"Yes, I did. I'm sure I will find him somewhere," I replied and started my search. I went up to his room and just opened the door, because he never locked it anyhow. Dad was known to forget his keys and lock himself out, so he just chose to keep it open. I startled him when I walked in. He had been taking a nap.

"Dad we have a coffee date today, remember?" I said, as he stood up from his recliner chair where he had been snoozing in front of the TV.

He jumped up. "Oh, I must have forgotten. I thought I wrote it down," he said, and looked at his calendar. He was excited to see me, as always, and grabbed jacket—and left his keys, of course.

We walked to the car and headed back to our usual spot. My dad always ordered the same thing, and the employees were used to seeing us. Dad ordered his tall coffee with room for cream, and I got my chai soy latte. I always offered to pay when I took Dad out for these types of things, but he stepped in this time and surprised me.

"I got a gift card that I would like to use for us today, Donell," he said and dug it out of his wallet.

"Okay, sweet Dad," I said, and let him pay the bill.

We made our way to a quiet table in the back that had lounge chairs. It was always our go to if it was available.

"Well, tell me what's new with you," he said.

I mentioned that I had met Debbie at the Native Youth Conference, and she asked if I was his daughter. He was pleased to hear that someone came forward to mention his name, but unfortunately, he couldn't recall the time they worked together. Then I took out my phone to show him the first episode of Dance Jam Kitchen. As we viewed it together, I could see his eyes light up with entertainment.

"Wow, cool. How did you come up with that? You are a pretty good speaker, Donell," he said, with a proud smile across his face.

"I learned how to speak in public because of you, Dad. And teaching yoga really helped too," I replied.

It didn't take much to impress him at this stage in his life. Anything I did, he would make an effort to let me know he was proud of me. I grew up with continued support from my father, and even when I got into trouble, he never turned his back on me. And granted, he took many of the responsibilities I had now to care for him for granted. But I had done the same while he raised me, and it was my turn to take the lead.

One thing he never forgot to ask me about was my injuries. For some reason, it was subject he never forgot.

"Tell me, what's going on with your knee?" he said.

I was still experiencing some sharp pain and wasn't able to do a whole lot other than walking. But it was better for both of us to keep that to myself. I didn't want to worry him or like discussing it, so I gave Dad my usual response.

"I'm healing and doing what I can, Dad. Don't worry about me."

And as usual, he replied, "I'm your dad, and I will always worry about you."

I had to give him that, and at least he was still able to play that part of being my father.

I asked him if he had any fun activities going on at the Ridge, and he mentioned, "They take us on field trips here and there, which are always fun."

I asked, "Oh, where are you going next?"

He replied, "Well, it's a surprise. We don't really know. We just sign up, and then they take us."

I was perplexed by his answer, but he said many odd things that didn't add up, and I just let it go. I just wanted to ask him about his day and what kinds of things he got to do, but with his dementia, he couldn't remember a lot of the time, and I felt bad when he realized it was getting worse with time.

Sometimes, the dementia would allow him to share stories of the past, and what life was like with Mom before I was born. He didn't speak of her a whole lot after she passed, and I appreciated this other side of him. He mentioned that day how he knew she was the one and wanted to marry her.

He began with, "Back then things were different, and your grandfather owned land, along with a farm and small logging company. He and your grandmother spent their days of hard labor up in the Yurok country of Northern California. Your mother and I had spoken about having a traditional Native wedding, so I asked for your grandfather's blessing in a traditional way. I offered your grandfather a goat, as a grand gesture that I was honoring old customs and was dedicated to your mother. This was how I asked for her hand in marriage, and for his blessing."

I was surprised to be hearing this news for the first time.

"Dad, you have never shared this story with me before," I replied. He took a sip of his coffee, and then placed it back on the table.

"Oh, really. Well, things were different back then, Donell, and that was the custom."

It was nice to hear him reminisce about her, and I wanted to know more.

"Did he accept the goat, Dad?" I asked.

He paused for a moment then said, "Nope, he didn't, but he still give me his blessing."

Hearing just this little bit of new information meant more to me than my father could understand. I don't know if he ever realized how little he shared about her with me after her passing. And perhaps it's not the best or most exciting story, but it came through his dementia, which made it even more rare and special. Dad had not been able to remember much about the present, or any future events to come, but somehow, he was still able to share glimpses of the past, and that was the gift I had to take from this disease. This was a day my father became the Storyteller. He shared a moment in time with me that I had never heard. Without that moment, I would perhaps have never existed, so this story for me is of great importance. It became part of my oral history, and one that I would call storytelling medicine.

CHAPTER 6
Traditional Foods

G ROWING UP, MY FATHER HAD RAISED ME like the classic tomboy and fully supported any physical sports I was interested in. Dad came to all my games and got involved in my sport activities any way he could. But over time, it seemed he enjoyed watching my games more than I enjoyed playing them, and that dynamic caused a few rifts and verbal fights between us in my teenage years. He even threatened to not let me drive his car my senior year if I didn't play basketball. Me playing sports became a reflection of him somehow, and I never did really understand why it meant so much to him. The time we spent practicing was bonding, and I was grateful he was involved. In the end, though, team sports just weren't my thing, and I preferred more being active in my own space.

The friendships that came out of my childhood sports teams were the real reason I kept playing, other than to appease him. And many of my friends had single moms, which made it easier for me to play matchmaker. Ever since I was a little girl I had hoped my father would find another mate. I missed having a mother, and I wanted him to be happy and have a special someone to share his life with. My girlfriends and I would devise a plan to set them up and then daydream about becoming sisters, and what it would be like to have our parents fall in love. Unfortunately, these dates always seemed to flop. Dad was overly picky and stuck in his ways. He was hoping to find someone just like my mother, and no one could possibly fill that position. He didn't date a whole lot during my childhood.

His career and taking care of me was his focus.

Regardless of his age now, I still entertained the thought of him finding someone. He was one the younger guys at The Ridge, and definite one of the best-looking fellas.

I asked him, "Any new ladies in our life, Dad?"

I knew there had been a few new ones around during the move. He looked discouraged and replied, "No, Donell, no lady would want to have me now. I wouldn't remember her. It's too late in the game for that."

I knew in my heart he was right, and that finding a mate now would be almost impossible. But I wanted to give him some comfort at the very least.

"Dad, you never know who you might meet at The Ridge. And sometimes a strong friendship is enough. It doesn't have to be romantic."

He agreed that he saw the value in that kind of companionship, and we let the subject rest. I really felt for my dad; he had been alone all those years. My mother was the love of his life, and he just never found anyone that matched up to the bar she set.

We didn't really get into my love life when we spoke, but Dad would occasionally ask me if I had any new love interest. There was no one to speak of, and I didn't share too many details about my romantic life with him anyhow. I still hadn't dated anyone exclusively or felt those special butterflies when you look at someone like they're magic. I was trying to keep to my number seven New Year's resolution: no relationships, don't settle for less.

However, that all changed, when I gave a particular dating app another go, and this time I came across a profile that really caught my attention. Levi was younger than I preferred but still in his late twenties, and I was really attracted to his pictures. I rarely meet anyone on here, but this guy seemed different somehow and a catch. I was surprised that he was in Spokane. Surely, he had to be on holiday and just passing through. We sent each other a few messages, and I could tell right away I would appreciate his conversations as much as his face. Several days later, we agreed to meet for our first date. I wanted to show him what nature the Pacific

Northwest had to offer, and we set a date for an afternoon hike. By now, the winter had come and gone, and spring had taken its rightful position.

I felt nervous the day of the date, and I was anxious to meet him and see how our energy would match up. He came by in the afternoon to pick me up and texted me when he arrived. I came out to the car, and when I opened the door, Levi was playing some dope EDM music, and that was a good sign. I was taken aback at how handsome he was. His pictures did not do him justice. He had these amazing brown soulful eyes, light brown skin, and a nice head of tailored short black hair. He had mentioned in our texts he was of Mexican and Apache descent. All I could see was a yummy mix of something wonderful. The attraction was strong from the get go, and it was clear we could both feel the pheromones.

He drove us to Riverside State Park, which is about twenty minutes from where I live and is my favorite place to go hiking. The conversation was effortless. I liked his energy right away and knew this would be a fun date.

He asked me, "What are some of your favorite EDM jams?"

I loved that we had this in common. "I love so much, but right now I'm really feeling Croatia Squad and Zhu," I replied.

Levi shared some of his favorite jams with me on the way to our destination, and I just sat back and enjoyed his company.

Levi was definitely dressed too warmly for our hike. We both laughed about his choice of attire that day. He was from California, after all, and to him, sixty-five degrees is cold. Residents of the Northwest have a broader understanding of the four seasons, and the spring weather was much colder to him than it felt to any of us. I took us on one of my favorite trails down by the river to get better acquainted. The trail itself is fairly easy. You just have to pay attention to not stub your toe on all the ground-in rocks. It has a few steeper moments, but it's not physically demanding for most. Within ten minutes from where it starts, you can already hear the river, the sounds of the water brushing up against the rocks and descending into shallower pools. When I come here alone, I choose not to listen to music. It's a distraction to whatever messages I need to hear from what's around me, whether it's the river, the animals, or even the plant life.

Levi asked me along the way, "Tell me more about your culture. I don't know much about my Apache ancestors."

I was happy to share, and I always began with my parents.

"My mother was Yurok and raised on the Hoopa reservation in Northern California. My father is Ottawa. His tribe came from northern territories and in Canada. They have been moved and relocated several times, leaving them spread out in Michigan and Ohio. My Otter Clan is in Oklahoma."

Levi showed interest in knowing more about my ancestors, and we continued to dive deeper into getting to know each other. He was very connected to his Mexican roots but wanted to learn more about his Apache history. It seemed we were both really enjoying each other's company, and the time was just flying by. I took him down to a steeper trail to get access to the river. I thought we could take a moment to sit and visit while taking in the view.

Levi asked, "So, how long have you been single? Were you ever married?"

I briefly responded, "It's been two and a half years since my divorce, and I've been single ever since. How about you?"

He quickly responded, "I have only been single for a short time, and I was with my ex for six years."

I wasn't pleased to hear he was recently single. From my experience, that situation comes with baggage, and I didn't want to be a rebound.

I asked, "So what happened with you two?"

He was a bit hesitant to answer, but then he said, "We grew apart, and I went from my last relationship straight into this one. I haven't had time to be single. And I finally plan on just doing me for a long while."

I could understand that completely, but I had just hoped the breakup wasn't so recent. We discussed some of our past, and what we learned from those other relationships. It was refreshing to meet someone that I felt comfortable enough right away to be so open with. Our connection felt natural and not at all forced or awkward. After about two hours of deep conversation, we agreed upon the fact that we were both hungry and decided to make our way back. As we both stood up, we locked eyes, and gave each other that look—the one where you recognize the connection. The look that tells that other person you want to be kissed and are waiting for them to make the first move. However, I never made the first move. It wasn't my style. Instead, I looked deep into his dark brown eyes and sent him messages that I wanted him to lock his lips against mine. He leaned down, wrapped his arms around my waist and gave me a soft gentle kiss on the lips. We both felt our energy connect. and it was intense and familiar. He pulled me in closer and kissed me with an incredible amount of passion. Levi knew my dance; it was familiar and effortless. It lasted only for a moment and felt like magic. I knew this one was different, and that he was special. From the words we had just shared, I understood that he had no intention for a relationship, and that our time together would be limited, considering he lived in California and he was newly single. But I didn't care. Any amount of time we could spend together was worth it to me.

On the way back, we picked up some Thai takeout, and headed back to my place to visit a bit longer.

Levi said, "I do have a buddy that I might have to meet up with later tonight."

I really didn't want him to go. I loved spending time with him.

"I suppose if you have to." I replied.

After our dinner, the kissing got more intense, and the passion between us just continued to grow. We had to hold ourselves back from going too far; it was our first date and we still were trying to get to know each other. Sex always has a funny way of complicating things, and I didn't want to ruin what we were possibly building.

That evening, in between the hard make out sessions, we spent our time sharing our favorite YouTube videos. It gives you a sense of each other's sense of humor and taste level, I suppose. My go-to vids usually consist of dancing, some superhuman physical activity, or animals doing strange or funny things. The time flew by that night with Levi, especially when we just sat there and gazed into each other's eyes. It sounds super cheesy, I get that, but this wasn't just lust. It was energy, and it felt very different from any other man I had met so far. I was quite content just getting lost in the moment, no sense of time, just truly embracing this new vibration of energy I was receiving from our time together.

Needless to say, his buddy didn't need his assistance after all, and Levi choose to stay the night. This was very unusual for both of us, but we didn't want this epic date to come to an end just yet. I had become accustomed to sleeping alone by now, and usually didn't like sleepovers with men I dated. But Levi was different, and I just couldn't get enough of him. Around one a.m., we crawled into my bed, and he wrapped his arms around me, snuggling me from behind. I loved his smell as he drew me in closer to his body. I could feel his body heat, and it felt familiar and comforting. His pheromones were driving my desire to be more intimate with him, but I had to resist. We fell asleep that night with him holding me, and we stayed in the same position the entire night.

I was surprised when I woke up that morning that I had slept so soundly with a new person in my bed. In the past, it had always been awkward for me, getting used to sharing my bed with anyone but James, and I never slept well. I could see that Levi was slowly waking up too, and I leaned into him for some morning cuddles.

"How did you sleep?" I asked,

"Actually, I slept really deep last night, and I didn't expect that," he replied.

"It must be my sacred space," I said, while giving him a soft kiss on the cheek.

"I suppose so, Donell, or maybe it's just you," he said, and returned the soft kiss on my cheek.

The deep eye-gazing started once again, and I rolled myself on top of his body, naked with the exception of his boxers. Then I kissed his forehead, working my way down to both cheeks, and then softly on the lips. He had his hands around my hips, pulling me in tight, then working their way down the small of my back and down to my backside. The intensity of our passion grew, and we found that magical dance once again between our lips. We took it steps further than we had the night before, getting to know each other's bodies a bit better, exploring the feel of one another's skin in a more intimate way. We still had not committed the deed, but every inch of me desired his touch, and I wanted to have the full experience.

Levi pulled away for a second and said, "Are we sure we want to do this?"

I really had no hesitation at this point, just pure sexual desire for him.

"Yes, I want to feel you. I know it's sooner than we should, but right now I don't care," I told him.

From that point, the flame had been lit, and he knew exactly how I wanted to be touched, as if he had done it for years. The passion between us was like nothing

I had ever felt before. This was a different kind of medicine for me, and I was addicted to his touch and his being.

We lay in bed till late that morning, after loving on each other for a while and then sharing some music. I made us some breakfast crepes filled with all the fixings, eggs, some sautéed veggies, and a few strips of bacon. He only had about ten minutes left before he had to leave, so we spent that time dancing and kissing to the new music we had shared the day before. By the time we parted, our date had lasted almost twenty-four hours, but it only felt like minutes. My time with Levi felt like magic, and I couldn't wait to see him again.

Levi had another few days in town before he had to head back to California. And I knew he might still go on some dates while he was here, but I tried to pay no mind to it. After all, he was a recently single man, and I understood that he needed to do his thing. I just hoped he felt our time together was as special as I had felt, and that any other women were not worth the effort and couldn't offer the connection that we had. We had joked around a lot about some of our previous dates and matches and kept the whole situation of dating very light. I had no intention of trying to secure a relationship with Levi. He had made it clear what his boundaries were. But even though I understood his position, I wasn't keen on him going on dates when I was right here, either. I kept that to myself, of course, and gave him enough distance to choose where he wanted to spend his time. We did see each other several more times while he was here. The sensuality of our intimacy grew with each time we exchanged our sexual chemistry, and so did my feelings for him. It was never just sex with Levi. From the start, it felt like something more, and I gave more of myself in an energetic way than even before. I knew he had to leave soon, so I chose to protect my heart for now. He would return in another month to reconnect and hopefully start where we left off.

He texted me somewhat while he was gone, just enough to keep me interested. The main line of communication I could depend on was our love for sharing music. It became an outlet to check in and let the other person know you were thinking about them. With each new song I received, I felt we were still connected somehow, even though we were physically far apart. I reached out in an effort to possibly be included into the life he had when he was back home. I asked to be friends with him on social media, so I could see the whole picture and see if there would ever be any place for me in it. But he had mentioned before, "I don't like social media. I needed to take a break from it, because it was consuming too much of my time. So I got rid of it and plan to keep it that way for a while."

I found that remark quite strange, but I trusted his words. He was a private person when it came to his personal life there, and I figured he would share more as we got to know each other better.

As time passed, my gut continued to tell me something was wrong here, and that Levi remained a little too private. He had an excuse for not responding to texts for a day or so, and since I didn't want to seem too needy, I accepted whatever he told me. When he was here, he would take his phone with him into every room he went, even to the bathroom. Against my better judgment, I continued to see Levi every four to six weeks when he would make his work visits in town. We became incredibly comfortable with one another, and I practically let him live with me when he was staying in Spokane. I had never given anyone I dated thus far a key or even told them the code to get into my building. I trusted Levi, and I wanted him to feel at home when he came here to work. I figured that, with all I had to offer, he wouldn't want to date anyone else, at least while he was here. If I could meet all his needs, then why would he need other female's attention? I understood while he was home he would do as he wanted, but I hoped that while he was here, I remained his only romantic interest.

He became my lynx medicine. When we were together, he was always present and a good listener. He was more aware than most of the world around him and how interconnected everything is. We took our deep conversations to another level and to a place I had never reached with anyone else but James before. He understood my perspective on life, and how I reached various belief systems within my journey. As the mental and energetic connection between us grew, our intimacy just continuously got better. The more time we spent together, the closer we became. I felt nurtured and protected for the first time since James, and it felt nice to have someone to hold me. He even attended a few of my yoga classes, which meant a great deal to me. I had always wished James would be more active with me and enjoy the bonding time of being physically active together. But that just wasn't who he was, and I suppose it wasn't fair for me to try and change that either. It took me a good year to realize that you can't change the ones you love, whether or not it's for their own good. I had tried to mold James into who I wanted him to be. At the time, I felt it was for his best interest, but really, it was for mine.

The last two and a half years of being single and dating a variety of men made me realize more of what I wanted and wouldn't settle for. I understood from the beginning that my time with Levi would be limited. He had no plans to move here, and never offered for me to visit him. I knew that I deserved better when it came to some of his strange behaviors, but I wasn't ready to let go of his companionship.

I couldn't shake the feeling I was a secret, and my gut continued to tell me that he wasn't being honest with me. But the incredible sex and a strong energetic connection had me hooked. He had become like a drug, or what some call love medicine, that I craved in an animalistic way. I had no interest in anyone else. He met most of my needs in ways no one ever had. Even though I didn't want to admit it, I was in love. And if he ever chose to put the chance of us being together on the table, I was all in. That realization scared me. I had tried so hard to keep protective walls up, but it was no use with how I felt about this man. There was love there, but I still had not expressed the words, and I didn't plan to, for fear that it might scare him off.

Our "situationship" continued into the fall, which had always been my favorite time of year at home. I love observing the magic of the leaves changing from greens to bright crimson reds, oranges, and yellows. The closest comparison to its sheer beauty is like viewing a live painting in the flesh, being created right before your eyes, as if it was being made just for you. My morning walks along the river had become an integral part of connecting with medicine tracks, because I would leave feeling grounded and connected to nature. This time gave me a chance in my day to just be, and not over think my "first world problems" or obstacles that continued to plague me. I could fully take a breath and try and absorb all the smells and sounds of the nature surrounding me. I observed the animals and their behavioral patterns. Perhaps, if I listened closely enough, I could understand their language and the lessons they could teach me. Seeing the magic in the simplest moments began a new healing for me with all that was still going on with my father, my divorce, and the relentless pain that wouldn't leave my body. This morning medicine was another gift that I had taken for granted the majority of my life. I could never go back to the way I used to be, and even though the road here was painful, I could see the growth within myself as I continued to heal from the inside out.

My body was doing a little better, and I could push a little more, feeling like I was on the road to recovery. I was still teaching yoga, but being careful with what I demoed, and my students understood my dilemma by now. I realized through this experience how much influence my ego had, and how I compared my abilities to others. Creator was providing me lessons in being patient and listening to what my body was telling me. Learning the hard way seemed to be my only option, but at least I felt like I was learning. And telling my students, "Let go of ego, and what doesn't serve you," was something I needed to do myself.

It had been a several days since I had heard from Levi, and I was feeling a bit down. There was no snow on the road, and but the temperatures had dropped to a brisk chill. I tend to stay indoors in weather like this, in fear of the cold and slipping on the ice to reinjure my leg. This morning was different that most, and I chose to stay home when I did my daily smudge. I lit a smudge stick made of sage that had only be used a few times, so it was still fairly big. I began fanning the smoke over my body, my face, and down my backside.

I spoke to Creator, saying, "Please heal my body. I am begging for my freedom of movement back. I'm sorry for not honoring what movement I did have before, and I will never take it or granted. Please continue to give me patience when dealing with this injury, and with the difficulties that lie ahead with my father. I don't understand exactly what I am doing wrong, but I promise to make it right. I want to make you proud, to make my ancestors proud of the path I have chosen. I pray for you to continue to send me signs that I am on that right path and making the right choices for why I was put here on this earth."

I set down the smudge stick and placed it back in my colorful abalone shell, to let it burn out on its own, as I always have. I walked away and began getting ready for my day. When I returned, the smudge stick had completely turned into ashes. I had never had that happen before, and I wasn't sure if it meant anything.

I recalled a series of disturbing and exhausting dreams I recently had about Nikki, earlier that week, that left me feeling very conflicted and upset. In the first dream, I was running an obstacle race, and glanced over to see her on the sidelines watching me intently. I became extremely irritated and made no attempt to acknowledge her presence, and quickly ran by. She then followed me into my next dream. I was in Las Vegas, enjoying a spa service at some swanky venue. When I entered the lobby, I saw her sitting at a table with several of my closest friends.

What the hell is this? And what is she doing here? I thought to myself, and I was filled with rage and adrenaline as I decided to confront this monster head on. Thoughts of personal attacks about her looks, or that she appeared to have put on some pounds, ran though my head. Filled with revenge, I wanted to really jab her with some hard blows and hurt her as she had hurt me. Or perhaps I might just walk up and punch her square in the face and give her a new makeover with my fists—my fists that literally read "Kind Soul," a tattoo I had chosen to get a few years back. I had never imagined I would use these hands for violence, but she had crossed the line. Quickly, the series of how to engage was playing through my head as I got closer to this conflict.

Do I just run straight up to her and pounce, like a wild animal attack? Or do I give her the option to speak first? I wondered.

But I chose to hold back, even in this reality. I unclenched my fists of rage and allowed my arms to drop. My subconscious wouldn't allow me to speak such words, to come from a place of hate. I found my voice after the anger settled. I sat down next to her and said, "Do you even understand or comprehend how much you hurt me? I loved and trusted the both of you, and I told you everything about my marriage. How could you possibly do me this way, after I have been nothing but a good friend to you?"

There, finally, I was able to say my piece, and it felt good to express my truth that had been buried so deep within me. She had nothing to say but showed me in her disposition that she understood the pain she had caused. What could she have said anyway? I don't think it would have changed a thing at this point.

She leaned in to hug me and caught me by surprise. I allowed it only because it felt genuine. During that brief hug, I saw and felt a release of anger leave my body. It came in the form of a dark smoke that had been residing within me and was fed through my anger and resentment. I had allowed it to reside there, and for good reason. But once it was the gone, and the darkness that came with it, I was allowed a new space for healing. I knew this was the first step of many that lay ahead to truly heal the feelings of betrayal and mend broken my spirit. This didn't mean I was over my suffering, or that I had truly forgiven her. But it was progress, and for right now, I could accept that and move forward.

I went to work and went about my day, feeling energetically exhausted from all my current realties. I couldn't wait to get home, looking forward to a night of hibernation with just my pup and me. But I was never able to get completely comfortable, because my stomach wasn't feeling right and I couldn't shake it. Throughout the night, that feeling in the pit of my stomach began to turn with such intensity that by eleven p.m., I was feeling paralyzed by the pain. I remembered that I had this feeling a month prior and thought it was food poisoning. It kept me up until eight o'clock in the morning, and then I eventually passed out from the pain and managed to sleep. This couldn't be food poisoning. Something was seriously wrong. I could barely make it to the bathroom, which was only a few feet away, hovering in pain and agony. By this time, it felt like someone was twisting my intestines inside out, and I was sick as a dog. I eventually made my way back to my bed and placed a bucket next to me on the floor. I stared at the clock in aguish, watching time pass by with no sense of relief. I lay down in the fetal position, crying and asking, "Creator, what's wrong with me? I feel like I'm dying, and I don't know what to do." It was two a.m. now, and none of my friends were awake to ask for help. I had tried to text a few and gotten no response. Then I realized that perhaps my appendix was going to explode, and I should Google the symptoms. The description said an extreme pain in the right side, caused by inflammation or a blockage of mucus, parasites, or fecal matter. If it ruptures, it can release dangerous bacteria into the abdomen resulting in peritonitis, or being septic. I absolutely hated going to the doctor, and I still didn't have a primary care physician. However, I knew what my body was telling me, and I needed to go to the hospital ASAP. I felt terrible leaving my old dog alone while I was gone, not knowing when I would be back, but I had no choice. I crawled out of bed to put on some clothes and made my way slowly down to my frozen car. There was no way I would have called an ambulance for help. The bill was going to be high enough as it was.

Once in my car, I just tried to focus on the road and making it there safely. Luckily, it was so late the roads were empty, and it allowed me to get to the hospital faster. I parked right out front at a meter, with a great urgency to get inside and be seen. I told the receptionist I believed my appendix were going to rupture, gave them my insurance card, and took a seat. Feeling miserable, looking incredibly pale with sweat dripping from my forehead, I was scared and alone, wishing someone I knew was sitting next to me to offer some comfort. I couldn't relax even just to take a normal breath. I was called back after about ten minutes, and immediately vomited into a bag while they ran some tests. The nurse confirmed this was the case, and then escorted me into a room in the emergency center to lie down, while we waited for more tests. I felt some relief being there, but I was worried about my car, my dog, and the clients I needed to cancel for tomorrow. I phoned my neighbor and Ronnie, but still got no response. I couldn't help but cry—not just because of the pain, but because I felt lost. I didn't have a special someone to be there. And there was no way I was going to tell my father. He would worry himself sick, and that would just cause me more stress. The feeling that my body was the road to recovery was gone now, and it felt like it was angry with me and punishing me again. Around five a.m., I got my MRI tests done, which were incredibly painful. Every adjustment I had to make was followed by a stabbing pain, but it was the best way to diagnose the issue. The doctor came into my room shortly after to tell me, "You have appendicitis, and I will be performing your surgery at eight a.m. We will put you on some meds now to ease the pain. Just try to relax, if you can."

I was anxious to get out of there. I had so much running through my mind about what needed to be done. Around seven a.m., I finally got ahold of Ronnie and my neighbor Craig. They agreed to come get my keys from the front desk to take care of Jackson and move my car. I was told by a nurse to stay off my phone. She said, "The morphine will make you forget, and do crazy things at times."

But I had to alert my clients that I needed to cancel, to get that off my mind for at least today. I had also booked an Indigenous food symposium in Arizona in five days, and now how was I going to be able to go? This event was so special to me, and my heart was set on gaining new knowledge of ancestral foods and sharing my own. The depression began to set in while I waited for my surgery and for this long horrible day to be over. I was moved into another room around ten a.m., still waiting for my surgery and so desperately wanting a drink of water. I should have guzzled it down before my arrival, but I had forgotten the protocol about surgery. I reached out to Levi, hoping for a response, when he actually called me. I was pleasantly surprised, because he rarely made phone calls.

"How are you feeling? I'm so sorry you are there alone," he said.

"I wish you were here holding me. It's what I need right now," I said. I could feel emotion behind his voice and that he cared

"I wish I was there holding you, too." It felt good to hear these words, and I felt some comfort in at least a phone call. He apologized for his distance and assured me that everything would be okay. I would share the rest of the conversation, and I do know it lasted awhile, but I honestly can't remember. The morphine was in full gear by that point. I had sent a lot of messages out, rebooking my appointments to other days, which became a huge mistake when I finally did make it back to work three days later.

Kathy, my turtle medicine and nurturer, showed up to my room to see me off to surgery and to make sure I was feeling supported. She was a gift that I felt so grateful for. I didn't ask her to come; she just knew I need her there. She understood why my father couldn't be there and stepped into a role that I will be forever grateful for. We waited several more hours before they actually took me into surgery. By that time, it was four p.m., and I had been there since two-thirty a.m. when I checked in. I was wheeled into the surgery room and given anesthesia. I remember asking the doctor, "Can I keep my appendix? Will you save it in a jar?"

He looked at me very strangely and said no but understood my sense of humor. The surgery was fast, and I woke up less than two hours after they had finished. The doctor came by to check on me and mentioned they had a harder time finding my appendix, due to the fruit bowl tattoo I have across my lower abdomen. We found it humorous, and I was relieved the surgery was over. My girlfriend Rose and Kathy greeted me in the waiting room and wheeled me out of the hospital. Kathy took me to get my meds at the pharmacy, along with a few snacks for the house. When I arrived back home, Jackson was happy to see me, but gave me some space with the understanding I was fragile. The morphine was still going strong, and I felt pretty great. I was moving around quite well and thought the surgery was a piece of cake.

Kathy and Rose told me, "You need to lay down and rest. You have to take it easy."

I was feeling pretty great for just having had surgery, and I brushed it off.

"I'm fine, guys, no need to worry about me. I bet I can go back to work in a few days."

Kathy left me to get settled in, and Rose chose to stay the night for few days, to help me with Jackson and getting around. She was my hawk medicine, and she felt the need to show her guardianship through protecting me during times of great healing. Rose had shown me over the past six years of friendship that she embodied the qualities of being a noble human being. I couldn't have asked for a better person to take care of me while in this state. I passed out hard that night into a heavy sleep, so happy to be back in bed, and so happy this nightmare would soon be over. Things could start going back to normal, and I would get back to work soon.

I woke up the next morning, somehow believing the worst was over and that I could just go about my day. But when I tried to sit up, an intense pain came over me, and I fell back, and with that came the tears. Oh shit, I thought, I am not even close to being okay.

I called for Rose to come help me. "Babe, I need to go to the bathroom and I can't get up."

I heard her giggle, and then she replied, "Oh no, babe. One second, I will come help you."

She rolled me out of bed and to the bathroom, then gave me some privacy. I didn't think I was going to need this help, but I was already so glad she was there. And taking Jackson out to the bathroom is a task within itself; I don't know what I would have done without her help. I realized how much I missed having a partner in times like these, and it made me think of James—how he would have been there to take care of me, and how different this entire experience would have been.

The next two days continued to be difficult. I couldn't sit up at all and chose to lay down most of the time. I decided to go back to work just for a couple clients that were difficult to reschedule. It ended in bouts of sheer pain, and I couldn't hold back the tears. I actually fell crumpled down to the floor and lost it for a second. I wasn't ready to be working, and I was foolish to be even trying. But the symposium was in two days, and I still had my heart set on going. I was trying to prove to myself that I was ready and could go.

At this point, I still had a weak appetite and felt gross from all the extra fluids they blow you up with for surgery. Glancing in the mirror, I could see the extra water weight dangling around my belly, giving that permanent look of extreme bloating. Food wasn't at all appealing, and I was still anxiously awaiting a bowel movement to get my system feeling somewhat normalized.

Four days had passed since I had heard a word from Levi, and I just couldn't understand why he was choosing to distance himself when I needed his support.

He even chose to ignore my communication through music, which had never happened before. But again, this seemed to be his routine, and I felt foolish to have invested so much of my heart in this man. Later on, my retrospective mind pondered whether this behavior was possibly what he had to do to keep himself from feeling too much. Regardless, it hurt that this was a time I needed him and he was choosing to create boundaries. I had to get out of the depression I was feeling from the pain meds and the self-doubt of my abilities to make this trip. Time to clear my head, stick to regular Aleve for the pain, and set myself in motion for the journey that lay ahead.

After all, I had made these agreements to myself and had to get into the right mindset. I came across a Native healer that lived in Tucson a few months earlier through social media. I had hoped we could connect during my travels, but he said that he wouldn't be around. He was traveling back from Seattle to Tucson for only one night, then heading to California to see his daughter. I was really hoping to connect with Tony. I had viewed his past work, and his words spoke to me. He understood our connection to this earth and all living things, and I needed his guidance and medicine now more than ever. Feeling very vulnerable and unsure of why my body failed me at this time had left me with enormous doubt. Was I on the chosen path? And if so, was this event part of Creator's divine plan?

One gift I didn't expect was that James would offer to take Jackson while I was away. It was one less thing to worry about. We hadn't seen each other for at least several months, and I really appreciated his offer. I knew that Jackson would be in the best care, and that he would be happy to see James.

My father phoned me the night before I was set to leave, just to check in and catch up. I still hadn't told him about my appendix. I didn't want his worry about my situation to add any unnecessary stress to his. But he knew in my tone that something was wrong. Those dad instincts were still in effect, even through the dementia. I was trying to hold in my emotional state and pretending everything was normal.

"How's it going, Donell? Are you excited for your trip to Arizona?" he asked with lots of enthusiasm.

I became overcome with emotion, just as if I was that little girl who needed to confess her truth to her father. I began to cry and explained, "Dad, I had my appendix out, and was in the hospital several days ago."

I could hear the shock in his reaction. "You got it out already? How are you feeling, and why didn't you tell me?"

I felt bad for keeping him in the dark, but this was the best option with his current situation. "I didn't want you to worry, Dad, and there was nothing you could do to help at the time. My friends and Kathy came and took care of me."

I could feel some sense of relief from him over the phone. He responded, "Well, you know I'm always here for you, Donell, and you can tell me anything."

In this special moment, it felt like I had my father back, the one who raised me and supported me my entire life. There were no signs of dementia, and it felt like we stepped back in time and, if for only that moment, he was being the man I needed him to be. I felt good about what we had shared, and I went to bed that night feeling anxious about the travel but ready to let go and leave it in Creator's hands.

The next morning, I was packed and ready to go. I made my way to the airport, feeling very unsure whether my body would hold up but knowing my spirit needed this trip. I was nowhere near normal but felt a stronger urge to go than to stay. I was told not to lift any luggage over five pounds, which made it incredibly difficult with security checkpoints and boarding the plane. I was lucky enough to meet a few kind travelers to help me out along the way.

When I arrived in Seattle around ten a.m., I was very unsure about my decision. I felt nauseated, with intermittent sharp pains when sitting in various positions, and the layover was a couple hours before I could catch my connecting flight to Tucson. Sitting on the plane had been uncomfortable and I had a hard time finding any peace, so the layover allowed me some breathing time. I chose to lie on the floor, and I didn't care at all if I looked strange, or that travelers had to walk over me at times. This was the only position at the time that kept me from tears. Still feeling self-doubt over whether I had made the right choice, I knew that the next flight would be even longer.

I finally felt some urge to eat. I gathered my things and made my way over the bagel sandwich place to take something for the flight. Heading back to the terminal, I was blinded by the sun beaming through a large window. And then I saw him: he had long black hair covered by a stylish black cap. He had kind brown eyes that could see into your very soul, and that strong and powerful Navajo bone structure that is undeniably beautiful. Tony was a beautiful man from the inside out, and it was exactly the sign I had been asking for. I had to process this sudden interaction within seconds.

I shouted out to him, "Tony, hey, is that really you?"

He turned to me, and his eyes widened as he began process this unexpected meeting.

"Donell, whoa, is that you?"

It took a moment for us to embrace, but when we did, I felt safe. I understood that Creator worked this divine alignment in my favor, leading my medicine tracks straight to Tony. And regardless of the amount of time we had, I was able to be in his presence and absorb whatever medicine he carried.

Tony ushered us back to the gate.

"Let's take a seat and catch up. I would like to know the progress after your surgery and how you are feeling, dear."

"Well, I'm struggling a bit, but I had to make this trip. And now, seeing you along the way, I know I made the right choice."

We both smiled and understood that our meeting was serendipitous. It had caught us both by surprise. The flight was getting ready to board, and I watched Tony get in line ahead of me. He stood for a few minutes, and then suddenly turned around and looked in my direction and made his way back over. He pulled a rectangular cedar box out of his bag, then opened it up to present me with an eagle feather that lay inside.

"I have been carrying this feather with me on my travels for some time. And Creator just told me you are the one I should give it to."

I felt overcome with emotion but chose to keep it in, being at the airport and all. Then I gave Tony one last hug.

"Thank you so much, you have no idea how much you have helped me. And I appreciate you, Tony."

He acknowledged my words with his smile, and we said goodbye.

Once aboard and just after takeoff, this flight was turning out to be quite uncomfortable as well. I had to sneeze a few times, which caused enormous amounts of sharp pain. I just wanted to take some Dramamine and pass out, and then I could wake up and be there already. After a few hours, we were landing in Tucson, and I was on a mission to get to my hotel as soon as possible to rest and relax.

I received a text from Tony. "Wait for me. I will help you with your luggage at baggage claim."

This was very good news. I was happy to not have to lift my bags and to speak with Tony some more. We made our way to baggage claim, and he offered me a ride to the hotel. I told him I had a rental car but appreciated the offer.

"I would like to take you to dinner tonight, after your settled, then, and share some stories with you."

I felt blessed to get a chance to continue to connect with someone I admired so much.

"That sounds wonderful. I will see you around six p.m."

I picked up my small red European-style rental car, which was perfect for the trip, other than the countless speed bumps that seemed to cover this city. I had never experienced a car like this before, being about the size of a golf cart and offering little to no protection in the case of a collision. I had booked my stay at a hotel that was also a casino, because they had offered a discount for those of us attending the symposium. I made my way to my room and was very pleased to see the king-size bed and soft ambience. I needed to rest from my travel, and in no time at all, I took a very long and much-needed nap. Two hours later, I awoke feeling better than I had most of the day and waited patiently for Tony to message me about dinner.

He picked me up later that evening and we headed into the city, where he found a sweet a little restaurant that had plenty of options, but, most of all, was quiet. Tony had brought an album of his family history to share during dinner. I loved hearing his stories of how he came from a strong line of ancestors who shaped him to do this work and understanding who his parents were and the hardships they suffered after the colonization. Then the boarding schools forever changed our people and caused an enormous amount of historical trauma. We faced the struggle between trying to hold on to our old ways, but still having to find our new place in this industrial world. I was moved by the words he had to share, and I felt so honored to be sharing these stories of our ancestral history. This wasn't the history

I was told growing up in the public school system. The truth that our country was founded upon is dark. Our ancestors, our relatives suffered so incredibly much for us to be here today. But our resilience is a gift, and individuals such as Tony are still carrying the light and truth that our ancestors had prayed for. I realized that evening that Tony was my eagle medicine. His connection to Creator was undeniable, and he had made it his life work to share this knowledge. He sacrificed various paths of his life to be a healer, to carry on that divine spirit and spread the message. The time I spent with my eagle was beyond impactful. He gave me the courage to stay on my chosen path, no matter how hard it gets, and the gift of an eagle feather to remember him by, so that every time I looked at it I could remember the medicine it carried. I was no longer afraid of the pain and could embrace the rest of my trip knowing I was meant to receive this medicine.

The next morning, I was up early and headed down to the lobby to see if any other attendees were gathering there. The organizers had mentioned a shuttle would be available for transportation to the event, but I had rented the car just in case. I saw three other Natives that seemed to be waiting for the shuttle; we were told the shuttle was running really late. From the looks of it, if we waited, we would show up to the symposium forty-five minutes late. I offered to take all of us in my tiny car but warned them it would be a tight fit. Everyone was pleased that I could be of help, and we set off to the event as a pack. The gentleman joining us was from Arizona, and he worked with traditional foods back home. The two young ladies were college students from California, involved with community gardens and Native American issues in their area. I enjoyed their company, and we had a great time getting to know one another on the thirty-minute drive through the desert.

Arriving twenty minutes late, the four of us rushed to make it to orientation in the main auditorium. Looking though the agenda, I was so pleased to see so many amazing speakers and opportunities to connect with people with similar passions. The lectures consisted of holistic farmers, traditional food programs, Indigenous chefs, students, seed savers, and elders with storytelling of our past food ways. Every meal was prepared by these Indigenous chefs, utilizing the best of desert and southwest cuisine. Up to this point, I still had a very low appetite and tolerance for food because of my surgery, so this traditional medicine came at the perfect time to nourish my recovery. I had never experienced traditional desert cuisine, and by the smell and presentation alone, I was hooked. The menu consisted of blue corn rabbit tamales, sautéed cholla buds, and corn fritters. My taste buds were heighted by these new flavor profiles that had never met my mouth, the gentle heat from the green chilies, and the delicate but sweet flavor of the prickly pear. My body recognized the love that was put into these dishes, which in itself had more healing power than the actual food. I appreciated this new palate of Southwest Native cuisine, and the timing of it all couldn't have been more perfect.

The next three days I spent absorbing as much information as I could, making new connections and healing my body with traditional food. I was able to spend one afternoon watching some elder women basket weavers making their creations. I sat there, in sheer awe, observing their patience and love that goes into weaving. These baskets were essential to our gathering of foods and were also used for the actual cooking. The energy in this circle was different from the rest of the conference; these women were holding a sacred space within themselves and the space around them.

It felt familiar and made me miss my grandmother. I remembered watching her gather her plants, and then spend countless hours weaving them into works of art. She had so much patience, and her intention during the entire process was pure. My grandmother was kind and resembled so much of our old ways. She was a small woman with that classic short roller-styled hair, her face adorned with thick-rimmed glasses, and a sense of style that had not changed since the seventies. I loved learning any form of art she wanted to share, and our time together was incredibly special. I didn't get to see her much after mom had passed, having to wait for summertime when Dad could fly me to Eureka. Our time together was limited but was always filled with magic; she loved to tell stories and I was blessed to listen. She fed me traditional foods of salmon, eel, berries, acorns, and an abundance of seaweed. My grandmother was incredibly gifted, and she shared those gifts with so many people in her lifetime. Spending time with these weavers really brought back all the old memories I had of my grandmother. And even though they never spoke to me, I felt connection and love from just being in their presence. This was elder medicine that I was receiving once again. I hadn't anticipated it, but it was worth the wait.

On the last day of the symposium, we were blessed to have cedar plank salmon, served and prepared just as my Yurok Tribe makes at home. This was the food of my people and I savored every bite. It took me back to my grandmother's arms and that little girl who saw magic in everything. The salmon is filleted in half, leaving

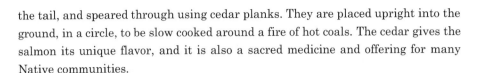

the tail, and speared through using cedar planks. They are placed upright into the ground, in a circle, to be slow cooked around a fire of hot coals. The cedar gives the salmon its unique flavor, and it is also a sacred medicine and offering for many Native communities.

I made my way through some of the other booths to stumble upon these striking Hopi women making Piki bread on a traditional Piki stone. I had never seen bread like this before, dark blue in color and paper-thin in density. She explained that these sacred stones are passed down through generations from mother to daughter. And in the past, a young woman was expected to demonstrate her skills of making Piki bread before entering wedlock. It was made up of blue corn, water, and ash, which allowed more nutrients in the corn to be absorbed by being broken down by the ash. This traditional food is mostly only seen in ceremony, so this was a rare and special treat. I watched her dip her hands in the batter and then rub the mixture on the hot stones. She would add strokes of batter, until it formed a large sheet. The dough cooked very quickly, and then she pulled it off, for another sheet to be made in the same manner. The previous sheet is layered on top and the sheets are then folded together and rolled into one. She was fascinating to watch, and this was really special tradition. We shared some stories, and I took her photo, with a promise I would send her a copy when I got back home.

This being my last day of the symposium, I took my time walking around the desert grounds, looking for the perfect place to pray. The landscape was so different from back home, with a vast variety of succulents and other plant medicine that doesn't grow in the Northwest The red dirt blanketed the earth as far as I could see, with grandfather rocks that held our libraries encoded with the history of our ancestors. I wanted to remember the way the air smelled, and the sensation of the dry heat touching my skin. The desert is something special, and I felt very connected to it in my short stay in Tucson. I began to recall that dream I had previously where I stepped through that mirror into this landscape. The scenery was similar to what I was seeing now. Perhaps I was experiencing déjà vu, and this was another sign that I was exactly where I needed to be.

After a few hours of walking and trying to absorb my surroundings, I found a space to pray. This space held more stillness than the rest. I lit the smudge stick filled with dried sage and began to immediately cry healing tears. I could finally reflect upon what this trip had meant to me and let go of any worry or doubt of my body's abilities to be there. I found another type of healing through Eagle medicine and the nourishment of these traditional foods. I made some peace with where my heart was at with the healing of my divorce. I knew that whatever was to be, I could handle it, and these were all lessons I needed to learn. I had been so angry for my body turning against me, but perhaps that was inevitable and it was good timing after all. I realized that I was blessed to have my turtle and hawk medicine step forward to take care of me during my recovery. I actually began to feel grateful that it happened exactly when it did and the way it did, and that this was part of the plan.

I arrived back home in the late afternoon and made arrangements to meet up with James to get Jackson back. He texted me he was there, and I came out to the parking lot to greet him. Jackson jumped out of the car, happy to see me as usual. I walked back with Jackson toward the end of the truck. I wanted to express my gratitude to James for his help, but I felt reluctant to be so open. We had stopped sharing any type of emotion for quite some time now, and I wasn't trying to stir the pot or make him feel uncomfortable.

But I found the courage, and said, "Thank you so much, James, this means so much to me. I really didn't expect you to help out."

He smiled at me, then reached out to give me a warm and sincere hug. We stayed in the hug for what felt like several minutes. This embrace felt incredibly healing; I had to hold in the tears and just smile. I didn't at all expect this gift, and it meant more than he could have ever understood.

We stepped away from the hug, and James turned to me and said, "I'm happy I could help you out, and I wanted to spend more time with Jackson. I could tell his health is declining quickly, and it was no problem."

We actually looked each other in the eyes that afternoon. And what I saw was my best friend again. It may have only been a glimpse, but it was the man I once knew. I saw the man that I trusted and had shared my entire life with. This moment allowed us to see the love was still there, just in a different form. It might have been the only time I would see him this way, but I felt blessed for at least that one last chance.

I came home from my trip to Tucson with so much more than I had left with. I was able to receive the medicine that I knew all along but had somehow taken for granted. I would use the fuel and knowledge that was given to me by my experience at the symposium and share it with the Native youth. Traditional food medicine had brought me back to life, and to where I needed to be. I had a responsibility to share that gift on this new path that was chosen for me for a greater purpose.

CHAPTER 7
Lynx Medicine

BACK TO REALITY, and three days later I had a stressful meeting with my dad and his financial planner. I had been anticipating this news for the last year and had wished it would somehow just go away. Pete was not just my dad's financial planner, but a trusted friend for many years. I appreciated his help, and he made my life a lot easier. We could form a team and give my dad collective advice that he seemed to take better in general.

We sat down in his office to look over some financial statements and future concerns. Pete offered us a beverage, and we got down to business.

"So, it's time to look at some other options for income. Don, your long-term care runs out a year from now, and will no longer cover the costs of your assisted living. When that happens, it will cost six thousand dollars a month to stay at your current address. This doesn't cover your other bills, or any services you require."

I felt a sense of panic, and the anxiety came shortly after. I couldn't believe the expense of this facility, and I didn't know what in the hell to do with this news. I wanted my father to live as he wished, but I couldn't afford to keep him there if his money ran out. We figured that at this rate, he would be broke after two years tops, and then what? I had never imagined being in this position. The added stress was unwarranted, and I was feeling beyond overwhelmed. I chose to wait, and to speak to Dad in private about some things we could do to save money right away.

Once we hopped into the car, I had to force myself to ask some hard questions and find some way for him to save some money now. I was hesitant and I'm sure he could hear it in my voice.

"Dad, what do you think about what Pete said?"

He didn't answer and just looked out the window.

"Dad, I know this is uncomfortable to talk about, but we need to save some money now."

He took a breath and replied, "What do you suppose we do, Donell?"

I hated having this conversation. I felt helpless and wished at that moment I had James for emotional support.

"Well, I think we need to cut back on your outings to movies and takeout meals. You can still go, just not as much," I said.

He looked down, and I could tell his spirit was saddened by all of this news. "But that's all I have look forward to, other than spending time with you," he said.

My heart ached, and I had no response to his words. I didn't want to take any of the joy he had left in this daily life. He had already lost so much, but I was left to make the hard decisions. I wasn't ready at all for this battle and decided to let it go for now.

"Let's visit this topic another time, Dad. Don't worry, I will handle it. Keep doing what makes you happy."

I had more on my plate once again, and it felt like it was piling up on top of the leftovers. I previously had scheduled a new treatment with Dr. Lenoue, in the hope that I would finally heal my damn knee once and for all. He explained that PRP, platelet-rich plasma, is a procedure where they draw your own blood and spin it in a centrifuge machine. Extracts of the platelet-rich portion of the blood is then injected back into the wound or soft tissue. The hope is that the body will utilize the platelets and promote healing itself, with no harmful side effects.

The treatment wasn't covered by my insurance, and it cost a hefty six hundred dollars, which I most definitely couldn't afford right now. I knew my hospital bills would be arriving soon, and I would have to take off more work after the injection. I couldn't afford this treatment, but I was also fed up with my body. I wanted to dance, to run, and to move without fear. I had committed to this appointment months ago, and I needed to follow through and worry about the money later. Dr. Lenoue had mentioned it would be painful, and I feared the worst, but I seemed to handle physical pain better than other forms.

I woke up Monday morning around seven-thirty a.m., feeling anxious and stressed about my injection in two hours. I wanted to just get this part over, so I could begin to really heal and move forward. This could be the answer I had been waiting for, and Dr. Lenoue was always on the cutting edge with the newest treatments.

I showed up to my appointment to be greeted by his lovely wife, Sarah. She was a nurse and would be taking my blood sample for the procedure. I had heard him say lovely things about her, and her energy felt comforting. They prepared the injection and set up an ultrasound machine to get a clear view of the injury and injection sites.

Dr. Lenoue mapped out exactly what tissue he needed to treat and then asked me, "Are you ready, Donell?"

I was feeling terrified but ready to try anything at this point. I said, "Yes, you can proceed."

I felt the needle go in, and I was surprised that it didn't hurt much at all. Then I felt my blood rush into the damaged tissue, and I was overcome with such an intensity of pain that I could not deny it or act tough. Tears of agony rolled down my face, as I grasped to hold Sarah's hand. She was telling me to breathe, but I could barely think straight. The pain had become so intense I couldn't control my body functions.

As I begin to shake uncontrollably, all the pain from my past confronted me. This perhaps was not just pain from this lifetime, but trauma from other lifetimes. I had never felt anything like this before, and I thought I had a strong threshold. But this pain was about to break me; I didn't know how much longer I could endure this reality. I wanted to scream, but I couldn't even breathe controlled enough to get one out. I wanted it to be over. My anxiety had taken ahold of me, followed by a trauma-induced panic attack.

Dr. Lenoue treated me using some acupressure points to calm my nervous system and stop the shaking. He said it seemed like I was suffering from PTSD, and I agreed that was a possible explanation of my experience. I thanked Sarah for being there for comfort; I actually really needed her presence. It took me some time to calm myself down. I wasn't prepared at all for that kind of treatment. Maybe the pain was intensified by all the stress I carried with me, I wasn't really sure.

I was finally ready to get on my feet and test out the leg.

Dr. Lenoue said, "Stay off it for at least few days, if you can, and come back and see me in a few weeks."

The worst was over, and I felt exhausted, not just physically but energetically.

"Thank you, Dr. Lenoue, I will make sure I do."

I did as he asked, and this time, I went straight home and stayed there elevating my leg until the next day.

I was scared of what to expect when waking up and getting out of bed the next morning. I learned to not set expectations on my healing, and I had to be patient with this new treatment. I removed the sheets to look down at my leg; it looked quite strange still and not at all normal size. The injection had made it swollen and misshapen to say the least, but I had get up and let Jackson outside. He was so patient with me and had gotten used to me not being as quick or as active. But his bladder was small these days, and I needed to hurry if I could. We took the elevator and made our way out the door. It was a cold and rainy day, and it took so much effort on my part just to get outside and let him do his business. In moments like these, I wished again that I had someone special in my life, someone to take care of me in these difficult situations and make life a little easier. I had already relied on my friends so much with my appendix out a month ago, and I felt bad asking for help.

Being forced to be off my feet once again left me mostly couch-ridden and a hermit. Then, once again, depression set in. I was feeling a little lost and, honestly, somewhat lonely. Levi continued to make little to no effort at times and was playing games with my heart. When he was here, our time together felt like magic, filled with deep conversations and lots of love medicine. We would pick up where we left off, and the passion we exchanged somehow still continued to grow. However, when he headed back home, the communication and connection changed dramatically.

I would ask, "Why haven't I heard from you in several days? Why is it so hard to respond to a text?"

His explanations of what he was doing didn't make sense, and part of me knew I was in denial. I began to internalize that maybe he was embarrassed by me in some way. I only met one of his friends in town and, of course, was never introduced to anyone back in California. I knew I should have let him go by now, and maybe he was treating me this way to make me do just that. He didn't know I loved him, but I had known for some time now. I allowed him into my heart space, and I took down the walls I had built because he had felt so different from anyone else before. I felt connected to Levi, not just on a physical plane but with my spiritual body as well. That was the one thing missing from all the rest, and now that I had found it, I had an extremely hard time letting it go. I believed if he could see my light, I would be enough for him to want to invest more. I felt torn and divided with how I felt, and how he made me feel one day, and completely opposite the next.

I had to release some of this heavy energy I was carrying and made an effort to go back to practicing some breathing exercises I had picked up in my yoga trainings. I closed my eyes and imagined myself with no injuries, being active and carefree. I breathed in deep from my diaphragm, breathing in light, love, and positive thoughts. This was countered by a release of that breath, holding anything that is negative or not serving a higher purpose, and leaving your body as you exhale. As the negative thoughts left my body, I envisioned my healing taking form, and the end result was my freedom of movement. I would never take my body for granted again and being injured for this long continued to humble me. I realized that these injuries were serving as lessons in patience and listening to my body. This treatment could potentially heal my body, but if this didn't work, it was on me to heal myself through a spiritual transformation.

The real work had just begun. I was just finally catching up to the fact that I had more power in healing myself than I could have understood until now. Throughout the next month, the PRP showed that some healing had occurred, and the fascia along the injury was stronger and more stable. But I wasn't fully healed. The pain was still there, and my body was telling me I had more work to do.

Meanwhile, I needed to keep feeding my passions by staying busy and growing my health coaching business. I was making an effort to post new recipes and food porn of my creations. I found the time to make a few more cooking videos of Dance Jam Kitchen, even with my limited movement. The effort had to continue to be there if I was ever going to make something of this career. The symposium had fueled me with new knowledge and ideas to implement with my vision. I wanted to help my Native community and their overall approach to wellness. But I wasn't sure how to approach this issue and really make a lasting impact. At times, I would be filled with self-doubt about my abilities or qualifications to make these changes. How could I possibly make a difference? What made my efforts special or different from what had been done before? Then I realized I had to at least try, and if I were patient, the path would reveal itself.

I had recently heard about the Nk'wu Nation, a group of Native American students at Rogers High School that had come together to form a drum circle. I contemplated some ideas that might get the kids excited about traditional foods and contacted the adult supervisor of the group. Jeremy was excited about my interest in the group and agreed we should work together. He asked me to come to their next weekly meeting, Thursday after school, and I could then meet the kids, introduce myself, and see if I could spark their interest.

That afternoon, walking back into Rogers High school felt so strange. I imagined the last time I walked halls like this was when I was a student, nineteen years ago. The group was gathered in Jeremy's office, waiting for me to arrive. That day, about six kids showed up, but I was told the group had a few more members. I introduced myself and opened up about how I wanted to use my knowledge of using food as medicine as a tool. The best concept we came up with was to host a traditional dinner for the community. We could gather these foods during the course of the year and get donations for the rest. The money would go back into the group to fund any Native youth conferences that they might want to attend. For me, it was a win-win situation. I could teach the kids about these foods and spend the time gathering them like our ancestors did. Some of the kids would never have had access to this process any other way. And later in the year, we would come together to prepare this dinner, and work with these sacred foods as group, providing something very special to those that attended, sharing the medicine that I was able to receive in Tucson.

I continued to meet with the kids on a weekly basis, getting to know their personalities and trying to earn their trust and respect. I believe it's a two-way street, and I treated them as adults. I formed a bond with one young lady in particular named Iaitia. She was not like her peers, and I could see the elk medicine within her form. She showed great strength, pride, and noble qualities I rarely get to see in someone her age. Being that she was close to six feet tall made her stand out from the crowd, but that wasn't what got my attention. She was proud of her Lakota heritage, and she already understood what her ancestors had endured for us to be here. By the way she carried herself, she was born to be a leader. I knew that this young lady's participation was vital to the group and that I could count on her to keep the other students accountable, leaving less pressure on my part. During the meeting, we set up some times to gather for that following year. We were already too late into fall to begin this project now. But the intention was set, and this dream would soon enough become a reality.

◄ ◄ • ► ►

I observed the change in the leaves as they continued to fall, the process of turning from such bright warm colors and full of life into lifeless, faded brown, dead plant matter in a matter of weeks. And Jackson's health had gone from a fairly healthy dog, with the exception of his small bladder, to such a severe decline that he had days he barely moved. He couldn't drink enough water, and would just pee it out as fast as it went in. He was sixteen human years old and had lived a beautiful life. But I knew that our time was limited and that he was suffering. The vet had mentioned on his last recent visit that the time had come to put him down, and I needed to do it before he had no good days left.

I made arrangements for him to be taken into the vet and euthanized before he suffered too much longer. The day before, all my girlfriends came over to say their goodbyes and love on him one last time. The next morning, I made him one of his favorite meals of fried eggs and kale. He ate it up with no problem and had some actual pep in his step. He had refused to eat the days leading up to now, but today he was showing some life. The guilt set in and I pondered if I was making the right choice, and whether I should wait. Was I being selfish by letting him go, or was I being selfish keeping him around when he was suffering? I had made an attempt to get into contact with James to allow him the time to say goodbye to Jackson. I didn't want to do this alone. I had never been in this situation before.

Time to drive to him to the vet one last time and say goodbye to my sweet boy forever. Oh God, I was freaking out as we got closer and pulled up to the vet clinic. He jumped out and seemed happy. He had no idea what was about to happen. I was pissed James didn't respond. Why didn't he want to say goodbye? This wasn't about me or us; this was his dog, too, for thirteen years of his life.

They took us back to the room, and the vet explained the procedure. They would give him a shot to first relax him, and then the final one to put him to sleep. They assured me he wouldn't suffer, and that I was doing the right thing. I had them leave the room for a moment to give us some privacy. Jackson was feeling restless, and I'm sure he was picking up on my anxiety vibes. I picked him up and held him on my lap and began petting his chest and the backs of his ears. I couldn't help but cry, feeling guilty for making this decision to end his life. I never imagined this day would come, or that I would be handling it alone. I pulled him in close, and shared what words I could offer.

"You are such a good boy. I don't know what I would have done without your comfort these past few years. I will miss you so incredibly much. You were all the company I needed."

The vet reentered the room and gave him the injection to relax. He fought it at first and then began to wobble around and lose his balance. I helped him find some calmness and a stable area to lie down. The final injection went in, and he closed his eyes. His soul has now left his little body. The vet left the room and gave me some space with my mourning. I was feeling the great loss of a trusted friend and companion. I allowed the endless tears to flow and kissed his forehead for the last time.

"Goodbye, my little man. I will miss you."

I headed back to the car, feeling paralyzed with a deep sadness but also some anger with no response from James. Jackson was the last thing that tied us together, and perhaps that's why he couldn't bring himself to be there. I was foolish to think he would make an appearance, but I still made the effort to let him know it was done. The text I sent him was,

> Jackson is no longer with us, and it was incredibly hard to let him go.
> I hope that you didn't chose to not come because of me. I would have
> given you space without me around. He was your dog too, after all.

I came home to an empty house, and it felt so different without him. It didn't take me long to figure out that I had never felt truly alone before, with Jackson there. But now I felt it and realized I would no longer be greeted with his smiling face at the door. Just another change to adjust to, one that made me feel lonelier than ever. I understood this day would come, but I didn't know it would feel like this.

But I received a gift that evening that I never expected and could have never anticipated. James finally responded to my text, and it read,

> I have no words for the sadness I feel. I loved him and Apollo like they
> were my sons. I couldn't come to see him, but I want you to know it's

not because of you. It's because of me and the situation I created.
There is so much more I want to say to you, but I just don't know how.
I'm so sorry, Donell, I'm just so sorry. Goodbye.

I had to read the text several times before I could begin to process what James had said. I cried tears of pain as well as tears of healing, and I found some new comfort in his words. James took some ownership of what happened, and for the first time said he was sorry, and I believed he meant it. Of course, I wanted to know more about what he couldn't tell me. But I had to let that shit go quick, and just accept his words for what he was willing to share. He gave me a gift that allowed me to find another healing with what happened between us. It opened me up to move forward, to continue to heal and trust the process.

As I got closer to approaching the new year, I went back to reflect on my New Year's resolutions to see if I had made any progress. I still hadn't come close to healing my physical body; the pain was still there, and I had to make smart choices when it came to any physical activity. But at least I could still go for my morning medicine walks and enjoy the fresh air. Resolution number four, giving back to my community, was at least set in motion with the traditional dinner planned for next year. This was a project I was so looking forward to and was anxious to begin. Number six, booking my dream trip to New Zealand, was still on the back burner, and a distant hope for when I could have the freedom and finances to be able go. I felt even further away from that goal than I had the previous year. But I wasn't going to up hope. This was to be my dream vacation, and only I had to the power to see it through. Number seven, no new relationships, was the resolution I felt the most conflicted about. Granted, I wasn't in a committed relationship with Levi, but it's what I have would have wanted. He was still in my life to some degree, and still felt the need disconnect at any given time. I even went on a few dates to try and see if I could get over my feelings, to cut that energetic cord that kept me connected to him. But no one sparked my interest after the first date. I compared their energy to his, and it felt pointless. I realized it wasn't fair to these men to not be even given a real chance. My heart still belonged to Levi, whether he wanted it or not.

The day I had been dreading arrived when I saw that some of my hospital bills had come in the mail. I had decent insurance and hoped it would cover a large amount. But to see that this one bill alone was five thousand dollars, even with my insurance, sent me into shock and my level of stress rose even higher. By the time I had opened them all, my appendix was going to cost me seven thousand dollars. I just couldn't understand how this could be. What was the point in paying for insurance if you still barely got covered when you needed it most?

At this point, I imagined my plate had gotten so full that the universe had sent me back for seconds. I didn't know how I was going to pay these bills, and the stress of it all just continued to build. I not only had to worry about my own finances, but once my dad's insurance ran out, I would take on his on as well.

The best stress release for me, with the exception of exercise, had been great sex, and I was in desperate need of it. I had no intention of looking for it—the only exception being with Levi. It had been an entire week with no communication on his part, and this was the longest he ever went with distance. I thought this was it, he and I were over. It hurt my feelings incredibly badly for him to end things this way, to offer no reason or closure and just disappear as if it never was. So, I was shocked when I received a text from him claiming his excuse for his disappearance was a snowboarding trip out of town. He said that he had no service and was away from his phone. He must think I'm really stupid to believe such a tale, I thought. I told him it didn't add up, and I was feeling like a secret again. He said he would be visiting in a week for work, and even though I wanted to see him, I knew it wasn't a good idea. No matter how upset he made me, his presence would override any cognitive thoughts I had about us. He had a spell over me and would always find a way to smooth things over when we were together.

I got a late-night text at midnight, and it was Levi, inquiring how my night was going. I wasn't sure what the angle was, or why he was asking me this. After I responded that I was at home in bed, I got a knock at my door about ten minutes later. I really didn't expect to see him at this moment. And I was still angry and hurt by his games, but I couldn't help but to want to love on this man. He pulled me close and kissed me just like he always had, like nothing had ever changed.

"I had no idea you were coming," I said.

He looked deep into my eyes and stroked my hair behind my ear.

"I wanted to surprise you, Donell," he said.

I felt mixed emotions about my anger and my love for this man. He had a way about him that seemed to override my rational thinking of what was healthy for me. Some might call it the "dick spell," you ladies know what I mean.

We stayed up late sharing stories and multiple orgasms. This came to be one of our favorite pastimes. Up to this point, Levi had been the only one that felt like this. When we were intimate, I felt an energetic connection that was undeniable. It was in this space that our connection felt like magic, and we could spend hours just staring into each other's eyes. His timing was impeccable, and he chose that night to actually express the words, "I love you," which filled an empty space in my heart that had been waiting so long to hear them. I had wanted so badly to tell him I loved him but was in fear he would just run further away. I wanted to confront him about his previous actions, but after sharing that moment, I couldn't find the courage. I didn't want the night we expressed our love to end in an argument. I choose to just stay in the moment and let go for now.

Levi and I spent the next few days together, in between his work and my work schedule. I strategically planned on making my interrogation about all my concerns and doubts that came from his behavior but was trying to find the right time. Then he mentioned he had to leave for a few days for a work trip in Seattle, which is less than a five-hour drive away. I wasn't pleased to hear this news and decided to wait till he got back. I had some things I needed to say, but I wanted him to be present and not in a hurry.

The second night Levi was gone, I got a phone call from The Ridge at one-thirty a.m., and I knew something was terribly wrong.

The nurse said, "Your father was having trouble breathing, and needed to be rushed to the hospital."

"What's going on? Do you need me to come down right now?" I replied.

The nurse said "No, we need to run some tests. You won't be able to see him right now. We will call you back when we have some results. "

I hung up the phone, got out of bed, and began pacing around my place. I was feeling so worried about my father, feeling helpless because right now, there was nothing I could do. And I knew my dad was feeling anxious; he hated being at the hospital. I needed to talk to someone, and I texted Levi.

"Are you still up? Can we talk?"

He responded right away and gave me a call.

"What's going on? Are you okay?"

I had already been crying, and he knew in my tone that I was not okay. I wanted to still get so much off my chest with us, but right now, I needed him. He spent two hours with me on the phone that night, offering comforting words and making me feel loved. He told me he wished he was there to hold me, and when he returned the next day, he would. We hung up the phone just after three a.m., and I slept for maybe an hour, awaiting the latest news on my father.

The hospital called me back around seven a.m. My father was now admitted and they had secured him a room. I could come see him when visiting hours began at nine a.m., and they would tell me what they had found. I cancelled my clients for the day and made my way to the hospital as soon as I could see him. He was in the ICU and had a fairly big room to himself.

My dad was so happy to see me walk into that room. He smiled and said, "Donell, I'm glad you're here."

I gave him a gentle hug and sat beside his bed. We waited for the doctor to come in and inform us about what they had found thus far.

It took several tests to reveal he had a blood clot on his mechanical heart valve that was causing him shortness of breath and a lack of energy. The doctor said the only fix was a stronger dose of blood thinner to relieve the clot. My father was already on Coumadin for his mechanical heart valve and wasn't happy to hear he needed more thinners. The Coumadin made his body very fragile and sensitive to injuries. When he had falls or hurt himself, he would bleed and bruise significantly. But, at least this wasn't life threatening, and he would be out of the hospital after a few days of being monitored after the injection.

His dementia was the hardest obstacle we had to face during his stay; he felt a lot of anxiety being out of his normal routine. I had to pay a caretaker to be there when I couldn't to keep my dad from escaping his bed and making a run for it.

He said to me several times during his stay, "I have places to go and people to see. Why am I here?"

Then he would remove his hospital gown, and declare, "Where are my clothes? I don't want to be in this. I need to leave; I have people waiting for me downstairs."

He made constant attempts to get out of his bed, and I would have to calm him down and get him to cooperate with me. I was the only one he would listen to, and even then, he kept trying my patience. When he thought I was asleep or not paying attention, he would move quickly to get out of his bed.

I would catch him in the act and tell him, "Dad, lay back down. You have to rest."

He would say, just so casually, "Donell, I was only stretching."

We both knew that was a lie, but I couldn't blame him for feeling restless and not wanting to be there.

He didn't understand what was going on, and why it was so vital that he stayed in bed. I had no other family around to come and see him, which would have definitely made things easier. And my friends, of course, did offer, but I didn't want them to see my dad this way. The days at the hospital were long, and we got bored, so I took it upon myself to entertain us both. My dad loved basketball and shooting hoops with me growing up, so I found some things for us to make bank shots in the garbage can of his hospital room. He seemed to really enjoy this activity, and it made the time go by faster for us both. His male nurse, who was quite good looking I might add, gave some assistance to my efforts. He had been dealing with my father's constant "jail breaks" and wanted to help keep him in his bed. He pulled out some syringes, still in the plastic, and said, "You can throw these away, but they cost about five dollars each, so don't tell anyone," and gave us a wink.

My dad found some joy in this activity, and I appreciated that his nurse added to our fun.

The longer we stayed, the more creative I had to become with keeping my dad comfortable and keeping him in bed. I picked up the photo album I made him for Christmas several years back, complete with pictures of his childhood and mine. It had memories of everyone he needed to see, and I hoped it would make him feel some peace. I also brought some essential oils of sage and lavender, and headphones for him to listen to Indian flute music. I placed one earbud in his ear, and I listened though the other. Then I rubbed some oils on his wrists and told him to smell their medicine as he wished.

"Dad, go ahead and sit back and relax. Close your eyes and imagine being home," I said.

The circumstances that had brought us to this point were beyond stressful and energetically draining. On the other hand, I was made aware of how we could still find joy in a space or situation we never wanted to be in. Sure, I was tired, and hadn't gotten a good night's rest in days, but my father was going to be okay. Our bond felt stronger than ever, regardless of his dementia. I could have never imagined finding something beautiful in all of this, but I had to, in order to keep moving forward and becoming the rock my father was for me.

After five long days for us both, my dad was released from the hospital, and I made sure he would have the essentials before returning home. I picked up some clothes and shoes from his room at the Ridge and headed to the hospital. He was so happy to see me and was ready to make it a break for it.

"Let's go, I'm ready to be home, and they said I could leave."

I understood his urgency, but we had to get clearance before we could leave. "Yes, Dad," I told him, "But you need to change, and I need to speak to your nurse before we can head home."

I assisted him with putting on his clothes, which he was so eager to get into. Can't blame the guy, I thought. Hospital gowns are the worst, and this change meant he was going home. The nurse arrived and explained what to expect for the next few days, and what to tell his nurses and caretakers at the Ridge.

Finally, it was time to take Dad back home, and to start to get things back to normal. I didn't tell him about my medical bills or how I was struggling with my knee. More than anything, he didn't need any added stress, and I wasn't going to burden him with mine.

The adjustment for my dad back to his normal routine took close to a month; he struggled quite a bit after his return home. The anxiety of being in the hospital, and the change in his meds during his stay had an impact on his behavior. He felt depressed, and he realized how fragile he had become. We were both very thankful that he had overcome the clot, but it felt like a matter of time before another issue would surface. That time in the hospital with my father really opened my eyes to the fact that our time was limited. This is something we all understand, but it's so easy to forget.

Levi just happened to be around during this time when I needed him the most. It was nice having someone to come home to after a long day of work and visiting with Dad at the hospital. Things were far from perfect, and I had so much I wanted to confront and discuss about us. I just couldn't bring myself to add to any extra stress, and this wasn't the time to figure us out.

Levi had become my medicine, and his presence for those several days made all the difference. I just wanted to be held and cared for. He was the only one who I would have shared this space with. I needed to share my emotions of caring for my father and my fear of losing him. Levi's lynx medicine continued to be helpful, as he was a good listener and knew how to calm me with just his touch.

Things were beginning to return to normal, or what I suppose would be normal in my day-to-day life. My body was angrier than ever, and I was feeling constant pain in my knee and calf. Dr. Lenoue and Kathy both told me they thought it was stress related. That with everything that had happened, in addition to the continued stress of my father, was being manifested to take form in this pain. This made sense to me, and I understood my role in creating my own obstacle. It had been almost two years since I was able to run, due to constant reinjuries, and nothing on the holistic side had helped much. I had seen orthopedic specialists that were clueless about what to do. They couldn't figure out exactly how to treat my injury. I began to give up hope that I would ever have my freedom of movement again. I prayed to Creator for help. I was feeling lost and needed the right medicine.

Then I came upon this book that I had bought a few months back but hadn't yet had the chance to read it. I love when you pick up the right book at the right time, and it immediately speaks to you. The author's words were written just for you, so that you could relate and do what's necessary to get out of your own way. I came across a book called *The Thirteen Original Clan Mothers*, by Jamie Sams. In this powerful book, Jamie explained the ancient legend behind the clan mothers and the gifts and lessons each one can teach us.

I connected instantly to her words, and we shared the same sacred number of seventeen. For me, it held a lot of significance because my sister was seventeen when I was born, and I was seventeen when she passed and my path took a darker direction. I even tattooed it on my body when I was twenty-seven; even then, I understood this number would continue to resurface in other forms.

I got into the first chapter and fixated on the power of her words and how they were speaking to my soul, as if she knew I was in need of healing and had tried everything I could up to this point.

> When we heal ourselves, others are healed. When we nurture our dreams, we give birth to the dreams of mankind. When we walk as loving aspects of the Earth Mother, we become fertile, life-giving Mothers of the Creative Force. When we honor our bodies, our health, and our emotional needs, we make space for our dreams to come into being. When we speak the truth from our healed heart, we allow life abundant to continue on our Mother Planet.

Healing tears ran down my cheeks like a river as I processed where I was at in my journey. These words gave me the introspective lens to see that I was actively participating creating my own prison walls that kept me from being active. I found myself to be lucky for the movement I had right now. And the freedom of movement that I had for so long—that in itself was a gift. These injuries had taught me I didn't appreciate my physical body and its abilities, and I needed to be slowed down. I came back to the conclusion that if I was ever going to heal, I needed to heal my spirit first. The stress was not going to slow down, so it was up to me to find a new way to find my center without being physical. I was going to use this time to put even more effort into my healing from the inside out. I thought I had done the work for the past two years, but clearly my body was telling me something else, and I need to listen. I needed to heal my heart, in order for new life force to take form and heal by body.

Then I came across the clan mother Loves All Things, representing my favorite color purple, and her lessons involved gratitude and healing. I saw myself in her journey, as she learned how to embrace painful memories of the past and look at them as gifts. Gratitude was her greatest teacher and her medicine for healing her past. She was known to bring comfort to others but was the hardest on herself. She had learned to forgive ones who had hurt her but hadn't forgiven herself.

I found myself in every part of this lesson. Was I in fact not loving myself as I had love for others? Did I express enough gratitude to Creator and my ancestors for me being here today? I needed to find my balance between strength and being gentle, just as Love All Things had. This was exactly the medicine I needed to keep me on track and trusting my process.

These aha! moments of clarity brought some other realizations about what I was doing with my personal life. I had lost my power with Levi, and he had the control of the communication. How could I let myself get so lost in a man who didn't want to be seen with me outside of town? How could I continue being a secret, and feeling ashamed of whatever truth lay behind it?

Then, maybe a week later, it all became clear with one visit from a regular client at the salon. She asked me about Levi and wanted to know if we were still dating.

I told her, "Yes, but it's complicated."

She asked to see a picture, and then got really quiet. "I have something to tell you, Donell," she said, "And I'm having a hard time finding the right way."

My stomach sank. I had to know what the hell she was talking about. I burst out, "What do you mean, Shelly?"

She didn't want to hurt my feelings, but I could tell her words of truth were about to.

"Levi dated one of my best friends for several months. They stopped about two months ago, because she discovered he had a girlfriend."

I was freaking pissed, but it made total sense. "Please go on," I told her.

"Well, she thought he was dishonest, and looked into finding him on Facebook. But she could never find him anywhere. So, she looked through another friend's profile, and there he was. Looks like a happy couple, and that they have been together for a long time."

I know at that moment she was speaking of the same girlfriend he said he broken up with right before we met. But he never did, and she had been there this entire time.

Shelly went on to explain, "She was blocked from finding him. And when she confronted him, it didn't go well."

I had looked for his profile before and had been unable to find it. So I asked a few friends if I could find her on Facebook so I could see it for myself. And there it was, a couples picture set in what appeared to be a vacation, posted as her profile picture. They had a life together, and from the surface, they looked really happy. She was a beautiful girl, and I couldn't hate on her, for she had done nothing wrong. I was the other woman, and I never expected to be in this position. In a matter of minutes, the truth was revealed in one picture, a truth I had felt but denied for almost a year. More pain set in knowing I wasn't the only woman; he had carried on a situation of sorts with this other gal while he was here too.

Not only was I not enough for him in general, I wasn't even enough for him in my own town. He knew how I felt about cheating, and I had told him everything about my painful divorce. My head began to spin, processing the countless lies he had told for the last year. All the excuses he made for his distant communication, and why I was never invited to be part of his life there. I thought he loved me, so how could he deceive me like this? I felt a lot of anger, followed by a deep wound that had been reopened. He was indeed a lynx, a keeper of secrets—secrets that came from his own deception.

I wanted answers and I wanted them in person, so I decided to wait for his next visit. I knew if I confronted him over the phone, he would hang up or just purely run away. It became incredibly difficult to play this waiting game and pretend I was emotionally well. But I wanted closure if at all possible, and the only chance of that happening was if I waited to make my move. He had planned on coming back in two weeks' time; I would just sit tight till then.

Of course, I informed my friends of the real truth behind his mystery. It was something we had discussed over the last year and had come up with various scenarios for his behavior. A few of them were shocked that I didn't confront him immediately and demand answers. Others felt I should try and message his girlfriend and tell her about our affair. But I didn't want to be part of their drama, and I chose to stay out of their business. My issue was with him, and him only. I was able to wait for him to come back, and that's how it needed to go down. I was most definitely anxious and nervous to call him out on his shit, but I was determined to do it.

He showed up late in the evening from a flight or some previous engagements he had. I really couldn't believe anything he said anymore, and that's probably what hurt the most. During the next two days we shared amazing intimacy, just as we always had. I knew it was wrong, but I chose to be selfish, fully understanding that once the confrontation happened, my love medicine would be gone for good.

My spirit had had enough, and it was time to make this happen, for I felt ashamed for allowing this to continue as long as it did. There was no hope for a future together, or even a chance to continue to nurture what connection we had created. Levi came to my yoga class that evening, which was a sweet gesture, and I loved seeing him there. But there was nothing that could change what had I to say, and no way to take back what had been done. I had fallen in love with a man that was taken, who had been dishonest with me since day one. I had no way of knowing what was real and what wasn't. He had lied about so much at this point; the fact that he told me he loved me was most likely just another lie as well.

After class we picked up some takeout from our favorite Thai restaurant, the one we ate from on our first date, and headed back home. I waited for him to finish eating and hoped he would settle in. But he could tell I had something on my mind and kept doing trying to look busy on his laptop, saying "I have a few emails to respond to." I wasn't sure if that was true, or he was just buying time.

Eventually he put down his laptop and spooned me on the couch from behind.

I found my courage and turned to him and said, "Do you have something to tell me?"

He quickly responded, "No."

I asked again. "Are you sure?"

He said nothing and looked down with the understanding that I knew his secret.

"I have seen your Facebook, and your girlfriend's, as well. Now do you have something to tell me?"

He knew he was caught red-handed. He wanted to run, but I had him trapped.

"I am surprised it took you this long to figure it out. I am really sorry, and I meant to tell you," he responded.

I was angered at choice of words. "I didn't find out because you lied, and I trusted you. I know you blocked me from finding it, anyhow."

My words were fueled by pain, but I chose to not raise my voice. I spoke with grace and just let the tears stream down my face. He started to cry and felt ashamed for the truth coming to light.

He said, "I meant to break up with her before we met, I just ended up chickening out. I don't want to hurt her, and I didn't mean to hurt you."

I heard what he was saying, but it was clear he didn't really care about her feelings or mine. This was a coward's way of dealing with matters of the heart, and he planned on having his cake and eating it too.

"If you loved her, you would be honest, instead of lying and keeping us both."

He asked how I had found out, and how long I had known. I told him it was fairly recent, not that it mattered.

"How could I not even be enough for you here? When did you even find the time to date someone else here?" I asked.

He just looked down in shame, and I realized he needed the constant female attention. I had thought something was broken with me, but I realized in that moment that something was broken in him.

We went further into the details of his relationship and the lies he had told to keep us both. He claimed he had only been cheating on her the past year, followed by a list of reasons to justify his behavior. This was an old trick I was familiar with; my ex played the victim when he was first caught cheating. I wasn't falling for it.

"I feel sorry for you, that you chose to live this lie," I told him. "Imagine what you could do with all the time and energy you put into keeping up this facade."

He didn't say much and continued to feel embarrassed by my words.

He had gone from relationship to relationship with no time in between to find himself. He could not be alone, and travel allowed him and easy option to seek attention elsewhere. His constant communication disappearances occurred when he tried to end our connection by being a coward. He had never planned on being honest with either of us, or any of the other women he had lied to. I felt bad for his girlfriend and that I had any part in this.

We did hold each other at times, with the understanding this connection between us had to be over. We stayed up all night connecting the dots, and he answered the questions I had to ask. I still ended up kissing him that night with all the love and passion I had before. I wanted him to miss my energy, my touch, and our connection.

Feeling love and pain at the same time is a strange occurrence. I felt foolish for the charade lasting as long as it did, but I wouldn't take it back. I knew I deserved someone who could see my light, where I was enough to keep their attention. I had to take my time with Levi, as both a gift and a lesson. He was my medicine when I needed him to be. I was loved and cared for during a time that weighed heavy on my spirit. I had always known our time together would be limited, and closing this chapter in my life, in this way, was not ideal or easy. I felt ending things in person for me, at least, would bring some closure. If I had reacted any other way, I would have not received any answers I was seeking. I wanted him to know the pain he had caused me, and the turmoil of emotions I felt from him not treating me as I deserved. This talk had to be face-to-face, raw and present. I didn't plan on ever seeing Levi again, so this was the way I chose to say goodbye.

In time, Creator would bring the right man into my life, and I needed to continue my journey towards healing. I chose to embrace the teachings of Loves All Things and went easy on Levi. I couldn't hold hate towards someone I still loved. But I also needed to forgive myself and be gentle with my own heart and protect it once again. The lynx medicine had served its purpose, and I received the good attributes along with the bad, just another lesson in trusting my gut and the process of the journey.

CHAPTER 8
Buffalo Medicine

NOT HAVING JACKSON OR LEVI in my life anymore left me feeling lonelier than ever. If I couldn't be held, I wanted to be holding something, if not someone. I didn't trust myself feeling incredibly vulnerable, so seeking some pet therapy was clearly a better option.

Grace had a regular client that came into the salon, and he had the sweetest Boston terrier named Olive. He would bring her in during his appointments when I was around, knowing I wanted to see her. She had been used to seeing me since she was a puppy, and we had a special bond. After hearing about the loss of Jackson, he offered to let me borrow Olive for a week. This was such an unexpected gift, and I was thrilled to have her company for any amount of time.

Olive was a special creature; she was small for her breed but showed more love than a dog three times her size. She was friendly with people from all walks of life and could be trusted to behave in any environment. Being raised around two young boys made her tolerant of kids, but gentle with them as well. I so loved this pup, and I knew the feeling was mutual.

I swooped her up the following week, and gladly thanked the family for allowing us to spend quality time together. She was the perfect medicine, and I knew I needed to share her gifts with my father. He was never a dog person, and claimed he had allergies. But I had a feeling she would have the same healing effect on him as she did on me.

We pulled up to The Ridge and waited for Dad to come out. He walked up to the car and was surprised to see a dog in his seat.

"Wow, who is this?" he asked.

I picked her up and let him get buckled in. Then I sat her on his lap.

"This is Olive, Dad, and she is a very special dog. She will be staying with me for the week. Is it okay if she sits on your lap?"

He smiled and looked at her darling little face. "Sure, if she will be okay and she sits still."

I took us to Manito Park to watch the ducks and sit back for a nice conversation. My dad missed coming to this place and would drive here frequently when he still had those freedoms. It was a treat for us to come here together, and now we had Olive's company to add to the mix.

We arrived at the park and took a short stroll through the grass and over to the small duck pond located at the opposite end. There were benches all around this area to enjoy the view and soak in the afternoon sun. We sat down and I picked up Olive and sat her on my lap.

"How are you feeling today, Dad? Getting more back to normal?" I asked.

He petted Olive for a moment and glanced around the pond, watching the other people enjoying the same view.

"I'm doing a little better, just miss some of the activities I used to do," he responded.

As kids, we seem to be in such a hurry to grow up. Then, once we hit a certain age, we feel the desire to reclaim our youth. That leads to eventually having to accept that fact that we are part of the cycle of life, and our days are numbered. I couldn't imagine how my father was feeling right now, but I tried to sympathize, knowing that one day I would be in his position.

"Well, I'm proud of you, Dad. You have done so much for so many people."

I spoke the truth. He had always been so involved in helping the community and the public school system. I was proud of his accomplishments and the dedication he had shown throughout his career. He was a healer of sorts, in his own right.

He smiled and said, "I hope so, Donell."

I held his hand. "Trust me, you have, Dad."

Then Olive jumped on his lap and began licking his face. She must have picked up on the moment and understood my dad needed a little extra love that day. Never in my life had I seen him let a dog do this, but he actually seemed to be enjoying himself. My dad didn't realize that he in fact also carried the dog medicine, and Olive was able to recognize that. His medicine had become strong through his efforts to serve humanity, with his consistent counseling for those in need, whether it was homeless kids on drugs, soldiers suffering from PTSD, or widowed spouses. The dog medicine doesn't come from owning a dog. It's about embodying the attributes of being loyal, giving service, and offering forgiveness within all of our human shortcomings.

We spent the afternoon just enjoying each other's company; we didn't need outside entertainment, other than good conversation. I loved that even though my dad was not the man he used to be, he was still very present on days like this. The dementia never took that piece of him away, and I was incredibly grateful, for that was still a gift.

After the week was over, I was sad to give Olive back, but I knew I could borrow her anytime I asked the family. She was such a blessing for us both, and I planned to bring her around my father as often as I could. She had offered me an incredible amount of comfort when dealing with losing Jackson. And the positive effect she had my father was indeed medicine for him, as well.

Mother's Day weekend tended to be a hard time for Dad and me in years past. Our tradition was picking up flowers, then making our way to spend time visiting my mother's and sister's graves. They were buried across the street from one another so many years ago. I knew Olive's presence could lighten the mood and perhaps make the day easier to bear, so she would come along, too.

Dad had mentioned earlier that day that he didn't feel well and wasn't sure if he would have the energy to come. I thought maybe he was just feeling a little depressed and was using it as an excuse to skip the tradition. Maybe he felt this would just add more unwanted suffering and bring back some pain from the past. I could understand his position, and the cruelness of the dementia had made him relive those losses all over again. He questioned the love and connection he experienced on this earth with my mother and siblings, worrying that perhaps he didn't show how much he cared, and for that he was being punished by loss of them no longer on this earth. Over the course of these last few years, he relived the five stages of grief all over again: denial, anger, bargaining, depression, and acceptance. He encountered them in no particular order, and some would resurface again. My father understood these concepts more than most, he had lived them many times, and found the best way to heal was to teach them to his peers, students, and patients. But things were different now, and I had to step up and do what he did for me all those years. It took about twenty minutes over the phone to convince him that he would feel better if he just got some fresh air. I assured him that we had to keep this tradition going, and I wanted to spend time with him today. He finally agreed and made the effort to meet me outside The Ridge.

As he walked out to car, I could tell something wasn't right, but I wasn't sure if it was coming from his mental or emotional pain body.

As he opened the door, he was greeted by Olive. I had wanted it to be surprise.

"Oh, wow, you didn't tell me Olive was coming today," he said, and was able to smile, probably for the first time today.

"I planned on her being with us today, Dad, for extra comfort, and she is always good medicine for us both," I replied.

I had already picked up the flowers on my way to get Dad, so we were ready to head to the cemetery. It was only about a fifteen-minute drive on the freeway, and it took no time to get there. I parked as close as I could to where I remembered the graves to be. But once we got out of the car, we struggled with finding them. Since my dad wasn't feeling well today, I told him to just wait with Olive, and I made my way down different rows of the cemetery in search of my mother. I had been here so many times before, I couldn't understand why I couldn't find the grave today. Dad didn't listen and got out to walk around and look. It was upsetting to him as well, that he was struggling to find her. After ten minutes or so of searching, I finally stumbled up her grave and saw my mother's name, Elvera Barlow.

"Dad, I found her," I called out, and motioned for him to come over with Olive. He had used up more energy than he should have, and I told him to take seat on the grass next to Mom. I went back to the car to get her flowers and some water for the underground vase. And I also had planned to pray today with Dad and placed my smudge stick in my pocket. Dad seemed to look a little under the weather, and I asked him if he was feeling okay.

"I'm having a harder time breathing than normal today, Donell. But I have felt this way for about a week now. I have had it looked into at The Ridge, and nothing seems to be of concern. I'm really glad I came with you today, and I didn't miss the tradition."

"I'm really glad you came today, too, Dad. I don't know if I could bring myself to come without you" I replied.

Before I could place the flowers in the vase, I had to use my knife to MacGyver it loose out of the ground. When not in use, the vase was placed upside down into a metal cylinder, and, over the winter months, became sealed tight. Once freed, I placed a bouquet of pink Gerbera daisies, purple amaryllis, and white gladiolus, and filled it with water. Then I sat down next to Dad and Olive and took out my smudge stick. I took my lighter to it, and once it took ahold, the smoke appeared and the smell of sage came with it. I fanned the smoke at my feet, and then up my body towards my face, while using my other hand to wave the smoke over my head.

Before beginning my prayer, I placed the smudge in front of Dad and fanned the smoke over his head. I chose to express myself with words.

"Thank you, Creator, for this day. I am grateful for my father and Olive being here. We miss our family so much, and some days it's still a struggle to understand why they aren't with us. I ask that you please continue to be patient with me, as I am trying to be on my chosen path. I want to make you proud, as well as the rest of my family. I am paying attention to your messages and am able to receive them as you see fit. And please watch over my father today, as he is not feeling well. Help him understand that he has messages awaiting him too, to see when he is ready."

My father chose not to speak but told me he liked what I had to say.

"I really like this smudging thing, Donell. It's really calming," he expressed. We spent some time reflecting and telling stories of the past, then sitting in silence and listening for hidden messages. I shared with him some of the magic I had felt when I would just sit and listen to the silence. And how Creator would send messages using the creature teachers as lessons, for me understand and put into motion in my own life. I personally don't feel connected to cemeteries. It holds the shell of the person you love. My experiences have taught me to be open, to find spirit wherever I feel the most connected. The dream world was one of those places, and it offered me a doorway to continue to connect with my family in other dimensions. My father was envious of this gift, but I assured him they were always around us and that he was never alone.

We got back into the car and drove across the street and into the other cemetery to pay our respects to my sister. Her grave was easier find, and it didn't take long this time to get her vase out of the ground. I placed another bouquet of the same flowers that I had given to Mom and filled the vase with water. Dad chose to speak this time, and I was pleased that he felt well enough to find the space.

"I cannot even begin to express how much we miss you, Laura. And not a day goes by that I don't think of you and the impact you had on us. I hope you felt enough love from me and knew that I would have done anything I could to protect you. You were always such a devoted mother and sister to Donell. I pray that you left this world in peace and did not suffer. We love you, we miss you, and look I forward to seeing you again."

I was proud that he chose to express such emotion when he was feeling like he hadn't wanted to come today. My father was one of the most expressive men I had ever encountered. I realized that I was lucky all those years that he was able to embrace the feminine energy along with the masculine, for I would be a very different person if he had not provided me with the dog and the buffalo medicine. This was one of those days I would hold dear to my heart. When we left the cemetery, I felt that we both had received a little extra healing because of this medicine he still carried within him.

I was still finding myself within the pages of *The Thirteen Original Clan Mothers* and now came across the journey of Looks Far Woman. She represents the full spectrum of pastel colors and stands as the doorkeeper to the crack in the universe. Her home lies within the dream world and is open to those who understand its value. Looks Far Woman safely guides us through our dreamtime, revealing our visions and ways to heal ourselves in this sleep-time reality. Through her teachings, this truth is revealed:

> *When we forget our ability to use free will, by forecasting what a future outcome will be, we can trap ourselves into projections, expectations,*

and loss of potential opportunity. The lessons we refuse to experience will usually catch up with us in later form.

I can understand that we have the power to change our path when we pay attention to what our dreams are telling us. I take my dreams very seriously, and I pay attention to what hidden messages might come through. They give me hope and, at times, complete freedom to alter the dimensions of the reality I am in. I could truly relate to this clan mother, for the dream world had always been a gift and a place of healing since I was a young child.

Little did I know that one of the most powerful dreams I had ever experienced was soon going to surface. But first, I had someone that needed to cross my path, for he would somehow unlock this dream into reality.

I received a sweet message on my social media from a Navajo man named Colby living in Oregon.

He wrote, "Hello, there. I don't ever do this, but I needed to say hi. I think you seem like a special lady and possess a beauty from the inside out."

I quickly checked out his profile to better understand what kind of person felt compelled to say such things. I was still very skeptical of men at this point, and for good reason. After just processing the deceit of my situation with Levi, I needed to be aware of any male's intentions. Colby seemed to give off a more wholesome energy, and his eyes brown eyes had kindness behind them. These days, your instincts are softened by what people choose to share about themselves on social media. But he did seem more genuine than most and might be someone I could call a friend. I chose to respond after a few hours, being in no rush, to see where this conversation was going.

"Well, thank you for seeing my light. You are very sweet to say such words, and I can see kindness behind your eyes."

We exchanged a few messages back and forth, getting to know one another a little better. I'm really not a big fan of texting and prefer a phone call, but it seemed impossible to get anyone on the phone these days. The lines of communication between people have changed so dramatically over the last twenty years. So very few take the time to call, and it's nearly impossible to understand tone within a text. To my surprise, he chose to call me, and I was pleasantly surprised he was making a real effort to understand me better.

We said hello, and at first it felt a little awkward, considering we barely knew each other. I knew he had an interesting story by just looking at his pictures. My brother Jason that had passed was Navajo, so learning more about Colby's experience within his tribe intrigued me.

He began, "I was raised the traditional way in a hogan, back in Arizona with my father and several siblings. Elders have told us the creation story of the first hogan, built by Coyote with the help of the beavers."

Hogans are the traditional and sacred dwellings of the Navajo people and are made using packed mud against an entire wood structure. I was fascinated by his words, and that he was raised in a traditional way. I had always wondered how different my life would have been if my parents had chosen the reservation life for me.

He went on to say, "After my mother passed, I was responsible to help out with the care of all my younger siblings. We didn't have electricity or any other conveniences that would allow us to watch TV and view the outside world. The household and schooling were very strict, and we practiced and lived our traditional ways."

I had never encountered anyone like this before. I could imagine that his life had been incredibly hard at times, but what a blessing to be so connected to your ancestors and culture on that level.

He said he hadn't experienced much of the outside world, like that was a bad thing. From my perspective, it sounded magical, and I envied that his family kept their traditions. There was so much we could share, being from to very different worlds but with similar values. I told him about losing my mother and siblings, and that I was now caring for my dad. He related well to my experience and had struggled with the loss of his father. And now he was caring for his two twin sons, with little help from their mother.

It's incredibly rare to meet a man that steps up as the single parent. The only other man I knew personally capable of this sacrifice was my father. Colby had not only impressed me, but also inspired me with the man that he was. The traits of being a good father were a very attractive quality to me. Just knowing these qualities allowed my heart to open up and begin some level of trust.

I had never planned on being a mother, but after having several dreams about my son, I changed my mind. I wanted to meet the little spirit I had created in my dreams; I wanted to be able to feel this kind of love only a parent knows. And if I got the chance to have children, it would only be possible with a man that embraced fatherhood.

The conversation lasted for an hour, and then he had to get the boys to bed. I looked forward to getting to know him better by sharing our stories and becoming better friends. I didn't know how to explain it, other than Colby had left an imprint on me. I went to sleep feeling good about what we had shared, and grateful to connect with someone so special.

That night I had such a powerful dream, one that I didn't need to write down. Looks Far Woman came forward and knew I needed her medicine by allowing me to see into my future and offering my truth.

I am lying in bed and I wake up to my father lying next to me. I realize this is not my bed, but his from our old house. I look around the bedroom and it's just as it was, and how he kept it, with the old antique rocking chair off to the right and the dark wood dresser at the foot of the bed. I turn to my father and his eyes are closed and he is looking very peaceful. I think he must be sleeping hard or in a deep dream. I don't want to wake him, but I have a strong urge to get out of bed. I walk over to the foot of the bed, and I see a Native American man lying there, sleeping on the floor. He has long black hair and strong bone structure. I get a glimpse of this man and feel connected to his energy. I don't know if we have ever met, but somehow, I feel safe in his presence. I then choose to lie down next to him and cover us with a shared blanket. This feels right, as if this man is my soul mate, and he has been waiting for me to find him.

When I woke up, I was startled by the events that just occurred, and what it all meant. The significance of it being in my father's bed had me worried. My mother had passed in that bed and in that room. What did it mean? Could his time be limited, and the dream meant he would be with her soon? And who was this man that I felt so compelled to lay next too? Why did he appear to me all of a sudden, and in the same dream space as my father? I tried to recall what he looked like, and then it came to me that he resembled the same features as Colby. This didn't make sense. I had just met Colby yesterday and didn't feel that way about him. I don't take all my dreams literally, but this one was different than the rest. There was a clear message here, and I needed to pay attention to what it was telling me.

I decided to make some plans with Dad and wanted him to take a trip for his birthday to Seattle. We could spend some quality time on the road, just like when I was little. He could see his siblings and grandchildren, and that would be really good medicine for him. He agreed that it sounded fun, but he was a little apprehensive about whether he would feel physically up to going. I assured him that he would be ready, and everything would work out. We had two and half months until July, which allowed him plenty of time to make a full recovery from the blot clot.

That dream had scared me into making these plans a reality, because I believed it meant his time was limited. His physical and mental capabilities to travel were dwindling, and we needed this time together. I wanted to see joy in face, and the love of having family around. He had spent so many years alone in our house, and I wanted to leave him with new memories. Whether he remembered them or not, it was still healing for us both.

I continued to communicate with Colby over the next few weeks and found his perspective on life refreshing and inspiring. I did tell him about the dream but chose to leave out the part that the man looked like him. I didn't want to freak him out or make him think I saw us in a romantic way. The truth was, I still didn't know, but I was staying open to the possibility of us being more than friends later on.

I was still very hung up on Levi, and trying to keep my mind straight was difficult enough. It had been a few months since we last spoke, and he sent me an email wanting to share one last playlist. This playlist was a complete library of all the songs we had ever sent. He must have gone to some trouble, compiling all of this shared music together.

> I can't believe how many songs we shared, and now they all remind
> me of you. I will miss our talks, our kisses, and looking into your eyes.
> I'm sorry for hurting you. This isn't goodbye but see you later. –Levi

It had been so hard not to communicate these past two months, and I was still in love with him and missed him immensely. Listening to these songs had proven difficult for me as well, with each one unlocking another memory of the magic we had shared. But I knew he wasn't going to ever change and be honest and loyal to one woman. We could have had an open relationship, but under the circumstances, he was already committed. Still feeling vulnerable, I had to stay strong and keep my distance, but I did email him back. I knew I shouldn't, but I justified it with our physical distance. And it concluded with saying we missed each other but would never see each other again.

Memorial Day was another holiday reserved for Dad and another visit to the cemetery. His depression over the last few months had never really improved, and he continued to feel more down than usual. Once again, he tried to cancel on me. He said he didn't feel well and experienced shortness of breath all weekend. But I knew he needed this medicine and that if I could get him outside, he would feel better. I swooped Olive once again for the weekend; she had helped so much before, and he loved to spend time with her. After some good convincing, he eventually gave in and said he would come, but didn't want to be gone long.

As he approached the car, I could tell in his stride that he wasn't well, and this was different from before. He had a hard time moving and struggled to walk the short distance. Once he got to the car and saw Olive, his energy was a bit lighter, and they greeted each other with warm cuddles. I was worried about if he could physically handle our tradition and felt bad for dragging him out of the house. But I knew if he missed this chance, he would regret it, and I felt responsible to push him as he had always pushed me. The roles had been reversed for some time now, and what if this was his last time to continue this tradition?

I remembered from our last visit to create some better points of reference so we could easily find Mom. I drove up as close as I could to her row and helped Dad out of the car. I had the flowers and the smudge stick ready for when we found her grave. I was happy that the flowers were easier this time around. The vase wasn't stuck upside down, as it was previously. However, Dad was in worse shape than before. I had to assist him to be able to sit on the ground. He didn't seem to trust his body or balance. I continued to worry about his health, but we were already there, and needed to finish what we started. I took out the smudge stick and lit the medicine, fanning the smoke at our feet and up our legs and all the way up to our faces. I then placed it into my abalone shell and allowed it to burn. Dad chose to speak this time, which made the fact he had come that much more important.

"Thank you, Father, for allowing me and Donell to be here today in memory of Elvera. We miss her so incredibly much, and I look forward to seeing her again with the rest of the family. I am grateful for Donell bringing me here and showing me how to smudge. My body is having a hard time today; please give me the strength to stay strong, Lord. I have been struggling so much physically and mentally, and I feel stuck in a hard place. I want so much to be the man I used to be, not just for myself, but for Donell."

Hearing those words pulled hard on my heart strings and gave me the sense that my father, the one who raised me, was still in there. We let the smudge stick burn for a while and sat there in the stillness. I chose not to speak and instead just allowed myself to feel what I needed to. I felt his grief for her loss, as well as my own. I wished there was some other way that I could ease any of his pain. I imagine that's how a parent feels when their child is hurting. Before we left, I gathered some of the ashes left over from the smudge stick and set them aside in a small medicine pouch. By the time we made the short walk over to my sister's grave, my dad's struggle for movement was clearly declining.

"Are you okay, Dad?" I asked. He looked really tired and a bit pale. I wasn't sure if this was a result of only physical pain or was coming from his emotional body.

"I am just having a hard time breathing today, and it makes me really tired. But I'm glad that I came today with you and Olive."

I arranged the flowers over Laura's grave, just as I had done with Mom's. Then lit the smudge stick and allowed Dad to have his time to speak whatever truth he wanted to share.

"Again, I want to thank you, Father, for allowing me to be here today. It's been so long since we lost Laura, but the pain never fades. She was an amazing daughter, mother, and woman. I struggle with the fact she was taken too young, and too soon. But I have to trust you know what it right, and I do look forward to being reunited again."

I chose to not speak once again, and just let Dad take the lead. Listening to him express his words was more than enough for me, emotionally speaking. I gathered ashes from her smudge and added them to my medicine pouch. I was pleased that my dad had made it today and that we got to share some healing words. He chooses to say the word Lord or Father, and I prefer Creator or our Mother. But when it comes down to it for me, it's all the same. And if it comes from love, I have no issues with it. Who am I to judge anyone's beliefs? The numerous church days we shared were never like this. We had found our way of expressing spirituality together. We left the cemetery in a different way than even before, perhaps with a little more closure and healing that we had received.

I had to take Olive back the next morning before work, having a day full of appointments followed by teaching an evening yoga class. I was blessed to get a cancelation during my lunch hour and used the time to read a book in the park by the salon. I had finished *The Thirteen Original Clan Mothers* and was halfway into *American Indian Healing Arts*, by E. Barrie Kavasch and Karen Baar.

This book also spoke to me right away, and I needed to learn its medicine. The book contained not just the plant medicine, but the ceremonies and prayers behind it. It walked you through the traditions that begin at birth, all the way through rites of passage, and into your adult life. I loved learning the different recipes for salves and healing teas, and the array of ceremonies tied to the different tribes and their meanings. I found so much beauty and strength in my ancestors' traditional ways, and I wanted to experience more for myself. I had read up to the middle age medicine path, and I found a section within its contents that sent chills down my spine.

> Middle age is a time when many healers find that they can devote themselves more fully to the Medicine path. Some admit that they've spent years exploring other life paths, ignoring the original call to healing that came to them in their youth. Whether it's because such a calling cannot be denied forever or because healers must have a wide range of life experiences before they can take possession of their powers, it is often during midlife that these individuals go through a requisite training to use their gifts to help others.
>
> Other Native healers first come into their powers at this time. Some individuals become more open to psychic and multisensory awareness after recovery from a serious illness or shock, such as surviving

lightning strike, or suffering a major loss or upheaval in their personal lives. Some Native people experience personal growth and change through an illness and the special medicines and rituals that are used to cure it.

This also might be a time when the healers and seers gain some added strength and intuitive capacity. They more frequently experience dreams that are filled with healing knowledge of certain plants, mushrooms, and minerals, or that foretell future events.

I felt as if the universe just slapped me across the face with this truth and had been waiting for me to recognize the signs and to wake the hell up. This felt like my journey, and that all the things that happened out of pain were actually meant to be used as gifts. I don't think I have ever felt so connected to an author's words than at that very moment. I could sum up my journey thus far within these pages. It also gave me hope that this suffering would transform to be my strength, and that I could use my wounds to help heal others, just as Dad had done.

I had twenty minutes left in my break, and I got a phone call from The Ridge. My gut knew instinctively that something was very wrong, and I felt panicked already.

"Hello, Donell, this is the nurse at The Ridge. Your dad was having a really hard time breathing today and was taken to the hospital in an ambulance. He was with his care taker, and they had just finished lunch."

I knew it would be bad news. I had just found some peace in my day, but that feeling left as quickly as it had come.

"Oh my God! Is he okay? Where are they taking him?"

The nurse replied, "He will be at admitted to the emergency room at Deaconess. Sacred Heart is full at the moment."

I had no issues with what hospital he was admitted to, but his cardiologist was at Sacred Heart. She ended with, "His caretaker Dianne is with him. Just get there when you can."

I couldn't help but feel panicked, and now I had to try to figure out how to cancel my appointments and yoga class and get down to the hospital. I made it back to work and had to finish one more client. I put out a group message to my gym and pleaded for a sub to teach my class, telling them my dad was in the hospital.

In the few hours that passed, I wasn't present with my client or anyone else. I needed to get to my father, and the waiting game was wearing me down. I ended up having to teach that evening, and it felt like torture. I didn't want to just bail on my students or the front desk, so I showed up in a physical form, but I clearly was somewhere else. As soon as class finished, I made my way up to the emergency room of the hospital.

Dad was lying in bed with his normal clothes on, awaiting some test results. Dianne, his caretaker, had waited for me to get there, and I thanked her for her patience.

I ask him, "How are you feeling? What happened with you today?"

He was actually very responsive and was acting fairly normal. He said, "I am feeling okay right now, but earlier my breathing became so difficult I chose to come here."

Then he proceeded to tell me about his lunch date with Dianne, and what he had on the menu. What caught my attention was when he mentioned, "I saw two women standing by the ambulance, Donell, before I got on."

I looked at Dianne and could tell in her body language that she thought my dad was crazy or that it was the dementia talking. But I understood what this meant and validated who he saw.

"I believe you saw Mom and Laura, Dad. We did visit them yesterday."

He was pleased that I could relate to what he saw. And I didn't at all think he was crazy, but I knew it was a sign, and I also knew to prepare myself for more change.

I called my uncle and aunt to inform them what was going on, and that I would let them know when I had more answers. Then I reached out to one of my Native mentors, Gerald, who lived in Illinois and was Ho-Chunk. He had helped and guided me with my path over the last year. I looked up to him for his wisdom and knowledge of medicine. I sent him a text that my father was in the hospital, and I was surprised I never heard back. This wasn't like Gerald, and I really needed his support.

I told Dianne she could go home and that I would keep her updated on any new results. We stayed in that room until about ten-thirty p.m. and were then finally moved into a regular room. I gathered his things and kept him entertained while he was wheeled to the next location. He was feeling restless, and I was hoping to find a way to calm him so he could settle in for the evening. It occurred to me he might enjoy me reading this book, and he could just sit and listen. After explaining to him what it was about, he was all ears and had nothing better to do, anyhow.

I had read into the old age chapter while he fell asleep, during the hours waiting for our new room. And now, I just so happened to be on a section speaking of the Yurok, Karuk, and Hoopa world renewal ceremonies. I thought Dad would enjoy hearing about this ceremony of my mother's tribe, whether he had known it before and forgot. It explained that everyone in the village was granted to participate in the sacred dances. The White Deerskin Dance was in honor of our first sacred animal, the deer. The Boat Dance was done on turbulent rivers, while the participants used long dugouts to catch and hunt traditional foods. The third dance, the Jump Dance, was said to create great power of renewal. The dancers wore woodpecker scalps that were fashioned into headbands and basket hats.

Dad was finding some calm in my words, and it took him less than an hour to fall asleep for the evening. I arranged for him to have a caretaker there first thing in the morning, and I chose to go home to sleep. I had no idea what to expect in the next couple of days, but I knew I needed to rest when I could.

I went home and couldn't find a way to let my mind or heart settle. I just kept reliving the day's experiences and worrying about Dad. I wished I had family nearby, or a partner to turn to for support. Just because I was used to doing this alone didn't make continuing to accept it any easier. The next morning, I cancelled that day of appointments, picked up the paper, coffee, and a scone for my dad and headed back to the hospital. The doctors still weren't quite clear what was going on and had to run more tests. Dad was growing impatient, just like before, and the dementia was beginning to skyrocket to an all-time high. He was back to taking off his gown and making attempted jailbreaks to escape his bed, only this time, his physical body was too weak, and he had only so much energy to spare.

We spent our long days at the hospital watching movies and visiting in between his naps. He became convinced that I was a famous actress and kept telling the staff I was on TV. They chose to amuse him and pretended to ask for my autograph.

I guess the fact that he was proud of me, even though it was an illusion he had created, still felt endearing. And at times like these, it offered us some humor in the situation.

As we approached another day in the hospital, I was feeling worn down and little lost, just trying with every fiber of my being to stay strong and hold it together. This was a time to access the buffalo medicine that my father had taught me, a time to find that inner strength to become the stability for him and the rest of the family. My Uncle and Aunt had made plans to arrive over the weekend, which would alleviate some of the weight, and be of help. I was looking forward to the company, and maybe it would lift Dad's spirits.

Earlier that day when I had visited with Dad, his thoughts were fairly normal, and he was responsive to my questions. However, that evening his behavior dramatically shifted, and it was like watching a sad film of a character you once knew and now couldn't relate to. He spoke of small children crawling up the walls of his room and coming in and out of his room. I had to remind him constantly of where he was, and that he was there to get better. Then he lost complete control of his bodily functions and returned to a childlike state. He was scared, and had no concept of why he was there, or how to react to anything around him. By seven p.m. that evening, he had worn himself out with the constant anxiety and fear he was feeling from being out of his element. I chose to read him a prayer out of my book, one that spoke to me before and that I hoped would calm his heart.

O Great Spirit,
Whose voice I hear in the winds,
And whose breath gives life to the entire world,
Hear me! I am small and weak; I need your strength and wisdom.
Let me walk in the beauty, and make my eyes ever behold the
red and purple sunset.
Make my hands respect the thing you have made and my ears sharp
to hear your voice.
Make me wise so that I may understand the thing you have taught
my people.
Let me learn the lessons you have hidden in every leaf and rock.
I seek strength, not to be greater than my brother, but to fight
my greatest enemy—myself.
Make me always ready to come to you with clean hands and straight eyes,

So when life fades, as the fading sunset, my spirit may come to you
without shame.

His eyes were closed by the end, and I don't know how much he had heard, but it felt good to share those words with him in that moment, because I needed to hear them for my own comfort. I took a seat, watching my dad sleep and pondering what the Creator had in mind for what was to come next.

Around eight p.m., I was surprised to be greeted by a female cardiologist. I had been told by his nurse that she would be there in the morning. Before revealing any results, she asked me a series of questions.

"Where is your father living, and does he have assistance? Did he have any previous medical conditions in the past six months? Do you have other family in town, or to help you?"

I answered all her questions without knowing I was about to get hit with a truth I wasn't prepared for. She explained the blood clot back in January never actually healed, and for the past almost five months, my dad's clot was destroying his mechanical heart valve, and it was leaking inside him. Surgery was not an option, with already having had two open-heart surgeries before.

I was feeling so helpless and began to cry while she continued to give me more detail.

She put her hand on my shoulder for comfort and said, "Your best option is to take him home, and call hospice. We will keep him comfortable on morphine, and I expect he has a month left before he passes."

There it was: my dream had been confirmed, and my dad was going to be leaving this earth very soon. She then asked if I wanted to relay the news to my father, and I said, "No, could you please tell him for me?"

She said, "Yes, of course, dear," and gently woke him up.

She put her hands on his shoulders, and with a gentle shrug said, "Don, this is your doctor. Can I please speak with you for a moment?"

He was groggy from the meds they had given him earlier to keep calm, and he had a hard time responding.

Then she asked him, "Do you know who that is?" and pointed at me.

He said, "That's Donell," and I was pleased he knew me still.

But then she said, "Is this your daughter?"

His response was, "No, she works at the hospital and tells people what to do."

She asked him a few more times, and he continued to say I was not his daughter. Each time I heard those words, I was cut with such a fierce force of pain, leaving me a dramatic scar of a new wound that I feared would surface one day. The doctor tried to see if she could get through to him and explain what she had told me. But it was clear he wasn't going to understand, and her effort was best left at letting him rest.

She gave me her card, and said, "I'm so sorry, my dear. Give me a call if you have any questions or need anything."

I was grateful to have had such an empathic doctor to give me the bad news. I felt like she cared, and that was at least something.

After she left, the emotions came pouring out of me. I lost it and I felt helpless. I messaged my family and a few close friends on the latest news, and then just sat in the silence of my pain. I chose to stay for another couple of hours, in case he woke up and felt alone. By eleven p.m., I had made up my mind to go home. I knew the long road that lay ahead was going to be exhausting on all levels.

The moment I walked in the door, I made my way to the couch and just cried my heart out. I began to smudge and pray, begging for answers and comfort from anyone who was listening. I quickly succumbed to a deep and dark state, for I had lost any sense of hope for my father's recovery.

Suddenly I wasn't alone, and I felt something touch my shoulder, and then the sensation continued all the way down to my hand. Although it startled me, this was indeed a touch of comfort, from someone who knew I needed it. I understood right away that this had to be my mother, and she had come to comfort me and tell me it was his time.

My tears took on another form as I cried out to my mother, "I know that's you, I understand he has to go. But I will be left with no one, now. How am I to be strong, when you are all gone? Why have you all have left me?"

I begged her to touch me again and cried out to her several times that night. I never got another response, but I felt grateful for at least the moment I got her touch one more time.

That night dragged on, and I didn't sleep or rest whatsoever. I was eager to get back to my father and begin the process of making arrangements for his final days on this earth. I walked into his room, and his eyes instantly lit up as he recognized me. He was trying to tell me something but was unable to communicate and was having what looked like seizures. The nurses rushed into the room to check his vitals and were surprised to see a sudden change in his condition. They said he had conversed with them a lot that morning, and even spoke to my aunt over the phone. I backed up and allowed them to get a closer look as to what was going on. Then I saw a panic in their faces, that something had gone horribly wrong. The nurse asked me if I would like to sit beside him, and of course I was happy to do so. But I didn't understand what's happening; he was supposed to go home soon. I looked into my father's eyes and I didn't see his spirit. His physical body was there, but his spirit was leaving.

Within minutes, Rose showed up and was shocked to see what was going down before her. I had mentioned she didn't have to visit, but she was intent on making an appearance. She sat on the bed and held my hand. We were both crying and feeling unsure about what to do.

I then turned to the nurse. "What's going on? And why does he look this way? Is he passing right now?"

She answered, "Yes, he is having a heart attack and will no longer be with us soon, my dear."

Rose and I looked at each other in disbelief, that within ten minutes of me being there he was gone. I continued to hold his hand until his last breath. I kissed him on the forehead and told him how much I loved him.

The nurse took off his jewelry and handed it to me. I looked down at his turquoise watch and put it on. I remembered him wearing this watch every day of my life, and I was going to keep it close to me. It all happened so fast, and I just couldn't bring myself to alert the rest of the family. I called my aunt and uncle and told them the news and asked that they inform everyone else. My uncle was very upset he didn't make it in time to say goodbye, and I tried to convince him it was for the best. My father would have hated being back at The Ridge in hospice care, and having his loved ones see him like that. I told them to still come up that weekend; we had a funeral to plan.

Rose was kind enough to be my messenger, using her hawk medicine, and inform my friends of the news. Then she cancelled the rest of my salon appointments for the week. The nurses had left us the room and told us to take our time and leave when we wished. Two other of my closest friends, Ronnie and Lindsey, also came for support. They greeted me with huge hugs and went over to my dad and said their goodbyes. My friends had always been so sweet to my dad, and even though he constantly forgot their names, he still loved them for loving me.

We spent close to two hours sharing stories about him and then collectively decided to head back to my place. I asked them to leave the room so I could say my final goodbyes to my father. I walked over to his body and kissed his forehead one last time. Still crying rivers of tears that were necessary I began saying my piece.

"I love you, Dad, and I am going to miss you so much. I understand you were fighting for so long, and you stayed to take care of me. I am happy for you that you finally get to be with Mom and the rest of the family now. I can't imagine ever having a more devoted and loving father than you. Dad, you are my greatest teacher, and you raised me to be a strong woman through your buffalo medicine. Please don't worry about me; I can stand on my own. I will look for you in my dreams, and in that space, we can be together again. I will make you proud, and I can't thank you enough for being the man of my life."

I was left feeling an incredible amount of pain, but in that pain, I already understood that he had waited for me. He didn't leave this earth until he saw me one last time, and I couldn't have asked for more than that. I had seen my other family suffer, and I had seen him suffer over the last few years. Perhaps him leaving this way was a blessing for us both. Neither one of us could heal when the other was suffering, and now he was set free. And then I realized within that experience that I was set free, and this felt like an even bigger life change than my divorce. There was so much to process, and I didn't even know where to begin.

I made my way home to be greeted by Britney and few other good friends for support and quality time. I appreciated their presence and efforts, but in all reality, I wanted to be alone. I wanted to connect with spirit and ask for answers or messages. The girls left after a few hours and gave me the space to finally breathe.

I messaged Gerald that my dad had passed, and he responded right away. He explained that after my last message, he had a vision of an owl. That meant that my dad would pass soon, and he didn't want to interfere with the process. He chose to give me my space and knew I would reach out when I was ready. I also wanted to reach out to Lori and let her know of my dad's passing. She and my father-in-law were so good to my dad over the years, and they deserved to know. I figured she would inform James, and I wanted him to know, but not coming from me. After that, I stayed off my phone and curled into a ball of deep despair.

I allowed myself to cry and to feel the pain, the loss of my hero and the one man that was always there to listen. I could have never imagined for my life to change course again so suddenly. But I had come to understand that change is inevitable, and you can either be dragged through the door kicking and screaming, while continuing to resist what is. Or accept that this was chosen for you, and do your best to move forward.

CHAPTER 9
Sweat Medicine

THE NEXT MORNING WAS BLEAK, and I was consumed with a deep sadness and so missing my father. I thought the best medicine would be a morning walk along the river, to pray and connect with nature. I brought my medicine pouch from the day we smudged and the smudge stick we used along with me. I took my normal route, to avoid the most traffic, and made my way down to the river. This time, I was stopped dead in my tracks by a crow before I could leave the parking lot. He was swooping over my head and being very vocal with his "kakaka." I thought maybe I was near his nest, and he felt threatened by me. But I went this way almost every day, and I had never seen this behavior before. I continued walking quickly away from him, and he continued to dive bomb just a few feet above my head. I didn't understand what he wanted, or why he felt threatened by me. I continued to increase my stride, as he was making me feel like I was in harm's way. He did it once more, and then I decided to turn around and give him my attention. He landed on light pole with no nest. We made direct eye contact and I understood then that's what he wanted. The creature teachers hold important lessons that we can learn from when we allow them the space to show us. He was giving me a message that I wasn't alone, and that I was connected, that I needed to stop walking away out of fear and just embrace what was chosen for me. After a few minutes of being present and giving him that time, the crow allowed me to walk away and let me be.

I was in need of some music medicine, and I used the rest of my walk to listen to the Indian flute songs that Dad and I spent hours absorbing in the hospital. The soft sounds of the wooden flute have such a powerful effect on calming my heart; it's what I imagine Mother Earth would sound like if she chose to play an instrument. The shorter notes carried my footsteps along the path, and I could hear the light wind and warmth of the sun in the longer notes that took more breath. As they continued to develop and take shape, the animals made their appearance and became part of the theatrical orchestra. Mother Earth took her position as the conductor and this song manifested into the magic that's all around us when we choose to pay attention. The delightful display of music in harmony with nature led me back to my medicine tracks.

I came to a quiet area along the river and headed down into a short but steep bank that allowed me some privacy. It was off the beaten path and felt nestled like a cove, as if it was by the ocean. The space was small but provided one single bench near the water to sit. Surrounded by a variety of trees to offer some cover, it had easy access to the water. I knew this ritual would feel different than the others, and I was anticipating saying my prayers. I lit the smudge stick that we had used less than a week before, waved the smoke over my head and body, and began to pray.

"Creator, I am asking for your guidance more than ever. My spirit has broken with the loss of my father. I understand he was suffering, and I got the messages you sent that it was his time. I am unsure with what direction you want me to take now, Creator. I know I want a family of my own someday, one that doesn't leave me. I do appreciate your guidance and patience with me. Please keep sending me signs that I'm on my chosen path. I am awake and I am paying attention."

I let the smudge stick burn all the way down while observing the flow and the movement of the river. The gentle harmony of the current, rushing over rocks around obstacles in the water, created another sense of calm within me. I closed my eyes and listened to its movement, trying to imagine myself in motion just like the water, and when I faced obstacles in life, finding a way to move with it instead of being resistant. This would make for an easier course, and it would be less painful and still allow me flow where I needed to and end up where I was supposed to be. I gathered the ashes from this smudge and mixed them with the ashes in my pouch. I felt good that I was able to receive some clarity on my "mourning walk," and chose to be on my way and head back home. I had important decisions to make about handling my dad's affairs, and there was no rest for the weary.

I messaged Gerald about the incident with the crow, and that I had just finished praying by the river. He had also just finished doing a ceremony for my father.

He said, "He is a powerful spirit, and he is so proud of you. He left this earth quickly, because he had important work to do on the other side. Your dad will visit you in time, when you are ready."

Then he mentioned that the crow was clearly trying to get my attention, and I needed to continue to listen for hidden messages. I felt so incredibly blessed to have someone like Gerald to guide me. I knew he was a gift from Creator to help me on my journey.

It's so unfortunate that when people die, you are not given time to grieve. Final arrangements for their burial, handling their assets, and bills all pile on with quickness, leaving you forced to make decisions when you have succumbed to despair and are not being present. But I did what I had to do and booked the funeral home for the following weekend. Once my uncle and half-brother arrived in the next few days, we could plan the rest.

I didn't mention my half-brother Scott before, because we don't have a relationship. I haven't seen him in thirteen years, and then he came down a few times to visit Dad in the last two. Our dynamic is complicated, but I prefer it this way after the confrontations we shared in the past. My father wanted us to be close, but it was too late for that. Somewhat recently, we had made a few attempts to connect, but they ended in arguments. I was thankful he wanted to help, but it was clearly going to be awkward for us both.

Even through the pain I was experiencing, I honestly felt more connected than ever to spirit. I imagined my entire family watching over me, and my father was now there to lead them. I had been given a gift to see magic in the smallest circumstances, and my senses of my surroundings took another form. I embodied the attributes of Listening Woman. She is the clan mother of the stillness and represents the color black, connected to the moon. Through activating her "Tiyoweh" or stillness, she is able to listen for those hidden messages from nature, the creature teachers, and the spirit world. And once again, the words from those pages spoke directly to my soul.

> In her state of heightened awareness, the clan mother understood all the steps of her passage and how each and every lesson had brought her to this moment of personally realized wholeness.

I felt these words as if I had written them myself, and I understood that Creator had a divine plan for me. She also taught me that people who lie and are dishonest are wounded. They haven't heard the voice that speaks to their "orenda," or spiritual essence. This made me think of Levi and what had transpired between us. I chose to reach out and inform him that my dad had passed. He was very responsive and tried to offer comfort in his words. He did mention he wished he could be holding me to take some of the pain away. A big part of me wished the same thing. Even though what had developed between us was special, the truth once revealed was deceitful and hurtful to the one he had committed too. We did say, "I love you," and I said goodbye. He chose to say "see you later," which held some significance to him. If I wanted to remain in this space of healing, I needed to embrace all of Listening Woman's lessons and stay open to any messages that could come forward.

I chose to visit my dad's apartment at The Ridge to retrieve some documents for his estate. I wanted to be there alone before my family arrived. I stumbled upon a large black leather keepsake album under his coffee table that I had never noticed before. When I opened it up to the first page, I was shocked to see what treasure lay before me. It was a copy of the same prayer that I had read to him during his last days in the hospital. I couldn't believe it. This was a for sure a sign I was meant to read it to him during his last days on this earth, and I set it aside to be used in his program for the funeral. The album was composed of old articles from college football days and some of his accomplishments. Towards the end of its contents, I found a letter, and when I opened it up, another gift was revealed. It was from my mother. It was dated Saturday, November 9, 1979. I wanted to get into reading its contents, but I chose to save it for my next morning walk. I grabbed a few more keepsakes and decided it was time for me to go. It felt strange being there without him, and the sooner I wrapped up his affairs, the easier it would to start the healing process.

The next morning, I set out for my daily dose of nature medicine and to practice my listening skills. I made sure to bring the letter and some sage to burn. The sun was shining down on face, and I could feel its warmth from a different place inside of me. I took my time trying to observe my surroundings. The various plant life, the light wind dancing in the trees, and the magic of the river and how it moves.

After about thirty minutes of walking, I found the place where I could be in solitude. This sacred space was down another bank. It had no trails other than to the river ahead. It was filled with a special life force that felt connected, and I knew it was time to read the letter. In the letter, my mother spoke of the work she is doing with the tribes down in California, and the struggles she is facing with her fight for the Indian program against the District Administration. She told my father several times how excited she was to see him in five days and that my other siblings that came before I was born were anxious to meet him. She ended her letter with, "Get well, my love, and get here soon. —Elvera."

I began to cry countless healing tears; it was such a gift to find this letter. This was the most of her handwriting I had ever seen, and I felt connected to these words, her words. She had no idea that in four years' time, they would have me, and by the time I turned thirty-seven, all of them would be gone. After I finished the letter, I wanted to pray and thank Creator for helping me find this treasure.

I chose to sit down on the one wooden bench that was located within the cove-like space. It was only about five feet from the water and offered a unique view of the river with the feeling of intimacy. The ducks liked to play around here often, and in the past, I had even seen a beaver or two just around the bend on the left-hand side. The large boulders to left offered even more privacy and added to the cove-like feel. For good reason, this had become my favorite place to pray along the river, and after some time, became quite sacred to me. I lit my smudge stick, fanned the medicine around my body, closed my eyes, and became still, just like Listening Woman had taught me. While in the midst of my stillness, I couldn't help but be distracted by a unique sound. I opened my eyes and saw two squirrels that were playing so hard, as if it was their happiest day on earth. They started at one end of the space and chased each other through the trees, jumping from one branch to the next, like acrobats in the circus in full display, and I was the audience. Together, they perched on the tree closest to me. Then, one took off and the other came down the tree and headed toward my direction. I kept thinking he would run off soon enough, but he just kept getting closer, until he was maybe only two feet away and starring me down, face to face. At first, I thought, he must think I have food, and that's why he found the courage to approach me so intimately. But the way he looked at me said something else, a similar feeling to what I felt from the crow the other day. I gave him my presence and smiled, and then he slowly returned back to his tree and with his mate. I realized in that moment that those two squirrels symbolized my parents reuniting. Reading the letter gave me a glimpse into their love and an understanding that they were finally together again. I felt some inner peace knowing this truth and left this space with more understanding of Creator's divine plan, and an understanding that I had used Listening Woman's medicine.

My family was set to arrive that late afternoon, and I scheduled us to meet at the funeral home at four-thirty to begin making arrangements. I had been dreading this all day, along with the anticipation of seeing my brother. When I arrived, my uncle and aunt were already there. We hugged each other and made our way into the home. My brother Scott came inside to greet us. It was good to see him, but awkward nonetheless, and we didn't hug. The funeral director showed us the spacious room to have his service, and then we sat down to go over the cost and details. I wanted my family to have a say in the process, and I made sure to include them in all the decisions. We agreed to call the service "A Celebration of Life" and use the time to honor my father and the work he did and appreciate the time we had with him.

I shared with them a special song, "Don't Worry About Me," by Frances, that I had heard on Spotify. The first time it found me, it had a profound effect, but at the time, I didn't understand why. But when I listened to it again after Dad had passed, I knew then it embodied our relationship.

I explained to them, "The premise of this song is about a loved one, whatever that relationship, is to not worry about you. And if you could take any of their pain away, you would. My dad had worried so much about me without understanding he raised me to be strong enough without him."

They loved the song and agreed it would be a special touch. When the director asked for a prayer of choice, I knew exactly the right one. I explained to my family the story behind this prayer, that it had found us both during different times of his passing.

My dad had made no prior arrangements for a burial, and I figured if he wanted to be with my mother, he would have arranged so. I believed he trusted me to do what I thought was best, and I told my family I wanted to cremate him, then take him on my travels and spread his ashes in sacred places. They were surprised at first but agreed. It sounded like a nice gesture, and I would provide them with a small urn. After we finished up the details, we decided to head up to Dad's apartment to look though old photos to use in his service slideshow.

I met with them again for breakfast the next morning. They decided to head back home right away, knowing they had to be back again in five days. Even though I don't feel emotionally close to them, I was thankful to have their help in making some my father's arrangements.

I reached out to Debbie over the weekend about my father's passing. She and I had met during the Native youth conference several months ago. I took her up on her invitation to come out Nespelem and taught a yoga class at the community center. She mentioned at that time that I should come out again and sweat with ladies there on Mondays. The sweat lodge had always been something I wanted to experience, but I had never had an opportunity. I knew this was exactly the medicine I needed, and I couldn't have planned for this experience to happen at more a crucial time. She told me to head up around five p.m. in two days' time and informed the ladies that run the sweat that I was coming. Debbie said to make sure to pack my medicine for offering, two towels, water, and snacks. I informed Gerald of my upcoming sweat session, and he gave me a prayer to say during one of the rounds.

> *Yo way oh hey, Yo way oh hey – 4 times*
> *Hey ya hey ya, Way yo hey yo – 1 time*

"I want you to say this phrase four times, to honor each of the four directions. This prayer will continue to protect you on your journey ahead," he said.

He was using his bear medicine to guide me on a journey of introspection during a new spiritual experience. And I continued to appreciate all the knowledge this bear had to offer. He understood I was in need of healing, and he embodied the medicine to help heal others.

I was feeling excited and anxious in anticipation of the sweat medicine. The drive to the Nespelem would take roughly about two hours, and this allowed me some time to get lost in my music and thoughts. I really didn't mind the drive: the bear medicine showed me how to utilize the alone time and solitude. I couldn't help but glance over at the passenger seat and imagine Dad's presence buckled in next to me and along for the ride.

I arrived in Nespelem around five p.m., and the current temperature was still at uncomfortable ninety-five degrees. I went inside the community center to greet Debbie and thank her for her invitation to the lodge. She walked me down to the sweat, opened the gate, and introduced me to two ladies that were waiting for me.

"This is sister Sharon; she runs the language program and the sweat at the community center. And this is sister Cindy; she is an environmental specialist for the tribe."

We gave each other warm hugs, and I took a seat by the fire to observe my surroundings. Debbie left us to get back to work, and I already felt so comfortable in this space and the energy within its walls.

Sharon explained this sweat was four rounds, and if it became too intense for me, I would be able to leave after I said my prayers.

"I will go easy on you, sister, being as you're not used it," she said.

I watched Cindy grab a shovel and protective gloves to remove four hot rocks from the fire to represent the four directions. They were taken from the bottom of the pile, where the heat builds to be more intense, and were bright orange in color. She carefully carried them into the sweat, beginning with the East being laid down first. Then she came back to the fire and picked up three more rocks, to make seven total, and laid them on top of the previous four. Each round, seven more heated rocks would be added to the lodge, making it twenty-eight rocks total.

Sharon grabbed a bucket of hot water that sat by the fire and transferred it into a larger bucket inside the lodge to be used during the ceremony. These ladies were seasoned sweaters and it showed. Their attire consisted of something you could easily slip off, and flip-flops, and bandanas. I imagined this was a ritual they had experienced their entire lives, and how amazing it was to have this medicine so early in life. Sharon said it was time and asked me to grab my offerings and walk over to the other side of the fire. The smudging pot was located just outside of the fire pit, in a circular metal container filled with some fresh cedar. Ashes from the fire are used to engage the medicine so the smoke can be used to smudge.

I watched Sharon go first. She removed her sandals and placed her feet over the smoke, one at a time. Then she began guiding the smoke towards her legs and then all the way up the body and to her face. She turned around, beginning once again at her feet and moving all the way up the back. Then she took her bandana and dunked it into a bucket of water filled with rose petals that sat next to the smudge pot. She used the bandana to cleanse her shoulders and neck as the very last step before entering the sweat. I observed Cindy do the same ritual as Sharon, and then it became my turn. I took my time, wanting to not take for granted any part of this new medicine, as this was an experience that I had patiently waited for.

Sharon encouraged us both to bring in a water bottle, and for me especially, since it was my first time. Our ancestors were very traditional in how they ran a sweat, but in modern times, some of those ways have become more relaxed. Most sweats don't allow water inside the walls, and in some cases, you were expected to fast for periods of days. Different tribes have their way of doing things, and I can understand why some have a different protocol, running their sweats according to how they were taught and what medicines were around. The animals we honor and the medicines used for each direction can vary as well.

The four directions have to be honored even before the sweat begins, and each direction represents an animal, a lesson, and medicine. The North is white and shared with Hummingbird. He is wise like our elders and tied to cedar medicine. East is yellow and shared with the Elk, who is an observer but can also show ignorance. His medicine is tobacco. South is red and shared with Coyote, who is known to be a trickster, but has his wits about him. His medicine is sweet grass. And West is black and shared with Eagle, who is well-grounded but can be overemotional. His medicine is sage. First round prayers are offered to the elders and our ancestors, with the offering of tobacco. Second round prayers are for the women, the protectors, and lavender or sweet grass can be offered. The third round is for our warriors, our providers, and we offer them cedar. The fourth round is the sage medicine and can be used to pray for others or ourselves. This is just a one way of running a sweat, but in this case, we just went with the flow and offered what we had on hand. My belief is that the strongest medicine when it comes to prayer is the intention you put behind it.

We entered the sweat, finding our place to sit, and Sharon asked Cindy to close the door to the sweat by bringing the heavy blankets down over the opening. The lodge was now completely dark, with the only light radiating from those hot orang rocks. Sharon explained a few things before we began.

"The sweat lodge resembles the womb of our Mother, and a birthplace of creation. When we choose to suffer and pray in here, our ancestors and Creator hear our prayers. There is no wrong way to pray. Just speak from your heart, sister. Before we begin, everyone, place your offerings for this sweat to Creator on the hot rocks."

She started the first round and thanked Creator for bringing me to the sweat, which meant a lot to me. Then she began to speak Okanagan, which is a Salish language with several different dialects. She had a lot to express about situations that were heavy on her heart. And even though I didn't understand the words she spoke, I felt her intention and was moved being able to witness such an intimate way to pray. Once she had finished, she used a long metal ladle to pour the hot water on the rocks. This created an intense steam, which intensified the heat dramatically. This felt symbolic of that release when you offer your prayers into Creator's hands and trust in his divine plan. I was new to the sweat, so she only did two pours instead of four.

Cindy's turn was next, and she also thanked Creator for me being there. I was amazed that I had just met these women less than two hours ago, and I already felt so incredibly loved. She expressed some difficulties in her life and asked for more patience when dealing with them. Sharon poured the water on the rocks, and the heat continued to build.

It was my turn, and I chose to start this first round to give thanks for the sweat and my new sisters. I wanted to express how grateful I was for being there, and for them making me feel so welcome. I chose to speak of my father, and how I was trying to handle the grief and loss using the tools he had taught me. The water works turned on almost instantly, and I became overwhelmed by my emotions in this sacred space. The lodge air grew thicker as the steam continued to spread throughout the womb within its walls. As I began to suffer from the intensity of heat building, the energy around me shifted. I could feel the presence of my family around me. It was as if they were taking part in this first sweat. They had come to offer me a forcefield of protection, one that I could carry outside these walls. The part of me that had felt so alone was now feeling protected by my family of guardian angels. Even though they weren't in the physical form, they had every intention of doing what they could to protect me from the other side. My father was the final link, and they had been patiently waiting for him to create a stronger unit to guide me.

Sharon closed the first round and spoke "ishkatompkin," which meant 'all my relatives,' and called for Cindy to open the door. We walked outside back into that intense heat, and it didn't feel too much cooler than the sweat. I felt depleted from not being used to the intensity inside the sweat and what had come to the surface during my first round. I needed to cool off in the outdoor shower and cleanse myself from the sweat that had been carrying pain, and to prepare for more suffering to come.

I sat down to join Sharon and Cindy by the fire, to take a quick breather and allow our bodies to stabilize. I explained to them more in detail what had happened with my father, and how blessed I felt to be there praying with them. I explained that part of me knew this medicine was calling to me and that they had now become part of my healing. We had entered the sweat as strangers, but I understood already we would leave the sweat feeling like sisters.

"It's time for round two," Sharon said.

Cindy grabbed the shovel and took seven more rocks out of the fire and placed them in the lodge.

Immediately upon entering, the lodge felt hotter. I could tell this round was going to test my physical body to its limits. Cindy started this round and prayed for her family and for some inner strength and guidance. The heat this time had a greater effect on me. My heart began to race and I felt a sense of panic. My sweat began to pour as if I was taking a shower, releasing itself from my pores like a faucet. I chose to lie down and try to slow down my breathing while calming my nervous system. The fight or flight panic button had been pushed from experiencing this whole new way of suffering.

When it became my turn, I made myself sit back up and prayed to Creator about the consistent pain I felt with my injuries. I asked to get my freedom of movement back, and to move without fear and pain. I said I had run out of treatment options and I knew the only cure might come from a spiritual place. I prayed for my family to find some peace with the loss of my father and to receive the understanding that it was his time. I had hopes that they could begin to heal once they recognized Creator's divine plan.

Sharon made three pours of hot water after my prayers, and the intensity reached yet another level of suffering for me. But I was determined to stay; I would not leave before we had finished the round. Sharon finished the round by expressing some very personal concerns and fears that followed with emotion. I had made it through round two and was eager this time to get outside.

I took another shower and embraced that cooler water running down my body. The sensation calmed my senses, and it felt like another release, leaving behind the suffering I felt within that round and the pain I had expressed. I sat back down by the fire, to engage with the sisters before entering the third round. They were curious about my nutrition background and the work I did with the youth back home. I explained my passion for using food as medicine and that I realized this gift could make a real impact in the Native community. I mentioned the Nk'wu Nation and our plan to serve a traditional dinner in the fall to the public as a fundraiser. We would begin our gathering and the foraging of these foods after their summer vacation. The sisters loved hearing of this work and offered to donate some of their traditional foods they had already collected earlier in the year. That spring, I had missed the chance to gather camas and bitterroot due to my father's first hospitalization. I had no free time in between handling his affairs and my own. But we were getting into huckleberry season, and even though school was out for the summer, I could still make the effort to gather for the dinner.

Now it was time for round three, and I helped Cindy bring some of the rocks into the sweat this time. The three of us got settled in and offered our medicine.

Sharon asked me, "Could you start this round, sister Donell?"

I knew this was the time to speak my prayer that Gerald had given me; I was ready to speak to my ancestors for the first time using my native tongue. As I began saying,

> Yo way oh hey, Yo way oh hey
> Hey ya Hey ya, Hey ya hey oh

I found myself finding a rhythm and then began singing the words into a song. Sharon began to say them with me, and those happy tears flowed like a stream of healing. We sang four rounds, for each of the four directions, and each round my voice got a little louder. This round of the sweat, while still intense physically, had somehow calmed me down. After speaking the language, I was feeling so connected to my ancestors while being in our Mother's womb. I understood why sweating continued to be a sacred practice of Native people and people connected to the earth. I felt love, I felt protection, and I felt connected to this sweat medicine.

Round four was the easiest heat-wise. I wasn't sure if I had gotten accustomed to the heat or if the pain that had left my body made it seem easier. I took one last shower and changed into comfortable shorts and a loose top for the rest of the evening. Debbie came back down to the lodge to share a few snacks. She had offered to let me stay with her in town for the night. I hugged my two new sisters goodbye and promised to return in two weeks.

It was about nine p.m. by the time I followed Debbie back to her house in Nespelem. It was dusk, and from what I understand, that's when the magic is the strongest. It comes after the sun has set and patiently waits for its turn to hold space in our Sky Mother. Dusk leads us into the night with mystery of the unknown and shows us there is no place for fear within our hearts. For without the darkness of the night, we would never see the stars. This is the time when Listening Woman could evoke her strongest medicine and utilize the power of moonlight and the stillness of the night to receive hidden messages. The moon has its time to shine, just as the sun does. There is a duality that exists in relation to all living things and how we are interconnected.

Once we arrived back to Debbie's house, we sat down to a cup of tea, and she asked me how my heart was feeling with Dad being gone. I explained how difficult it was to lose my Buffalo, but that I had had a dream that prepared me some to understand that it was his time. The pain was there, but he wasn't suffering anymore, and I could take comfort in that. She mentioned once again how she remembered working with him long ago and admired the relationship and bond we had between us, and how unusual it was to see a single man provide for his daughter and become such a positive role model within the community.

I felt very moved but what she had to share. I knew I was blessed to have him all these years as my father. Dad had brought us together; it wasn't intentional, but somehow this had become one last gift he left me before moving on to his place among the stars.

Before heading to bed for the night, Debbie said, "I have some freshly picked sage from the area. It's on the front porch. You are welcome to take whatever you like back home with you in the morning."

I thanked her for her generous gift and for allowing me to stay the night. It didn't take long for me to fall asleep. I closed my eyes that night with a newfound gratitude for these sisters and the medicine they had to offer. I had been guided to these women, and this place was going to be an essential part of my healing and my medicine tracks.

The next morning, I woke up early, picked up some of the fresh sage Debbie had offered and made my way quietly out of the house. I had to be back in Spokane by nine a.m. to meet with my dad's lawyer, so I hit the road just before seven. The sunrise had just begun to take the stage in the morning sky. With each new day comes this reawaking of warm light that allows us to adjust from the night before. It begins with a gentle illumination of warm red, yellow, and oranges, until finding its resting place in the bluest part of sky. Just the air alone is filled with magic, and, being fully present, I was able to see it more clearly than ever before. The two-hour drive home went by in a flash. It gave me a window of time to try and process what had happened during the sweat and how different I felt coming back home after receiving the sweat medicine. I imagined my father was sitting next to me, just as he was there on the way over, but this time, the rest of my family was in the back seat along with him.

I arrived at the lawyer's office right on time, where we were joined by my father's financial planner and dear friend, Pete. He gave me a warm hug and offered some condolences. I sat down with the two of them to go over my dad's affairs and make a plan of action to get everything in order. As soon as the paperwork started to pile, the energy shifted within me that had felt so settled. During this meeting, I became heavy, feeling suffocated. My mind was in no place to process all that was expected of me. I was in mourning, but this is what being an adult is about. I was grateful for the freedom I had to take a few weeks off from work and process all that needed to be done. The cycle of life is painful, but it is a cycle, and at some point, this part would be over.

My family was set to arrive a few days later, and I needed to prepare for that, as well. I seemed to be the main contact between us all, and I really didn't want to be. It would be nice to see some of them again, and I wished it were under different circumstances. It's unfortunate that a lot of extended families tend to only see each other for weddings and funerals. This was a truth that we shared, but Dad would be happy to see us coming together regardless.

The night before the funeral, we got together for a family dinner at one of Dad's favorite restaurants. I was happy to see my ex-brother-in-law and my niece and nephews. He had remarried a few years after Laura passed to lady from church, and even though it was weird at first, I was happy the kids had a mother figure. I understood in my heart that Laura would have wanted this for him and for the kids. My uncle and his wife, along with my other aunt and oldest cousin, made the trip, along with my half-brother, Scott, and his significant other. This gathering was to honor my father's life and share stories about how special he was to each of us. Times like these bring families closer together, which is exactly what my father would have wanted.

I spent that evening bundling the fresh sage that was gifted by Debbie to make smudge sticks for my family. I wanted them to experience smudging and share what it meant to my father on his last days on earth. That evening was also crunch time to rehearse my dad's eulogy. I wanted to be able to express myself without becoming too emotional. He was a great speaker and had taught me how to engage an audience. These circumstances were different, but I had a responsibility to make a lasting impact on the loved ones who came to honor his life. During that time, it occurred to me, this just might be the most important speech of my life. How can I wrap up my dad's accomplishments and the impact he had, not just in my life but for those around him? Everyone had been turning to me for comfort and strength with his passing, and with this eulogy I wanted each person to find their own peace.

I continued to dig deeper down into my past life events and the time that we shared and came to a profound realization. My father had been preparing me for his departure my entire life. Through his loss of my mother and siblings, he found healing in helping others that felt his pain. He taught them, along with me, how to grieve in a healthy way, and now I was experiencing his greatest teachings. He gave me the tools, and now that he had gone into the spirit world, I would grieve in a healthy way. I did the work necessary to connect my heart to spirit and had no intention to walk the dark path I had when Laura passed. I thought about that card she sent when I graduated, how she was worried about my bad choices and where my future was headed. I wondered if she understood her time was up before her body gave out, and how her family would handle the grief. This time would be different for me, and I would handle my father's passing as I wish I could have handled my sister's, for my father had never stopped teaching me lessons, even in his dementia and after he left this earth. His continued patience had allowed me to find my way when I was ready. What an incredible gift I had just received. This was my truth and what I would share tomorrow at the funeral.

I awoke early to beaming sunshine rays that came with a gentle life force through my bedroom window. I allowed my body to catch up to my mind, while remaining still in reflection on the day's events. Today, I would be joining loved ones together in honor of my father's life, and we would celebrate his accomplishments and share stories. This rare moment in life could be beautiful, with the understanding that he was with my family and no longer suffering. I was looking forward to honoring him in this way. I hoped that those who attended could feel it too, and their peace would be found at the right time.

Grace arrived early to meet me at the funeral, to set up for the service and to greet distant relatives. I had purchased frames with Lindsey a few days before and filled them with special life moments of Dad. I wanted to make sure to include all the family, and that everyone could see the time that they had spent together. My girlfriends had been such a blessing and helped with whatever they could. They were my sisters, no doubt, and loved my dad almost as much as me.

I stayed by the entrance to greet anyone who came to attend; it's what he would have expected of me. Dad was all about the meet and greets, handshakes and proper introductions. A shuttle from The Ridge arrived, and several residents came to pay their respects. These were my dad last friends and kept him company the last three years of this life. These elders formed a line and, one by one, greeted me with a warm smile and gentle hug. There was sadness in their eyes and some heavy energy in their hearts, but I was ready to offer them comfort. This was Dad's work, and now I was helping them grieve him being gone. It almost felt surreal at times, and I would have to pull myself back into my body. I never really imagined how this day would feel, and now that I was here, it was honestly more beautiful than I could have ever expected.

What I really didn't expect was the gift of being reunited with James's family. His mother, stepfather, sister, aunt, and uncle all came to support and celebrate Dad's life. It moved me, and I was able to feel their love that I had missed so much, these past three years. This was another kind of healing, the love and support were still there, and it meant more than they could have ever understood. His sister mentioned that James had planned on coming, and I really believed in my heart he would, although I had never heard from him after my dad passed, leaving me feeling incredibly disappointed. I had even saved something of my father's to give him, if I ever did get the chance to exchange words in person. Perhaps he would feel judged coming to my father's funeral, and the guilt would override his desire to be there. However, my friends and family would have welcomed his presence with open arms. The time had come to begin the service, and I realized he wasn't coming. It hurt, but I had to accept that this was the path he had chosen.

Indian flute music was playing while everyone was taking their seats. I choose to come in last and sit up front next to my dad's distant cousins, whom I had never met. My dad's chaplain, Connie, from The Ridge would be leading the service this afternoon. She was very kind, and my dad really seemed to like her and attended her services regularly.

Connie welcomed everyone, followed by an opening prayer and a few scriptures. She shared a few stories about the time she spent with dad.

"He liked to critique my sermons some days and would tell me to slow down my delivery. This was followed by positive feedback and a warm smile."

This made me smile with a faint giggle. I wasn't surprised my dad would take it upon himself to offer his input. She then presented a slideshow of pictures that my family and I had gathered together. It was a beautiful display of his life, and we tried to capture his essence the best we could. I even included a picture of him walking me down the aisle on my wedding day. He was proud, and it was a special moment for us. Everyone seemed to appreciate the slideshow and could find the beauty in my father's time on this earth.

Connie read a few more scriptures and then gave me the signal to come up and say my eulogy. I felt nervous, anxious, and overwhelmed with emotion, but I had only a few tears left in me at that point. I had cried so much over the past few weeks; the river within me had run dry.

I walked up behind the podium, took a breath, and began to speak my greatest truth, my dad's eulogy.

"My father was a healer, a teacher, mother, and a role model. He raised me to be a strong woman, but also taught me how to be gentle and show emotion. He was my buffalo medicine, and embodied stability, great strength, and resilience from outside forces. No matter what adversity he faced throughout his life. he took it head on and moved forward with grace. My father's life work impacted countless students, teachers, and the community. I was aware of this growing up, but he was enough just being my father. We spent many holidays together, just him and me. We shared stories, moments, and countless fights. I gave him a run for his money during my teenage years, but he still kept his patience. He taught me the lesson of patience up until his last days on this earth. His dementia was painful to watch, to see him suffer and struggle with everyday life. But within that, he taught me how to be a better daughter, human, and someday maybe a mother. Our relationship changed, as we had to change roles. Once we accepted those roles, it allowed some healing and new perspective. The dementia brought us even closer, and he shared stories with me I had never known before. Stories about his childhood and when he first met my mother. I could see the beauty in what memories he still had, and he felt joy telling those stories. I assure you, friends and family, he is exactly where he needs to be, and he left this earth when he was ready. My family was waiting for him on the other side, and now they are guiding me, and they are guiding you."

I took my seat and felt good about speaking my truth and the dynamic of our relationship. Connie then asked if anyone else would like to say a few words, and several people had some things to share. I was most proud of my childhood best friend Lindsey, who would never do public speaking or put herself in front of a crowd. As I mentioned before, she was my crow medicine and had never lost her spiritual strength, so it made sense this was a time she chose to speak. She was the only one of my friends he still remembered, and that meant a lot to us both. As she quietly walked her long limbs up to the front, and I could tell she was nervous as well as emotional. She smiled at me and shared stories of our childhood, and how my father had been her role model. He never gave up on her getting her GED, and it meant so much for him to come to her graduation. I knew my father was there, and so incredibly proud of her for speaking her words. Once again, even in his passing, he gave her the gift of courage to speak in front of a crowd.

My cousin Casey came up next and read a letter her son had written to his Uncle Don. It was a really sweet sentiment, and my dad my had become a huge fan of her son's baseball games. My aunt shared a few words, followed by my few of my father's past work colleagues and current friends. I enjoyed their shared stories and the kind things they said about him. The common theme I wasn't expecting was their admiration for the relationship we had with each other, and how proud my father was of me and the work I had been doing. They validated the bond between us and could see the complexity of our relationship.

Ronnie and Grace offered their beautiful voices and chose to close the funeral with a duet, singing "Amazing Grace." With their own unique twist and flair, they made this song just another special gift. I had the most amazing humans in my life to offer such a sacred moment, and I knew Dad appreciated the gesture.

Connie concluded the service following the prayer that I had shared with Dad in the hospital. Following the service, I was overwhelmed once again by supportive friends and grieving relatives. I had to be that rock, to take that role, whether it was chosen for me or not, and I embraced it the best I could.

Our family spent the evening together gathered in Dad's apartment, sharing stories, food, and pictures. I gave some of Dad's most precious treasures to certain family members to take back home. We didn't argue or fight about any of his belongings, which is a blessing, no doubt. Everyone seemed to leave with some special things to remember him by.

We scheduled a family breakfast the next morning, before everyone had to head back home. I chose a great brunch place by the river, so that afterward, we could do a little ceremony together. I poured some of Dad's ashes into each of their hands and lit the smudge stick to be passed around. I wanted to leave them with some peace if they hadn't found some already, and I began to speak.

"Thank you, Creator, for bringing us together, even though it's under painful circumstances. We are standing here together in honor of my father's life and the impact he made on each one of ours. We might not understand sometimes why people leave this earth when they do, but I get that you have a divine plan. I was told Dad had work to do on the other side, and I believe that to be true. I am grateful for having the father I did; he prepared me for this day. Send our love to the rest of the family, and please protect my family here as they travel back home. Aho."

It was the first time many of them had ever practiced smudging, but everyone seemed to like and understand its importance. I said goodbye to everyone and ended up hugging my brother Scott for the first time in sixteen years. It wasn't forced, and I could tell it was something that he needed to receive from me. Dad had always wanted us to be close, and maybe this was the first step towards mending the past. I felt relieved for this chapter to be over, even though more work was ahead. This was progress, and it felt like one more step toward healing, and that was one more thing to be grateful for.

I had spoken to Levi the week of my father's passing, and he mentioned he would be in town that weekend. I knew that it was wrong for me to consider spending time with him, but at that moment, I really didn't care. I wanted to be selfish, to be held and to be loved on by the one person who knew how. Levi was still the only man in my life that could play that role. Having to lie to my friends about what I was doing didn't sit well with my spirit. I felt guilt and shame for deceiving them about what I was doing, and also for choosing to be with him even though I was now aware he was taken. I never would have imagined being the other woman, and I had no intention of continuing in that role. But in the moment, dealing with the grief of losing the only other man I had in my life, Levi was medicine. The mornings I woke up next to him were less painful then the ones without. This had to be a one-time exception, and I prepared myself once again to say goodbye. I told him this was circumstantial and that, while I still loved him, in my heart I knew it was wrong. He understood and was just happy to have a few more days together. This was our last time of any physical contact, and I had no intention of continuing any communication. When we said goodbye again, I felt the pain just as before, knowing it was over, but that I had work and healing to do involving my spirit, which allowed no place for deceit, or continuing a love affair based on infidelity.

I suppose it was best I was still single and not having to nurture a relationship. I gave myself a week to get my dad's things moved out and his apartment empty. Without his insurance plan, it was like paying for a daily hotel. On moving day Lindsey, her husband Andy, Grace, and my girlfriend Mena all volunteered their services. I felt so grateful for the help. I didn't know how I could have pulled this off without them. Andy picked up a moving truck and the girls and I began loading the bigger items onto roller carts. We had to take the freight elevator, and then wheel the cart down a long hallway through the residence. After a while, it became a game, and we would take rides on the empty cart. We invited the older residents to take part, and some did not find it amusing.

The four of us shared a lot of laughter that day, which was the medicine I was in need of. It was hard to see his things go as the apartment became empty. But having to explain to the residents how Dad had passed so suddenly was even harder. Bless their sweet souls for caring, but it was wearing on me after a while. I donated some of his items to The Ridge's general store and the rest of the furniture to Lindsey and her family. They would take good care of his belongings, and they would have them to remember him by, as well. It took me a few more days to clear everything out and get it ready for another resident. I left the keys on the counter, took one last look at the place, and closed the door. Walking down the hall to the elevator, I felt relief that this part was over and I could take another step forward toward healing.

One week following his passing, I had several dreams about Dad, but upon awaking I couldn't remember them well. What I did recall was that in my dreams, he still had dementia. I was hoping to see my father as a healed man in the dream world, not still suffering from his past. I called Lindsey for some comfort and to tell her about the dreams I was having. She had comforting words and then had her own story to tell.

She said, "I believe, after your father's passing, that I now have crows as guardians in my life. After the funeral, the kids, Andy, and I went to play in an open field by their school. This place is known for lots of aggressive hawks, and I sometimes worry about the little ones. A large hawk was circling above my two youngest, and out of nowhere, this crow swooped down and aggressively cawed at the hawk to get it to go away. This happened a few more times, and we realized we should probably go, and that this little crow would tire itself out trying to protect us. As we walked away, the birds began to separate. Then Tollin had to run back to get her ball she left behind. The hawk came back and dived about ten feet above her head. Meanwhile, the crow came back again and took action to get the hawk to back off. It was the strangest thing, and we felt protected by that crow. "

I loved that she had shared this story with me, and it made sense, for she already embodied the crow medicine.

Father's Day was coming up on Sunday, and I chose to request Olive's company for the weekend. I knew I would want to be alone and allow myself to feel what I needed to, and little Olive was the only companionship I could nurture during this time. On Father's Day, I took her on our usual walk to the park and down by the river. On the way back, I made the attempt to visit the park bench I had been avoiding, the bench where my father and I had spent many days in open air, enjoying a nice lunch or a just good conversation. I took my time sitting down and getting comfortable being in that space again.

The salty tears began to roll down my cheeks while remembering that day and the last smudge we shared. Oh, how I missed my father, his constant phone calls, and his bad jokes. This was the first of many holidays I would experience without him. And I had used his lessons to get through the hardest parts of my grieving so far. I couldn't believe in three weeks' time how much had changed. Now my life was completely different.

After wrapping up what I could of my dad's affairs up to that point, I booked myself a trip to Maui. I needed to get away from my life at home, and I wanted to experience his birthday in a new environment. We had planned our road trip to Seattle during this time, and there was no way, now, that I was staying home. Maui had always been a place of healing for me. I felt connected to the land and the energy surrounding the islands.

Maui had been a favorite destination for James and me during our marriage, and I hoped to one day retire there or move there for part of the year. I love the other islands as well, but Maui had pulled me in closer than the others. I felt more at home there and knew my way around the island fairly well. When I booked my stay in Kihei, I choose to stay on the opposite side of town. I didn't want it to feel at all like the vacations I had shared with James. I found a charming Airbnb studio apartment that would be perfect and give me just enough space at a reasonable price. The décor was updated and a bit modern, but still with an island feel. This was the perfect place for me to get lost and allow myself to feel as I wished, whatever that was.

The first two days I spent basking in the sun and taking long walks on the beach. My body still wasn't healed, so this Hawaii trip would include no running, which was a first for me. I just kept to myself and felt content with being alone. It allowed me to write, read, and breathe in this healing environment. There was so much incredible plant life to take in, from the variety of flowers to the palm trees. My eyes never tired of the vastness of the sandy beaches that extended beyond my vision. I was mesmerized by the movement of the ocean, its sheer power as the tide rolled in and back out again, and with observing the smallest creature teachers that inhabited the beach and the ones living in the ocean. Maui is a playground of life; there is magic that can be seen at all times.

I woke up early the morning of July 3. It was my father's birthday, and I wanted to get to the beach before anyone was around. I had been waiting for this moment and took my smudge stick along with some of his ashes to spread. I had stumbled upon a different trail to the beach during the last two days, finding a sacred space that was more like a cove where I could be alone. I listened to the song "Don't Worry About Me" several times. I let the words soak into my thoughts and into my heart.

> Even if I fall down when you're not around,
> Don't worry about me.
> If I fall, you fall,
> And if I rise, we rise together.
> When I smile, you smile,
> Don't worry about me,
> Don't worry about me.

It was time for ceremony and to speak my truth. I stood up and lit my smudge stick and spoke out loud to Creator or whoever was listening.

"Today is my father's birthday, as you know, Creator, and it is the first birthday I haven't been able to spend with him. I miss him so incredibly much and am struggling without his presence. I feel lost at times and question if I am on the right path. I am free now to find a new home, and I have no idea where that should be. My family is all with you now, and I can feel they are protecting and guiding me as well. I am in need of your guidance, Creator; please send me a sign that I am on the right path. I want to make you and my ancestors proud of my time spent on this earth. Thank you for being patient with me and allowing me to say goodbye to my father in his final moments. I will never lose my connection to you again. Please continue to communicate your divine plan. I am open, I am listening, and I am willing to do what you have planned."

I allowed myself to cry as hard as I needed to, and the amount and salt in my tears matched the ocean currents. I walked closer to the water and spread Dad's ashes. I wished him a happy birthday and took my place back on the beach, sitting there and quietly reflecting on all the events leading up to now. The grieving tears were replaced by healing ones, and I felt a sense of calm carefully listening to the tide come in and recede back out. I closed my eyes as the gentle morning breeze caressed my face and wrapped around me like shawl of protection.

Moments later, I was caught by surprise and approached by a man that came out of nowhere. I believed I was alone and, feeling very emotional, I wanted to be. He appeared to be a local Hawaiian man in his early thirties; he looked like someone who worked with his hands. They showed years of heavy labor and told a story.

He smiled and said, "I would like to offer you some fresh coconut water, no charge."

I was a mess, my eyes were puffy, and I was in no way feeling like having a conversation with a stranger, or anyone else for that matter.

I replied, "I appreciate it, but no, thank you," and ushered him on his way. I spent another hour on the beach, giving myself time to grieve and calm my emotions. I walked back a different way than I had come, deciding to head back and get ready for the day. Then I heard someone calling out to me, about one hundred yards away, and I turned to see the same man that spoke to me before.

He said, "Good, I caught you. I want to offer you this coconut water I cut for you."

He handed me the coconut and smiled when I accepted his gift.

I took a few sips, and said, "Thank you, that is very kind of you to offer."

It was clear he wanted to talk to me for some reason, so I stuck around to see what else he had to share.

He mentioned, "My name is Don, and I am local here. I have never seen you before, you must be visiting."

I was surprised to hear his name, and replied, "My name is Donell, and I am on vacation from Washington State."

He looked perplexed, and by what I had shared.

"No, really, your name is Donell?" he asked. "That can't be."

"Yes, really, my name is Donell," I replied.

He explained that his daughter was named Donell. The hairs began to stand up on the back of my neck; this meeting was the message I had just prayed for. This man was telling me that he and his daughter had the same names as my father and me. He offered proof by taking off his shirt and showing the words DONELL tattooed on his chest. I had prayed for this, and this man felt compelled to track me down even when I turned him away. This was a clear sign that told me Creator was listening, that I was connected and that I had followed my medicine tracks.

I chose not to explain the circumstances of why I was there, but I thanked him once again for his kind gesture and asked to take a picture of the tattoo. During the walk back, I tried to process what had just happened and how grateful I felt for that message. It validated that I was where I was supposed to be, and that my father was truly was by my side offering his guidance and protection.

The rest of the week I spent in Maui continued to offer me the time I needed to feel a sense of calmness. Just that meeting alone with the man on the beach was enough validation for me to understand I was on my chosen path. Spending countless hours on the beach, soaking up the sun's rays and getting lost in my thoughts, became another form of medicine. The tropical heat would build with such intensity during the afternoon and force my body to release the salt water from my pores. As I began to sweat, I was reminded of its medicine and the profound effect the sweat lodge had on my healing that had no boundaries.

CHAPTER 10
Mother Nature Medicine

B ACK TO REALITY, back to the grind. I had a lot of projects in the works, besides everything pertaining to my father, with a live cooking demo set in a few weeks and a few nutrition talks. I needed to get organized and grounded, whether I wanted to or not.

I was able to arrange a field trip with some of the Nk'wu students at Rogers High School for an afternoon of gathering mushrooms and elderberries for the dinner. The group of us met us at an ideal location that offered these foods, along with Jeremy, their advisor, and our mushroom expert, Dave. None of us were really familiar with the varieties to gather other than morels, so he was indeed going to be handy. Before we set out to gather for the day, Dave shared a bit about what to look for while gathering.

"This location is ideal for King Bolete mushrooms, which can grow fairly large, with a thick stem and cap, and they are mostly found under spruce, hemlock, and oak trees. The other mushrooms we can gather in this area are called English puffballs. This variety is rounded and very smooth and can be as small as a golf ball but vary in size. They are also white in color and easy to identify. If you come across a variety you are unsure about, come and get me, or gather just one and set it aside. There are so many types of mushrooms that are not meant for our consumption, and they can be very harmful. "

We said a prayer and thanked the Creator for providing us these foods and allowing us the chance to gather. Then we handed the kids a few buckets for collecting, and they set out in their own preferred groups in search of these edible treasures. I took a slower pace, still nursing this going-on-a-year-and-a-half injured leg. I had some days it would cooperate better than others, but I had to be careful when hiking on uneven ground and steep terrain. Regardless, it felt amazing to be out in the fresh air with the kids, observing them making the connection of how our ancestors had to gather food. Each day was spent with the intention to feed their families and communities, and if the work wasn't done, they didn't eat and couldn't survive. We take for granted our access to food in the modern world and have lost that understanding and connection to where food really comes from. Generations today have come to believe food comes wrapped in plastic, with no concept of what real food is or how it is cultivated. Through these types of activities, the kids learned first-hand and made these connections through their own shared experiences.

Iaitia was able to make it that afternoon, and she chose to stay back with me so we could spend some time together. I sometimes forgot that she was seventeen; her elk medicine made her appear much older in the way she carried herself and what she took interest in. She wanted to hear all about my recent travels, but my focus was to encourage her to come sweat with me in Nespelem. She expressed the pressures of being a teenager and how it's a constant battle to stay on her chosen path, to not give into peer pressure and try to fit in by making poor choices involving substance abuse or being subjected to an unhealthy environment. I understood what it was like to walk this line, and I explained my past and how easy it is to lose sight of what's important. I described how I handled the grief of losing my sister, constantly escaping my emotions through unhealthy outlets, but that my father and our Creator never gave up on me and remained patient. She agreed to come with me to my next sweat after I returned from California, I couldn't have been more thrilled. The sisters would love her, I knew. She was one of those people that I felt honored to braid my sacred energy with.

The kids seemed to making good progress and had filled their buckets full of edible mushrooms for our traditional dinner. We even came across a few elderberry bushes that were at the perfect ripeness to be picked. These purple berries are very strong medicine for Native people and possess countless health benefits. They are rich in antioxidants, anti-inflammatory and antiviral properties, and when made into syrup are a perfect flu medicine. It is very important that they never be eaten raw and must instead be cooked to avoid a chemical that is bitter and could be toxic. After a few hours, we had reached our goal for the day. This fieldtrip was a success and the kids were able to gather and spend time in nature. And I had some quality time with Iaitia and was able to get my own quick dose of nature medicine.

Another birthday and another year of life snuck up on me the following week. I was crazy busy at the salon and distracted by getting ready for my trip to California, leaving in two days' time. But I was finally ready to give myself a gift that I had been patiently waiting for, a dream that had been on my New Year's resolutions for some time. Just after midnight, I booked my ticket to New Zealand, set to leave three days before Christmas. At the time, I had no plan, other than knowing I didn't want to celebrate the holidays here. This would be the first time without my father, and I wanted to escape that reality and feel something completely new and different. This was to be a special time in my life reserved for healing, getting lost with no concept of time, and embracing being out of my comfort zone. I had the option to be gone for two months total, but other than that, no restrictions. This type of travel was completely foreign to me, as I had never had this kind of freedom before. Traveling alone this length of time and distance would also be a new experience, but I was up for the challenge. I would worry about the details of my stay and what I wanted to accomplish later. For now, I had my ticket and had achieved the first step of putting this dream into motion.

I woke up early on the morning of my birthday, just after sunrise, and made my way down by the river to be in solitude before day walkers were out. It was seven a.m.; the blue sky still had traces left of the pastel pink and purple hues that came with the beginning of new day. I made it down to the water to find my sacred cove to sit. I observed the river's ability to have movement within stillness in the same shared space. I pondered how that synergistic energy could be applied to my own self. Did I have the ability to be calm in motion, and stay grounded when finding a new path? These profound thoughts seemed to affect me most when I'm down by the river, perhaps because I can turn off the outside static.

I took out my smudge stick and I prayed for being grateful for another year of life. I prayed for the medicine I was receiving and the medicine I would need later on. I then spoke to my father and told him how much I loved him and how much he was missed.

I made my way back to the trail and all the way around the park to the other side. On that side, there were two drawbridges and a waterfall, and even though I have seen them countless times, it never loses its impact. If you stay long enough, sometimes a strong gust of wind will transport the water's essence into a cooling mist all the way up to the bridge. This area has become a main attraction in Spokane, and I take full advantage of its beauty, living so close by. I wasn't sure about what I felt like doing for the rest of my birthday, but I decided to head back and get ready for the day anyhow. When I arrived back home, much to my surprise, I found birthday balloons, flowers, and other small gifts placed in front of my door. There was no card, but I had a strong feeling, from the choice of gifts, that it was from Levi. They appealed to our sense of humor, and it made sense that he would chose such things. I had cut ties in our communication after the funeral, but clearly, we both still had strong feelings for each other. I wasn't sure what to make of it, and it went against my better judgment, but I chose to text Levi, "Thank you for the gift, it was very thoughtful."

He responded right away, "You are very welcome. Happy birthday, Donell."

This meant he was in town, and I was in danger of relapsing, so I left it at that, at least for now.

I chose to make an appearance for reggae night with Rose and Ronnie. The girls know I can't turn down reggae music, and I thought it would lift my spirits. Dancing has always been a form a medicine and a good way to release stress, considering I hadn't been able to release it in my other favorite physical form for a while. Surprise, not surprise, we made it a late night, and I came home more buzzed than I'm used to. I don't drink very often, and I chose not to accept many of those free birthday drinks.

That evening, I had continued to think about the gifts Levi had left for me that morning and how badly I wanted to see him. I wanted to ask the girls' advice, but I knew I would be judged, and for good reason. The more alcohol that went down my gullet, the more my willpower went out the window. My sexual desires continued to increase with each hour I spent in that bar. I was craving his touch, the way he smelled, and the magic I felt when he was inside of me.

Around one-thirty in the morning, I said goodbye to the girls and began to walk the short three blocks home. I sent a text to Levi. "I am pretty buzzed and am heading home for the night."

His immediate response was, "Oh really, is that an invitation you giving me?"

"Well, of course it is. After all, today is my birthday."

Levi was there within thirty minutes, and I left the door unlocked for him to make a faster entrance. We locked eyes, and the magic was revealed once again. He picked me up and threw me on the bed. The passion was intense and within a few minutes of lip locking, it took another step forward. He removed his shirt, while I unbuttoned his pants. He stepped off the bed to remove my pants, tossing them on the floor. As he began to crawl up toward me from the foot of the bed, he opened my legs and began kissing my inner thighs. As his lips drew closer to giving me my birthday gift, I could barely contain myself. I held onto the bed sheets with a tight grip and then moved my hands onto his head. No one was ever able to touch me the way he did, and that was part of my addiction to him. He gave me the release that I needed—several, in fact.

Our late evening ended with incredible sex, using several of our favorite go-to positions. And by three a.m., we called it a night, and I fell asleep with him spooning me from behind. I did feel guilty about knowing the truth, that he was still not an available man, but it was my birthday and I justified it. These are the things you tell yourself when you know what you're doing isn't right, but you want to take the selfish route. Somehow, I was still under the "dick spell" and clearly still in love with this man. As soon as were done living in that space, the guilt and a stamp of shame would come back to haunt me. This had to be the last time. I had said it before, and in my heart, I had believed it. No more excuses. As long as I continued to allow him the opportunity, he would take it. And that didn't sound like the type of man I should be investing in, in the first place. We sometimes can't help who we fall in love with, but we do have choices about whom we spend our energy on. People can be medicine for a short time, or a long one, but either way, you just appreciate the time you have. This was it. I had to let him go for good this time, and with that, maybe I would be allowed the chance to meet someone that I was enough for. For the very last time, we said goodbye. It was emotional, but not as difficult as the times before. I was determined to stay the course and be the honest women I needed to be—to not use what we had as a crutch, and to make the best choices for my continued growth and healing.

◀ ◀ • ▶ ▶

Two days later, it was finally time to make the thirteen-hour drive to California, and I needed the time to clear my head and perhaps break his spell. I broke up the long drive into two days, making an overnight stop halfway, in Bend, Oregon.

I passed the time listening to Adyashanti's nondual teachings of living a spiritual path and exploring infinite possibilities. I had originally purchased the five CD set for the road trip to Seattle I had planned to take with my father. At the time, he seemed more open to other ways of expressing spirituality, and this could have been a bonding exercise for us. Adyashanti's approach is compared to early Zen masters, and his teachings offer a variety of subjects that come from a non-judgmental perspective. I wanted to get on the road early so I could make it to Bend with some of the afternoon to play and stretch my legs. I estimated the drive would take just over six hours, which wasn't too bad for my first day out on the road. I chose to enter into Oregon on US 395, passing through the Tri-Cities, which is known to have the most desolate landscape in Washington. Not much to look at this way, other than open fields of agriculture and farming. I chose to stop to get gas and stretch my legs in Kennewick, and then get onto US 395, which would lead me to I-82 and take me into Oregon.

The scenery began to change dramatically the closer I got to crossing the state border. Oregon is abundant with plant life; the constant rain showers keep the plants happy and thriving. But today, the sun was shining and I could feel her rays beaming through the windows of my car. The time passed quickly, and it looked like I would be in Bend by two that afternoon. I went straight to my motel to drop off my luggage and change into something more stylish.

Time to head into town and check out what Bend has to offer. Within ten minutes I was parked on their main strip of downtown, full of trendy shops and restaurants. I stumbled upon a few specialty stores and picked up a few gifts for my friends back home. Then the hunger monster within made an appearance, and I asked one of the store clerks for a food recommendation. She mentioned today was the afternoon Farmer's Market, and they would have some great options. It happened to be just around the corner and was connected to the infamous Drake Park.

This posh market had an abundance of food options, lots of fresh produce, baked goods of all sorts, with options of being gluten free and catering to other dietary restrictions. It was fairly busy, filled with families and locals. I purchased a rhubarb pastry and a homemade kombucha that came with the recommendation and headed toward the park.

Drake Park is enchanted to say the least. It runs along the east side of the Deschutes River and is a popular destination, not just for the locals but for a variety of bird life that also called it home. I followed the river trail for the next hour, making my way around the thirteen-acre park and taking in what it had to offer.

Bend is clearly a hip town, full of health-conscious individuals that live active lifestyles. The locals are friendly and actually smile and say hello when you look their way. I could imagine this was a very peaceful place to live and to raise a family.

I spent the rest of the evening back at the motel, mapping out my next day of travel. I had another seven hours of driving till I reached my camping site in California on the beach. I had to allow myself several hours of daylight to set up camp and check out the site, so I called it an early night meant for an early rise.

On the road again by eight a.m., I had to stop for gas and ice for the cooler before leaving Bend. Getting prepared for another long day of travel, I decided to insert the first CD of Adyashanti's teachings. The tone in his voice immediately captured my attention, and I could feel the intention behind his words, even though he mentioned to question everything, including his own lessons. He wants to support the self in letting go of attachment to things, and most importantly the ego of one's self. The more I listened, the more what he was saying resonated with my journey and with me. His words were like another language, one that I could understand because I was living this truth and it made sense. I imagined he was speaking directly to me, as if we were having a face-to-face conversation.

> Awakeness is inherent
> In all things and all beings
> Everywhere
> All the time.
> This awakens relates to every moment
> From innocence
> From absolute honesty
> From the state where you feel
> Absolutely authentic.
> Only from this state
> Do you realize
> That you never really wanted
> Whatever you thought you wanted.
> You realize
> That behind all your desires

Was a single desire
To experience each moment
From all your true nature.

My head was spinning, and I found it hard to process all the connections I was making considering this more introspective approach. Maybe what had transpired with loss of James, my father, and the disconnect of Levi were gifts that I had asked for, and no longer served my higher good. My relationship with my father had grown as a result of James leaving me. Our divorce, once the dust settled, allowed me more precious time with my father. We went back in time when it was just the two of us, switching roles. Once the point was reached that my father had suffered enough, he made his peace with Creator and moved on.

I had feared he would forget who I was for a period of time, while still living on this earth. But he had left just before that journey began, and it saved us both a world of hurt. Levi was there to love on me when I needed someone, to break down some of the armor the divorce had created. He allowed me to trust and open up to the possibility of love, even though it began in a place of deceit. We were never meant to be together, but it had served its purpose for the time we had.

I thought about the thirteen years I had spent with James, and how we had grown together. But the last two years, expressing absolute honesty, I had to admit we had grown apart. The fire and the light between us became dim and was not being nurtured. At the time, I was working on my healing and trying to be a better partner, but leading up to that, I pushed him away physically and emotionally.

I wanted to experience each moment from my true nature, just as Adyashanti had said. And to do this, I had to let go of my past and certain situations that kept me from where I needed to be. Being alone and taking this road trip to California, to connect with my ancestors and the land, would allow this to new awakening to unfold.

I knew in my heart space and in my gut that I was heading to exactly where I needed to be. The next six hours seem to fly by, as I couldn't get enough of his teachings and was eager to learn more.

I entered the redwood forest by two p.m. that afternoon and became instantly mesmerized by the size and magnitude of those cedar trees. I pulled over to take a few quick pictures, but the images were nothing compared to what I saw before me.

Some of these trees had been there for thousands of years and were up to two hundred and eighty feet tall and twenty-three feet across. The coastal redwoods can reach three hundred feet and are known for being the tallest living things on our planet. I was incredibly humbled to be standing here in their presence, and I could smell their medicine. I placed my palm upon a tree's trunk and could feel that exchange of life force from within its roots and its connection to the earth. I can only imagine all the diversity they have seen, being that the oldest living beings and dating back to more than three thousand years ago.

These trees are sacred and lived alongside my ancestors; they have witnessed the way we used to live in harmony with our Mother. They saw our struggle to protect her and to keep our traditional ways. In that moment, I was feeling beyond blessed to be here, and I couldn't wait to get to camp to take it all in.

I still had a drive ahead of me to make it to the Prairie Creek Redwoods that were located at the end of the national forest heading towards Eureka. I was able to reserve the very last campsite at Gold Bluff Beach Campground; it was all that was available with the busy summer camping season. I reached the dirt road the directions mentioned, and it became quite clear why no RVs or campers were allowed at this site. I had a hard time seeing any distance through all the dirt in the air as I slowly made my way down. The road was narrow and only had enough room for one car at a time. I hoped no one would come along that I needed to make room for. I felt anxious about a slow leak in one of my tires, praying that it wouldn't be flat in the morning. The assistance out here was limited, and I don't know what I would have done if that transpired. The road took me from a high elevation down to the ocean level, and I drove on a gravel road the rest of the way in. Finally, I made it the campground, and I saw that it was nestled right on the beach. What a sense of relief to finally be here. I could set up camp and make my way to the ocean.

I got my tent set up and my food properly packed away from any curious wildlife, meaning bears. I grabbed a warm blanket, my journal, and my smudge, and made my way down toward the ocean. It was a rather foggy day, and I'm told that was pretty normal around these parts in the summertime. The ocean was beautiful, and the tide was strong, but I couldn't see very far out into the view. Walking up and down the beach, the wind in my hair, feeling the sand in between my toes—this felt like living in my true nature.

I found a quiet spot with a little less wind to smudge and catch up on my journaling. I sat on that beach wrapped up in my blanket for a good couple of hours; I didn't need anything other than the seclusion I found in this space. I was proud of myself for making the journey alone thus far. It would be the first time I had camped alone. I had only camped a handful of times during my childhood, and with my sister involved it became more like "glamping." She took care of everything, from premade delicious meals to even providing blow-up mattresses for a better night's rest. James and I spent a few trips overnight in the great outdoors, but it never lasted more than a few nights and I always had him to take care of the "man duties." This time, for the first time, it was just me, no one else to depend on for warmth or shelter. This newfound independence came from something that was painful but would push me out of my comfort zone to make me stronger.

When I arrived back at my tent before dark, I realized that the weather was much colder than I had anticipated. With wool socks on my feet and a warm hat to keep the heat in, I got all bundled up in my warmest gear. I planned on staying in my sleeping bag for the rest of evening, and then began to rest my head on the hard earth floor.

"Oh, crap," I exclaimed out loud, as I realized I had forgotten a pillow along with my small travel air pad. I wouldn't be sleeping well tonight, considering my forgetful packing.

Utilizing my lantern, I spent the rest of my evening looking through the wedding photo album I had brought of my parents. They were married in the Redwoods back in 1975, and I had made this specific journey to spread my dad's ashes here. I loved that they had a traditional Native American wedding and joined their lives together in such a special way.

My mother was dressed in her best, wearing a white deerskin dress adorned with dentalium and abalone shells that hung toward the bottom like fringe. Her white buckskin moccasins came up to her shins and were beaded with the four specific colors for this marriage ceremony. On her head, she wore a traditional Yurok basket hat that was even more unique than most. It was made back in 1930 and woven out of bear grass, maidenhair fern, and porcupine quill. The designs created by these materials was called an obsidian blade and snake nose design. Dentalium shells and four woodpecker scalps adorned the top of her hat, also representing the four directions and a symbol of wealth for the Yurok. My father was dressed in a maroon and white ribbon shirt that screamed that seventies fashion back then. Around his neck lay a bear claw necklace, complete with fur and intricate beading that went all the way down the back of the regalia. He was Otter Clan, and his tall hat was made of otter fur with one single bear claw that dangled in front. Down the back of his hat lay intricate beading of blue, red, and white that formed together into diamond shaped designs. They were beaded on a separate piece of material in the shape of an otter tail, and when attached to this hat, the resemblance was quite clear.

The pictures showed they washed their hands together as symbol of purification and cleansing. This ceremonial washing clears away the memories of past loves and evil spirits and represents a new beginning. In attendance were a flute player, a solo guitarist, and drummer to contribute to their part of the ceremony. At the end of the service, a Karuk Indian leader conducted the medicine ceremony to bring everything all together.

Once the ceremony had commenced and the prayers had been sent, it was time to celebrate, and that meant a feast. The wedding album revealed lots of smoked salmon, acorn mush, deer meat, seaweed patties, and an abundance of berry-related dishes.

As I lay in my tent, I couldn't help but dream of one day when I might meet my own handsome brave and we could get married the traditional way. This was the second marriage for both my parents, and maybe I would receive this gift, as well, on the second time around. After what happened with James, I never imagined getting married again. But if this were an option, I would feel very differently, and might jump at the chance.

It was nine p.m., and before I could settle in for the night, I needed to find the restroom and relieve my water consumption for the day. It was so cold out there, but if I didn't go now, I wouldn't get any sleep. I grabbed my headlamp and put my shoes on, then headed toward the campground restroom. To my surprise, not even twenty feet away, I saw a large male elk, standing directly in front of the bathroom door. I froze in my tracks for a moment and then took another path leading off to the side. He had caught the attention of other campers around me, and we got our cameras to capture his movements. This campground is known for elk sightings, and new mothers liked to bring their babies down here, this time of year He was standing his ground; his medicine teaches us to balance our pride with noble intentions. This very independent creature came at a time when I myself was experiencing a newfound independence. In this instant, I was the closest I had ever been to an elk, and it felt beyond special to be sharing this space with him. He didn't seem to mind us, and everyone was smart enough to keep some distance. After about forty-five minutes, my bladder had reached its holding point and it was time to find an outlet. With the elk still holding the fort down at the bathroom, I chose to pee in the bush not too far away from my tent. Then off to bed; I wanted to get an early hike in before heading toward my next accommodation in Crescent City.

I was up with the sunrise; I didn't sleep much considering being without all the comforts of home I had forgotten. My body was sore from all the driving and not being used to sleeping on the ground. I put on a few more warm layers and made my way out of the tent to witness a new picturesque landscape awaiting its recognition. The fog had not set in just yet, but the mist danced above the hillside and mountains tops. The sky was clear and soft blue, with traces of pastel purples and pinks that appeared as brush strokes in a live panting. The air was clean and brisk, and as I inhaled it deep into my lungs, it felt like medicine. I let go of any physical discomfort from the trip and allowed that fresh air to take its rightful place.

It didn't take long to pack my things and take down my camp from the one night I stayed at Gold Bluff Creek campground. I passed on the shower; it was too cold for me to even reason with making the attempt, and I planned on showering in Crescent City that evening.

I started the car to see my low tire pressure light come on, and that had me most definitely worried. I needed to make my way out of this secluded area and to a gas station to fill my tire, pronto. The cooler temperatures overnight must have contributed to its slow leak, and I couldn't see much help around these parts, especially this early in the morning.

It took about thirty minutes of driving before I was able to make it back to Klamath and the only gas station around for a long while. I felt a huge sense of relief that the flat tire gods had taken pity on me and let me pass this time. I filled the gas tank as well and purchased a hot chocolate for the road, and I was set for today's adventures.

I stopped by the Trees of Mystery, which was on my way back towards Crescent City. It was a main tourist attraction in the Redwoods. Normally, I like to avoid tourist traps, but this opened back in 1946 and emphasizes educating the public about the magnificence of these trees.

Walking towards the entrance, I was greeted by the forty-nine-foot-tall Paul Bunyan statue, along with his thirty-five-foot blue ox, Babe. Over a loud PA system, he said, "Hello. Welcome to the Trees of Mystery." The trailhead began right away and took me through the Kingdom of Trees. This area is dedicated to the natural resiliency of these trees and how they were able to thrive here for so long. I learned that that fog, which I had witnessed several times while being here, was indeed essential to their life force. These giants pull moisture from the fog into their needles at the top of the tree, which doesn't receive efficient circulation.

Moving on and up the trail, I stumbled upon the Brotherhood Tree and had to take a moment to pay it my respect. This tree is over two thousand years old, nineteen feet in diameter, and two hundred and ninety-seven feet high. I believe these are living beings and deserve respect, for the human race could not exist without their constant sacrifice of providing shelter, along with the air we breathe. Upon leaving, I placed a small offering of tobacco and thanked this tree for all the years it had provided oxygen and life force on this planet.

The trailhead continued to climb higher and revealed many other types of tree species I was unfamiliar with. The Cathedral Tree was beyond magnificent; it is composed up of nine living trees growing as one. These trees came together to form a natural looking cathedral formation, giving you a sense of a church service in the woods.

The end of the trailhead led me to the Sky Trail, where guests were invited to take a gondola ride up to the very top and experience these beauties in another way. The ride moves eleven miles per hour and makes a few stops to allow the guests to take pictures and have a moment to appreciate the view. I loved seeing these trees from the tops; looking downward gave me a better understanding their sheer size and scale.

Once the gondola reached the top, I stepped out and walked over to a large viewing deck with provided binoculars. It felt like I was on top of the world, and in this crack in time, I felt here alone to share this experience with Creator and myself. I took in a few deep breaths, and my lungs were happy. They appreciated this fresh clean air in this space. The view extended beyond my vision, surrounded by the redwood forest and mountain ranges way off in the distance.

I spent some time on the deck looking at the maps of the different parts of the forest and determined my next destination was Jedediah Smith Redwoods State Park. This park would be closer to Crescent City, and I could get a nice hike in and maybe cool off in the river.

Jedediah Smith Redwoods is only a few miles inland from the Pacific Ocean and contains seven percent of all the old-growth redwoods left in the world. The ten-thousand-acre park offers twenty miles of lush trailheads and scenic views.

I reached the state park just under an hour and pulled into a campground that offered some parking for visitors. The camp was nestled along the Smith River, which happens to be longest major free flowing river in California. After a decent walk through the trails nearby, my body was calling me to water and that river. The afternoon sun had worked up a sweat on my outer layers, and I needed to decompress from all the physical activities of the day's adventures.

The beach was incredibly rocky and required sandals for most, and most definitely for someone like me who had tender feet. I laid my towel about ten feet away from these two tattooed ladies that looked about ten years younger than me. They had two adorable dogs with them and seemed really friendly. The dogs came over to say hello first, and then we introduced ourselves. The ladies were from Portland and on an extended road trip, living out of a van and camping along the way. I enjoyed their energy and conversation, plus, being around more tattooed females for me is always comforting. Being covered from head to toe seems to draw attention, whether it's positive or negative, but I have become used to it. My tattoos tell my story and represent different times in my life, both good and bad. Some of them remind me of my emotional scars and the life I had with James. A part of me wished that, at some point, I could remove or cover a lot of the work he had adorned me with. Then, I would no longer be defined by my past and would become a butterfly with new wings. But, perhaps, I was still in the caterpillar stage. This was to be a work in progress, and I had hopes that, one day, looking in the mirror, I would no longer see the connection, and neither would anyone else.

My legs were tight and screaming at me from all the day's activities. The cold moving water would become my natural ice pack and help with any inflammation. Time to make my way down to the river and prepare to embrace it for as long as my body would allow. Dipping in my toes, and then my whole foot one at time, I walked in slowly until it reached my waist. The river was brisk, and the cooling effects of its power took over my senses. This medicine created a space for healing and invigorated my entire body. As if I'd hit a recharge button, I was feeling reborn with a fresh pair of strong legs.

This river was such a blessing, and I felt so grateful to be able to seek refuge in her constant cooling movement. Our connection to the water is quite simple, being that we are made of mostly water. It's unfortunate that clean water to drink has no longer become a God-given right, but for some, a luxury. My ancestors understood this relationship and always did what they could to protect the water. We don't give water the respect and recognition it deserves for its healing ability and essential part in creating life on this planet. The Powers That Be take this precious gift for granted and treat it as an obstacle or a way to fill their pocketbooks. I began to think about what was going on at Standing Rock, and how much impact a movement like this can have. To make a stand as one people for the protection of our water and our precious resources could create the largest ripple effect the world had ever seen. The last few days without Wi-Fi or reception had me feeling clueless about the latest events. Even though the escape from the outside world was indeed a good thing, I felt guilty about not being informed and sharing the latest details. I was ready to hit the road one last time for the day and make my way to Crescent City.

The Ocean Front Lodge sits only thirty feet away from the Northern California coast. I couldn't have been more thrilled about this location, with little traffic in sight and plenty of seclusion. Checking into my room, I was blown away by my accommodations for the next three days. I had planned on treating myself with this room and had picked one with an indoor Jacuzzi. Normally, I would never splurge on a room like this, but it was only one hundred and fifty a night, which was fairly cheap for me for these accommodations, but, I suppose, pricey for Crescent City.

Without a shower in last twenty-four hours, I knew where I was heading first. I filled the Jacuzzi with some bubbles from my shampoo bottle and grabbed a book. The next hour would be spent soaking in this tub, allowing my body and mind to decompress from all the days before. This felt like a taste of heaven, a gift to be treasured, and I had every intention of utilizing this space and time.

After my soak, I was feeling so refreshed and relaxed, and wanted to take time now to get caught up on the happenings in Standing Rock. I got myself dressed in comfy clothes and crawled up on the perfectly made bed. I had trouble connecting to the Wi-Fi out here, but after several attempts on was online and ready to dive in. The best access to the movement was coming from live feeds and the water protectors that were sharing the details through Facebook. The national media and outside sources were of no help in getting the word out; it was up to the private and underground media to cover what was really taking place. By the end of August, the camp had been in effect for over four months. By this point, thousands of water protectors had gathered down at Standing Rock to join the movement. Word had spread of the Lakota prophecy behind the Black Snake, and what harm and danger would come if the pipeline was laid over the Missouri river. Indigenous people do not take these prophecies lightly; they are sacred teachings that have been orally passed down from our ancestors, as a clear warning of what's to come. This 1,200-mile pipeline would run a half-million gallons of crude oil each day through Lakota sacred lands and precious water sources. An Environmental Impact Statement was never done, and the Energy Transfer Partners seemed to think that was acceptable. Their current construction had already desecrated some sacred burial sites for the tribe. Through my Facebook feed, I witnessed friends going through an incredible amount of mourning, as well as trying to hold back their anger, as they had endured such a traumatic act of pure disrespect. How would the Dakota Access Pipeline employees feel if someone came to their families' resting places and dug up their graves, all for the sake of money and greed? These corporations have no regard for the true inhabitants of the land or those who have fought for centuries to protect it. I saw history repeating itself, and I felt infuriated with the system and how little it values our Mother. All I knew was that I needed to find a way to get down there to help. I didn't know when or how, but I felt called to give service to those water protectors down at Standing Rock.

Waking up the next morning, I felt refreshed from a good night's sleep and excited to get back into the Redwoods. Today marked the fifty-fourth Klamath Salmon festival, where I planned to be surrounded by Yurok tribal members. This was a rare opportunity to meet some elders that could have known my family and seek some stories or unknown information.

Unfortunately, this year would be different from the rest, with the prized and sacred salmon not being served at the festival. For first time in fifty-four years, the tradition would be broken due to poor water management practices. The dams that were built back in the fifties and sixties had, over time, created these conditions, producing deadly aquatic parasites that could potentially wipe out all the Chinook salmon. For my tribe, this is their livelihood and their way of life. The consequences would greatly impact their economy, considering they are fisherman, as well as having the daily need to feed their families. Not to mention times like this, where we would not have the salmon for special ceremonies such as the festival.

My grandmother had told me stories about how Creator had to prepare to bring humans onto the earth. He called out to all of the creature teachers and asked if they would sacrifice themselves to feed the people. Our brother Salmon, known as "ney-puy," stepped forward and offered himself, and then the water came forward to provide a home for the salmon. The one request of the Creator was that the bones of the first salmon run be put back into the water from which they came. This tradition would allow the salmon to return each year and is an essential offering to their continued sacrifice to feed us.

These old stories and memories of my grandmother, and the time we spent in this area together, came flooding back on the drive to Klamath as I passed by these giant cedars. The absence of salmon this year was devastating, and I couldn't imagine how the tribe would handle this situation. But I was here to reconnect and build to new relationships, and I could do my part by through prayer and educating others on the issue back home.

Before I left for the festival, I carefully packed my Yurok basket hat, similar to the one in my mother's wedding photo, in my backpack. It's less intricate and delicate than the one she wore in the picture but just as spectacular. I didn't know if the women would be showcasing them today, but I wanted to have mine on hand, just in case.

I arrived at the festival around nine a.m. I wanted to get there early to not miss out on any of the day's events. I parked about a quarter of a mile away and walked toward town. I could see classic cars all lined up and down the main street. There were vendors set up and down both sides, selling their cultural crafts, works of art, and other treasures. The parking lot behind the community center has been filled with food vendors, serving up huckleberry dishes, Indian tacos, and classic hamburgers and such. But, of course, there was no salmon to be seen this year. I hoped I could still find a way to enjoy a plate before I left California.

I made my way around to the podium to wait for the MC to announce the festival. The tribal council chose a highly respected elder to begin the festival with a prayer, and then they would make announcements. Everyone quieted down and bowed their heads as we listened carefully to the elder's words. He mentioned that before we were given the name "Yurok," we referred to ourselves in our native language as Oohl, meaning Indian people. He spoke of a time when our people lived in over fifty villages in our ancestral homeland, and how we thrived living the way Creator had intended. And once the colonization began, our ancestors endured a constant struggle to keep our traditions, ceremonies, and language in existence for future generations. This oral history led into saying our respects to the elders, the veterans, and the volunteers that helped continue to keep these traditions alive.

He then addressed the issue of the loss of salmon numbers and the matters at hand to save the Chinook salmon for future generations. A prayer was said for our brother Salmon, that his numbers be restored and that he make the journey back to feed the people next year. The festival was now ready to commence, and the parade would kick off the day's activities shortly.

I missed the free veteran's breakfast that was served at eight a.m., along with the start of the annual Ney' Puey 5K run but arrived in time for the parade of floats made by the local schools and members of the community made their way through town. I figured I would check out some of the vendors while waiting for the stick ball game to commence. My eyes were drawn to a man's booth that sat on the corner of a busy area and across from the main stage. He had two large tables displaying his antler carvings and beadwork. It stood out from the rest, as I had never seen anything like it before.

He introduced himself. "Hello, my name is Dale. These are all my carvings and I am a Karuk tribal member. What tribe are you from?"

Dale looked to be in his mid-forties, but it's hard to tell with Native people. We tend to age well when we are in good spirits. He had a longer-than-usual grey and black beard, considering most Native men can't grow beards very long, and stylish black-rimmed glasses with a beaded baseball cap covering his long hair that was pulled into a ponytail. His eyes were warm, and I felt a good energy from him, right from the start.

"Hello, my name is Donell, and I am Yurok and Ottawa. I am just loving your work." I pointed at one antler in particular, and said, "This one is speaking to me."

"Ah, yes, that is one of my favorites. It's called a sturgeon backbone design," he replied.

The design ran long and narrow and was made with two vertical lines down the center. Triangles that began upside down ran down all the lines, resembling the sturgeon backbone.

"Okay, then, I would like to purchase this treasure. It's definitely one of kind!"

"Well, thank you for appreciating my craft. Every piece I carve has a significant meaning to me. Before you leave, I would also like to give you some medicine I gathered."

Before me, there was a large, dark brown, abundantly rooted type of plant with no leaves, but the top was covered in a hair of sorts. I had never seen anything like it before. The strong root system revealed its home deep within the ground. I could tell it was medicine but had no understanding what it was used for. This unique plant had caught my attention during our conversation, because of its sheer size and its placement just behind all his carvings. He took out his knife and removed a chunk from the plant. He passed the medicine into my hands, and we exchanged a warm smile.

"This is bear medicine, or what we call Kishwoof. It smells like black licorice, and you can use it for sore throats, nausea, and many other ailments, or for ceremony."

I was touched that he chose to share his medicine with me, and I was excited to share this treasure with my sweat sisters back home. I stayed and chatted with Dale for another thirty minutes, and we shared stories and took a few pictures. He was a good man and had so much passion for his culture and continuing the traditions of his people. When we parted ways, I understood that every time I looked as this work, I would be reminded of this day and his special gift of medicine.

Making my way through the other vendors, I came upon a booth that offered healing salves made of wormwood and acorn flour for recipes. I introduced myself to the striking woman behind the booth and shared my passion for traditional foods and medicines. She was very warm and responsive, and happy that I had come all this way for the festival. Margo was striking for several reasons; she had medium-length sliver-white hair, with the darker grey that popped from underneath. Her skin was radiant, with so few wrinkles it made it impossible to tell her age. But it was her chin tattoo of three distinct black lines, called the "one hundred and eleven," that I admired most.

Margo said, "This is a symbol of beauty, and it represents my commitment to continue the traditions of my ancestors."

"Well, I think it is quite beautiful and looks so natural on you, sister," I replied.

We spoke about what recipes she liked to make with the acorn flour, and I mentioned I would try a few unique twists and pass them along to her. This excited Margo, and we exchanged information and a picture before parting ways. I was thrilled by the connections I was already making at the festival, and the day had just begun.

The first "werhiperh" or stick ball game of the day, with the youngest players going first, was about to start. The stick ball game has been around for hundreds of years and was used by some tribes to settle disputes without going to war. The game is played on a large field, and the teams score by getting a ball that traditionally was made by a rock covered in hair from one side to the other. The tools used for this game vary from tribe to tribe and can change with the region. Some tribes use two hickory sticks with netting that resembles more of a lacrosse feel. But in Yurok country, they have one stick called the "herhiper," and the ball is called a "tossie" and typically is cylinder shaped and made from wood. Then two tossies are tied to string, one at each end, and that becomes ball in the game. The players are not allowed to touch the tossie with their hands and can only use the sticks to maneuver the ball. While the game is in action, the boys not handling the tossie wrestle with one another to keep their opponents from helping them score. The wrestling makes it all the way down to the ground, and back in the day, it could get more aggressive. They use the herhiper to flick the tossie down the field to the opposite side to score. The game is made up of four fifteen-minute intervals, and it appeared to be a killer workout.

I loved watching the little ones go at it. They were still getting used to the game and were not as invested in the wrestling component. But these boys were eager to learn, and I could see their progress as the game continued on. It was late morning now, and the fog had dissipated for the day, allowing the sun to take its rightful position. The ever-present cool wind that seemed to always be in this area kept the players comfortable. I was bundled up a little bit, but thoroughly entertained. This was a rare crack in time, and I couldn't imagine being anywhere else. It felt so good to be surrounded by my tribal members.

Earlier that day, I had noticed a beautiful woman in a wheelchair wearing her traditional Yurok basket hat. She had a great energy about her, and we smiled at each other in passing. When I saw her again, I took it upon myself to make a proper introduction. That's what Dad would have told me to do, and I could feel him there hoping that I would.

She had long dark grey hair that hung below her waist, adorned with a traditional Yurok basket hat on her head, and she was dressed in a turquoise blouse that brought out her dark brown eyes and glowing skin.

We introduced ourselves, and I told her of my grandmother and why I had made the journey out here. She was pleased to hear my story, and it felt like we had made some connection. I pulled my basket hat out of my bag to see if she had anything she wanted to share about its care.

She mindfully handled it by balancing it by its outside rim carefully with the palm of her hands. She explained, "This hat is a flying geese and mountain design, made from spruce root and bear grass."

Then she showed me how to put it on and wear it properly, and I knelt down so she could place it on my head. She reached for my hand as I stood back up and connected not just her eyes but also her heart.

"You must always treat this hat with respect, and care for it as if it was a living being. These baskets require water, just as we humans do, and it's good medicine to wear your hat in the rain. This brings life to it, and it will take shape to sit perfectly on your head. When wearing this hat, you represent our people and our ancestors. Carry yourself with pride and humility, and above all else with gratitude for the Creator."

Before we said goodbye, I hugged this woman for the time and the knowledge she had chosen to share with me. I wore my basket hat from then on, along with a smile on my face, for rest of the day.

This day couldn't have gotten any better until I received a text from a distant relative that I must make a stop at Paul's Salmon before returning back to Crescent City. Robert claimed there would be authentic Yurok smoked salmon, and my only option in the area. I left the festival and high tailed it for my salmon fix. Right off the road in a small pullover, I saw this very quaint little white shop, aged but with strong character. Salmon were cooking on cedar sticks smoking around the fire, nice long fillets cut top to bottom and leaving the skin and tail on, pierced right through the center. This for me was food porn and a beautiful sight; I was drooling and possibly salivating like Pavlov's dog experiment. This was what I had been waiting for.

I walked into the shop, and a Yurok man in his fifties came out to greet me.

I mentioned, "Robert is my distant cousin, and he told me I needed to come try your salmon."

"Ah, yes, he is good man and distant relative of my wife's, too, so we must be family. What can I get you today?"

"Well, I wish I could get a lot of salmon, but I'm traveling, so just enough for lunch today, I guess."

He handed me a paper towel with two large cuts of smoked salmon, and then said, "No charge. You are family, and there is always more if you are still hungry."

I was so touched by his gesture and wanted to offer cash if he was willing to take it. But I understood to just accept the gift and say gratitude, for this was my favorite traditional food medicine.

I walked back outside to join the men at a picnic table who were eating their share as well. We introduced ourselves, and they told me they were locals, one from the Karuk and the other Yurok. Considering our feast, we didn't say a whole lot, but it was nice to enjoy their company during this meal.

The Yurok man from the shop came back outside to fatten me up.

"This is for the ride home," he said. He laid another large slab of his precious salmon onto my paper towel and told me to have a safe journey back home. I just couldn't believe the hospitality out here in the Redwoods; it felt like a home away from home. And finally being able to eat that prized salmon! It gave me physical nourishment, but the gesture behind it was just as special. Not a bad way to end the day, with a fully belly and an understanding that I connected with the right people along the way.

The next morning, I allowed myself to sleep in. This was going to be my last full day among the Redwoods, and I had been waiting for the right time to spread my dad's ashes. I was able to make it to the Jedediah Smith Park Boy Scout Trail by nine-thirty a.m., with only one other car parked in the area. It made for good solitude but also made me feel very vulnerable. I packed my bear bell, my knife, and some mace, just in case I stumbled upon a predator of sorts.

However, I welcomed the presence of Bigfoot, if any chose to make an appearance. Hiking this five-mile trail in one of the most pristine old-growth areas reminded me so much of my grandmother and the stories she would tell me about Bigfoot when I was a little girl. From my understanding, Native people had always coexisted with these living beings and showed each other a mutual respect. Back in the day, my grandparents owned a logging company deep in Yurok country and experienced several encounters with the creature turning over their logging equipment. Grandma's stories are documented in old books and commentaries, sharing all her accounts and experiences. I have had dreams that he has come to me as a protector and spirit guide as the result of the imprint her stories left on me. I even made it permanent by getting at Bigfoot portrait tattoo on the back of my left leg, with my grandmother's name, Vera, written in cursive underneath.

The air was a bit cooler, and the trees still offered a lot of shade. I just needed to find my pace, and I would warm up in no time. The air was so fresh; with each inhale and exhale, I got a new dose of medicine. The trail opened up from larger groves and then backed into meadows carpeted in a variety of ferns. Each turn around the next corner revealed another display of Creator's magic, and, once again, I couldn't imagine being anywhere else.

I used all of my senses to see any signs of the creature teachers around me. There is so much to learn by observing their traits and behaviors, and this sacred space was abundant with so many. The birds were singing, and the wind was softly making its own music as it kissed my face and moved through my hair.

This hike at times didn't even feel real, but more like a dream. I had never imagined what this day would feel like, but now that I felt it, I didn't want to let go of that feeling of connection, of being present, and allowing myself to be open. Hands down, it was one of my greatest gifts so far on this journey.

An hour and half into the hike, I came upon a stream that opened up into a small waterfall, surrounded in beauty. This sacred space sat nestled deep within the Redwoods, and the only way out was the way in. My body was warm from the trek, and I removed my jacket to bask in the sun during my stay. I found a good place to pray and gathered my medicines from my bag, along with my dad's ashes. It was time to return him to back to the woods, to the guardians of these sacred spaces, within the forest where he married my mother and where my ancestors had thrived.

"Thank you, Creator," I prayed, "for allowing me to come to this special place. My journey to the Redwoods and Yurok country has been incredibly healing. I felt very guided and protected by you and by my ancestors. I want to pray for safe travels home, and for all my loved ones that have supported this journey. I pray for the salmon, that it can make the journey and return in numbers next year, that people will wake up to the world around them and understand that everything is connected. I want to send extra prayers to the water protectors down at Standing Rock. May their voices be heard and may the powers that be see the light and open their hearts. And now, as I spread my father's ashes, I want to give thanks for the life you gave us. I want to thank you for aligning us to be together for the last thirty-seven years. Without his continued guidance and strength, I would not be standing here with you today. Dad, you can now become one with our Mother in this space and a protector of these woods."

I spread his ashes into the earth and some into the shallow pool just below the waterfall. I had completed my mission, and this was the perfect day to bring him here. After spending another good hour in solitude, it was time to head back to the trail. I needed to ice my knee, as well.

I left that day with the understanding to just be grateful my body allowed this trek; it was the farthest distance I had achieved since the injury. My relationship to my body and its abilities had transformed into understanding what work I needed to do from within. The act of slowing down allowed me to begin to heal my wounds and nurture my spirit. I left California with more peace in my heart than ever before. I fully received Mother Nature medicine, and it offered me a renewed strength for the next chapter to reveal itself.

CHAPTER 11
Dream Medicine

THE MOVEMENT DOWN AT STANDING ROCK continued to grow. By the end of August, and five months into this stand, an estimated three thousand water protectors had gathered already. On August 24, 2016, water protectors made it to Washington, D.C. in person to demand that the Environmental Impact Statement be done before the Dakota Access Pipeline could proceed any further. At this point, seventy-seven tribes had sent resolutions to Washington against DAPL, showing their support for the Standing Rock Sioux tribe.

I turned to social media, which still seemed to be the only source documenting these crimes, for the latest updates on the happenings around Sacred Stone Camp, which had become the epicenter where everyone gathered. The water protectors stated that the water tanks had been shut off and the portable toilets were not being emptied, in addition to five hundred yards of cell service being compromised in an effort to keep them from sharing information. The powers that be had urgency in getting the pipe laid down before any more time passed, and it was quite clear that they would stop at nothing to get their precious Black Snake into our Mother. Glancing at the regular news, I was disgusted to see some of the mass media implying the water protectors were behaving in ways not considered peaceful. This was a very dishonorable attempt on their part to confuse the general public about a concept meant for the greater good and the future of our planet's resources.

I felt very conflicted about this matter, because I had a sense of guilt for not being there already to help. I made donations early on in the cause, but my "orenda" spiritual essence was telling me it was not nearly enough. I had just gotten back home and had already arranged to leave for Seattle in five days' time for another healing session with Alex Turtle. He and his wife had previously lifted my curse and helped begin my path towards my Medicine tracks. But my orenda told me that, after that, I needed to get to Standing Rock, if even for only a few days. My clients could be rescheduled, and this freedom I had was a gift to be used.

The decision was made and within minutes I booked my ticket to fly into Bismarck, North Dakota. I would then rent a car and use that vehicle for my sleeping accommodations. Leaving any other details to be handled later on, I had plenty to prepare for to get ready for Seattle and then leaving for Standing Rock immediately upon my return.

The next five days went by in a flash; I worked my tail off squeezing in all the clients I had rebooked to make the journey to North Dakota. The blessing in this industry, and in being self-employed, allowed me to make this happen without too much added stress. I also had my clients' continued support in my journey thus far.

Before I knew it, I was back in my car and on yet another road trip destined for Seattle. The four and half hours would pass quickly, with this travel being a breeze compared to California. I still had one last Adyashanti CD to listen to and utilized the quiet time in my car once again. This last lesson spoke of the ego, and how it relates to opposition and separateness. Adyashanti explained,

> We will want to be right, and believe only what we see and feel to be true. When we realize that this reality is the dream state, only then are we actually free. And there will always be duality, polarizing with our beliefs. Both sides are equally true, it doesn't matter which one we believe is the right choice.

These words resonated with me so hard that I had to listen to them several times before pulling over to write them down. The lessons in ego are something I always struggled with, and I was not sure I would ever fully make peace with them. However, I was more aware of what drove them and how reactive they could reveal themselves to be in times of stress or suffering.

I loved to be right, to be first, and to have the last word. And my type A personality drove these behaviors; this archetype was sufficient and productive. I thrived on a competitive mind-set that continuously fed into this cycle of attachment to concepts that were fueled by ego. I was just playing a role that I believed at the time was necessary. The pain and the past didn't break me but allowed me to strip down the layers of who I thought I was. I wasn't aware or awakened to the effect this cycle had on my spiritual stagnation. This new introspective medicine, I was receiving told me, this wasn't living in my true nature.

I arrived into town in the early evening and met up with my niece for some much-needed girl time. I swooped her from work, and we grabbed a bite at this great vegetarian place called Café Flora. I am, of course, no longer a vegetarian, but Jewels is and I still loved the cuisine. I missed her face, and when in her presence I received the butterfly medicine she developed from her mother. Every time we get together, I sense my sister Laura is there enjoying our continued connection and sisterhood.

After dinner, we drove back to her new apartment and spent the evening looking at old family pictures. Some I had never seen before of my mother and sister, and this was a gift, no doubt. These moments, too few and far between, to share old stories and fond memories was another form of medicine.

The next few days were spent spending quality time with Jewels and reconnecting any lost time while making new memories. This was all leading up to my last day in town, and the main reason I had made this trip. I stayed overnight in an Airbnb in Edmonds so I could catch the morning ferry to Kingston.

I was looking forward to a quiet night in and catching up on the latest details at the movement down at Standing Rock. What I saw, I wasn't prepared for. The act of violence and pure ignorance that had just occurred sent chills down my spine.

The DAPL pipeline workers had worked through the night and dug up another ancestral burial site of the Lakota/Dakota tribes. This land had been documented by the court just days before as an archeological site. The morning of September 3, 2016, the water proctors got word and gathered in prayer at the site, joining together in a peaceful protest. I am aware that some of warriors spoke with words of anger, but they never retaliated in violence.

This time it wasn't just the police present, but a hired security team GS-4 that appeared to have the same authority as our law enforcement. Words became heated between the two groups, and the security team chose to take violent action. They went down a line of women, elders, and warriors standing at the front lines in peaceful protest and maced them right in the face. This was then followed by unleashing attack dogs into the crowd, resulting in multiple bites on several victims. The local law enforcement sat back and watched this atrocity unfold, offering no help to the people they were hired to protect. I watched several videos of what had happened, and I couldn't help but cry for my people. This is how our ancestors were treated not too long ago, and now it was history repeating itself. This event left me feeling more worried about my journey there in a few days, but I had to go and help in any way I could.

The medicine I would be receiving the next day in my healing session with Alex would offer some protection, and I had been waiting for another dose. I slept hard that evening, and the morning came quickly. I headed down to catch the ferry to Kingston by ten a.m. I wanted to explore the town and grab a decent breakfast.

I filled my belly with a delicious salmon and spinach crepe, and I was set for an amazing day. The address was in the middle of nowhere, and I passed it on the way in. But it looked like a community environment, with several small structures and lots of cars. I saw several people sitting in a circle outside of the main house, and after parking my car, I walked over to introduce myself. They all had a warm and inviting energy and made me feel very welcome. Alex came outside shortly after and gave me the play-by-play for our session.

"It's good to see you, Donell. It's been quite some time. We will get started here shortly. I have someone preparing our space, and she will also be sitting with us during your session. I'm teaching her the medicine, and I hope this is okay with you?"

"Well, yes, of course," I replied.

"Okay, good. So, tell me again, why are you here today? What brought you to see me again?" he said.

"I'm in need of some guidance, as well as some healing with my body and spirit. I will be leaving for Standing Rock in a few days and would also like to ask for some protection," I responded.

I could see an interested look in his eye as he processed what I said. Then he turned to me and responded, "Sounds like you need a tune up, my dear."

We both kind of giggled and exchanged of warm smiles within that moment, and I knew this medicine was already working.

"Okay, I have to go prepare. I will have my assistant call you in when I am ready," he said, and then walked off into a domelike structure for ceremony.

After about ten minutes, his assistant came out to tell me he was ready, and to follow her into this space. The walls were made of natural materials, and I wondered if it was a combination of mud and other resources. In the center lay a sacred place for fire, surrounded by a well-groomed dirt floor. The only light came in from the small entrance at the door. Alex was sitting there in a calm and peaceful stillness, and he motioned me to sit down next to him. Before he began this healing session, he opened up a cloth on the floor to reveal several sacred treasures. Then he carefully and with strong purpose placed an eagle claw, a feather, and an animal fetish of a bear on the floor before him.

He grabbed a stick and drew a small circle behind all the treasures and then asked his assistant,

"Grab some ashes from inside the fire and lay them down inside the circle."

She grabbed a small scoop shovel and placed the ashes directly on top of the circle and took her seat on the other side of Alex. He filled his pipe with sacred tobacco and, once it was lit, began to close his eyes and allow the medicine to begin. I tried to focus on what I came here to do and what kind of obstacles had continued to set me back on my journey.

After a few minutes, Alex began to unfold my current reality to me. Once again, he knew things that only someone connected to spirit could know. He took the pipe out of his mouth and began to speak with intentional words.

"A certain person who used to love you and be close to you, and now is no longer in your life, has put a curse on you. This person is jealous and doesn't want you to succeed. Their magic is dark, and you are not to blame for their bad intentions. This person doesn't want your voice to be heard or the work you do to become successful."

I was in somewhat a state of shock to hear I had yet another curse to lift, but I knew exactly whom he was speaking of. And it made total sense that Nikki would still for some reason feel this way about me. She never reached out or made any attempts to make amends. I had been informed she was the reason James didn't come to the funeral. She told him he wasn't allowed to come without her, and she had no intention of making an appearance. I couldn't understand how someone who claimed to love me at one point could be so cruel. To keep James from grieving with his family had nothing to do with me; it was a gesture to honor my father's life. I deserved, at the very least, her blessing to allow James to be present on that day, and she took that away, too.

Understand that some curses are just bad intentions that a person has toward someone else, and not crazy witchcraft. Even though there is that, too, among us, I knew this dark magic lived within her heart. She never wanted me to be happy, regardless of taking my old life away from me to become hers. For some reason, she was still fueled by jealousy, though I'm not sure why. She got everything she wanted, and I truly made the effort to not cause unnecessary drama for either of us. I can honestly say I handled the situation with the most grace I had within me. The only logic I could conceive of was that the dark space within her was now her main source of energy, at least when it came to how she felt about me. Through an introspective lens, I identified that I had to leave any expectations from our past friendship behind because that relationship no longer existed within her heart space. And if I continued to try and forgive her, I also had to accept the fact that she would never view me in a positive light or want me to succeed in this lifetime.

Alex watched me process what he had said and understood that I was aware of exactly who he was speaking of. I didn't have to go into details; it was clear that we both understood who was responsible for this dark magic. Then he took the stick again, and in the dirt drew a black arrowhead with distinctive designs inside of it. He also drew out a crooked and crazy feather that looked like it had seen better days.

Alex explained, "This black arrowhead symbolizes this person's bad intentions put onto you, and the markings on it are meant to close your throat, meant to keep your voice from being heard, and for others not to listen. I am not sure quite yet about this feather, but I do know I need to pull it from you. After our work is done here, continue to live with love in your heart. And if this person does become ill or have some bad luck, do not play into it. Just let it go."

I understood what this meant, and I knew to pay close attention to his words and lessons. I only wanted to practice good medicine, and it was never my intention to put ill will on others, even in these situations.

"Before we get started on this, I have to tell you I see a man standing next to you wearing a tall fur-covered hat. He must be of great importance to you," he said, looking a little surprised.

"Oh, you must be speaking of my father. He wore a tall otter hat when he danced in his regalia," I responded.

My father was present; he wanted to partake this time in my healing session and to lift this curse. I felt a greater sense of protection with his unexpected presence there and was ready for whatever would manifest once the medicine was lit. Alex placed more tobacco in his pipe, and I closed my eyes.

He told me, "Open your hands and rest them on your knees."

I felt the tobacco medicine being blown on my face and down throughout the rest of my body. When the aroma of sweet and earthy notes reached my nasal passages, I became in a meditative state. I envisioned that the smoke took shape once inside my body as a blue light of healing and left behind a new imprint to take its place. He directed energy from my center down to my arms and out through my hands, where he would use extra force behind his breath to push it through my fingertips. Once he reached my back and chest, the flow of movement had slowed down. He was struggling to remove some blockage within this area. He asked his assistant to go inside and fetch his war bonnet. I don't know the visual details of what took place in that moment, because I never opened my eyes. What I did feel, though, was a release of pain and suffering, and with that came the salty tears of healing as I felt heaviness leaving my body.

Alex then told me I could open my eyes, and I saw him standing before me, a stronger presence than ever before wearing his war bonnet. This one in particular had intricate beading of the colors of the four directions: red, black, white, and yellow. The extension of eagle feathers represented honorable and selfless acts that he had earned through using his medicine. Each one bore significance to the keeper and represented an extension of their beliefs. Once the eagle feathers are bound together, it is said the person wearing the bonnet embodies the eagle medicine of great wisdom and strength. Alex was out of breath and appeared to have just gone through some intense physical activity.

He turned to me, still panting, and said, "That was some strong magic, and I almost threw my back out releasing that curse from your body. I needed my war bonnet for the extra protection, and I felt all those scars and injuries you have had. You need to be more careful with your body and pay attention."

He went back to his seat, and said it was now time to reveal the objects he had pulled and send them back. He began to dig under the ashes that had been laid on top of the circle, in search of these items. He drew out the black arrowhead; with the same exact markings he had drawn in the dirt earlier. And then came this crazy crooked feather, just like the one he had explained. He placed the items down on the dirt floor, so we could examine them further.

"At sunset tonight, I will send these objects back from where they came, and the person who sent them will receive their karma if they continue to come with bad intentions. But we don't wish this on anyone; it is their choice what becomes of this."

Then he reached out to assistant, who handed him a cup of an unusual tea. He passed it to me and said, "I have prepared a special tea for you to drink before you leave. This will help protect you on your travels."

I was honored that this had been prepared for me and drank it feeling lots of gratitude and comfort. It tasted like plant medicine that I wasn't familiar with, but it was good all the same. I thanked Alex for his time and the work spent on my healing and made my way back out the sacred space.

Walking back to my car, I did feel a sense of relief, a feeling that now I could actually physically heal my body with no more negative energy blocking my path. The curses set upon me, as well as my own role in not paying attention to what my body was telling me, had been lifted. Alex had prepared me to embark on my next journey to Standing Rock. I felt more protection because of this medicine and felt ready to make the trek with no expectations. I scurried to catch the one o'clock ferry and then immediately drove straight back to Spokane. My flight for North Dakota would leave in two days, and I had to work at the salon to make up for lost income once again.

The morning flight came early, and I was feeling anxious about getting there and being part of the movement. On the flight over, I sat down next to this lovely woman who I could tell was feeling a lot of suffering. She had a small frame and looked to be in her late forties. She wore a smile on her face, but behind it was hidden pain and self-doubt. We introduced ourselves and began a casual conversation.

"Hello, my name is Karen. Nice to meet you," she said.

She went on to explain she was on her way to visit a girlfriend and was in a hard place in her life at the moment. What I didn't expect was after I shared some of my story, about my divorce and my father, she completely broke down. By allowing myself to be vulnerable to Karen, she allowed herself to open up to me in a way that felt very special.

She began her story. "I have been married for twenty-nine years now, and my husband and I have three beautiful kids. The last few years have been really hard, after I went back to work and started feeding some passions of mine. I finally began to feel like my old self before I met my husband, and it felt good to have some new independence. During that time, we grew apart and our communication is minimal. And I never imagined I would fall in love emotionally with someone else. But I did, with a long-time dear friend of the family. Know that nothing physical has happened, and that I have never even told him I feel this way. But I do know I love this man, and we could never be together, for this would destroy my family, and I just need to stick it out with my husband."

I carefully listened to her words and watched the steady tears make themselves present as she shared her truth with me. I thought about how James and Nikki had developed feelings behind my back, and how deceived and betrayed it left me.

"Karen, I understand what it feels like to be you and feeding those new passions, resulting in growing apart from your husband. But I also understand what it's like to be your husband, and to have your spouse leave you for a dear friend. What I can offer you is to be true and honest with yourself and do what is right for your spirit. Your husband deserves to know how you are feeling, and he can have the option to fix it or to move on and let you go. Out of respect, he deserves this chance before any physical activity takes place between you and this other man."

Karen took an intentional breath, one that told me she was processing what I had just said.

She began to explain, "I don't ever plan on acting on it. I will just have to stop communicating with the man I'm in love with and accept this is my reality." She looked defeated, and I could feel this decision would not make her happy or anyone else in the long run.

I said to her, "I understand that you feel the safest with that choice, but both you and your husband deserve to be happy. And sometimes we have to let people go or give them the option before we hurt them even deeper. I urge you to try and talk to your husband and be honest with your feelings. I hope that you can find some peace in all of this, but these things tend to get more messy than anything else for a while."

Karen thanked me for listening and offering her comfort when she clearly needed to talk to someone. The announcement was made that we were getting ready to land and to prepare for arrival. We looked at each other, shocked that the time had passed by so quickly, and within that time we had shared our truths.

What I really didn't expect was that, after we landed, the lady at the end of our aisle by the window wanted to share. She never spoke the entire time of the flight but chose to share with us her experience of observation.

"I have to say, I listened to you two talk the entire flight, and it moved me. What you shared in that time was really special and valuable for you both, and for me to hear. It's obvious that this conversation was meant to take place."

Karen and I looked at each other and smiled; this was indeed just that, and I knew this was the flight I was meant to take. A good start to my journey so far, and I hoped that Creator would continue to bring the right people around me.

I arrived in Bismarck around three p.m. and picked up my sweet rental Jeep, which was fancier than I had expected. But it would be my sleeping cabin for a several nights, and I needed to the extra room. I drove to the closest grocery store to pick up some more food items for the camp and some additional supplies the elders had asked for. It felt good to be getting close to being at camp, and I could now settle in for my one night at the hotel. I never planned on leaving for camp late that evening, not really knowing where I was going or knowing any landmarks for reference. I was also aware of the racism that existed in these parts, which was growing at a rapid pace with the movement and causing more friction between the Native people and the white residents in this area. Not to mention the high numbers of Indigenous women that go missing, never to be found, in these parts. As a Native woman traveling alone, I needed to play it safe and drive only during the daylight hours. Off to bed early; tomorrow was the day I had been anticipating and I would head to Standing Rock first thing in the morning.

Arising at six-thirty, I was up with the sunrise, wide awake, feeling anxious and excited to get on the road. The camp was estimated an hour and half away, but the GPS system wanted to take me the usual route on Highway 1806. I had been advised by some close friends to not take the main highway and to use Highway 6 as an alternate route. The local Morton County Police Department had set up a checkpoint along the main highway, requesting identification and asking what your business was being out there, along with a possible search of your car and belongings. If I could avoid this interaction, it would be ideal, so Highway 6 was the route, and getting lost was worth the risk.

The drive out in this country was stunning, from the rolling hills to endless plains filled with tall grasses and abundant life. This drive allowed me to take in the sheer beauty of the gifts this part of the country had to offer and to clear my head and my heart, so I could enter camp ready to give service. About forty minutes into my drive, I no longer had service on my phone, and the only GPS working wanted to take me on Highway 1806. I continued to drive on the highway longer than I should have, arriving in Fort Yates and missing the turn into Cannon Ball. I stopped into the local elementary school for assistance, and they were happy to print out a more detailed map for me.

Back on the road, I could see I was getting closer to Standing Rock, and Oceti Sakowin camp. I passed the casino and saw the signs that I was in Indian country and on the right path to camp. The rain began first as a light drizzle and, meanwhile, the sun dipped behind some dark clouds. As I rolled into the camp entrance, I was greeted by all the flags posted into the earth, representing three hundred tribes that had made the journey. They stood tall and were blowing in the wind, commanding a strong presence. It was incredible to see how many water protectors had traveled here, and all for one common cause, to protect our Mother.

The security team ushered me to park by the kitchen so I could unload all the donations in my car. Then I would re-park for the night to camp. I pulled into a good spot, turned off the car, and took a huge decompressing breath, feeling a huge sense of relief to be here, grateful I had made it safely.

Just moments after that, the rain turned into a torrential downpour and the wind picked up with gusts that were already causing havoc. This was a storm, and it was coming in with a fierceness I don't think anyone seemed to be prepared for. The weather from just minutes ago had changed dramatically, and it wasn't ideal to be outside. I grabbed my raincoat and ran into camp searching for the main kitchen. I found the staff to be overwhelmed by recent developments of the weather change and trying to keep the tarps from being weighed down by the rainfall. I was amazed to see the amount of donations and generosity that had made it out to camp. But the first priority was to keep the food dry, and I made myself available the moment I stepped into that kitchen.

I introduced myself to the woman who was running the kitchen at the time; she was heavier set and had the most beautiful eyes. She was an attractive Native woman in her late thirties and possessed that natural leader mentality. She said they needed help with prep for dinner and lunch, but to keep a constant watch on the tarps to keep them from collapsing. My first task was to dice about forty onions for tonight's dinner, which normally would have caused a river of tears but with these weather conditions, it became less dramatic.

The storm continued to build with a greater intensity. Tents around camp were collapsing and blowing away while everyone was trying to seek shelter. I could see all of this unfolding from where I stood chopping these forty onions, all while keeping a close eye on the tarps above us, and carefully finding ways to release the water without soaking the food or us in the kitchen. The storm charged all afternoon, and about every thirty minutes, a new tarp was ready to be cleared. The group of us volunteers got better with our approach and made a good team with the task at hand, considering the circumstances.

The amount of work needed to feed hundreds of people for one meal was unreal, and I had never cooked for a group of this magnitude, but the ladies there had a system and devoted themselves to feeding the water protectors. It was clear that some of them had been here for months, running on little rest or sleep, opening the kitchen by seven a.m. for breakfast and closing around eleven at night. No one at camp would go hungry if they had anything to do with it; this was a community where we all took care of each other.

A large semi-truck container fridge had been graciously donated to the movement; this became a significant help for the kitchen staff. The option to keep all the fresh produce, meat, and other perishable items cold was such a blessing to our cause. After I finished the onions, I was asked to go fetch some more produce out of the semi for a few items for the kids' lunches to be delivered in a few hours. The cooler was filled with so many generous donations from all over the globe. It was clear this movement down at Standing Rock had touched the hearts of many, and I knew that I was blessed to be here and I would make the most of my time.

Back to the kitchen, with major prep work to do. The protocol to prepare food in these conditions was far more complicated and needed to be done in a sufficient way. To clean the produce, I had to fill up sanitized buckets with clean water from a large water tank located near the kitchen, then carry the heavy bucket of water back to wash the food. Everything had to be done a little differently out here. We needed to keep a very clean and sterile kitchen while being out in nature and still adjusting to the storm. There was a group of men that volunteered to wash dishes all day to keep up with the constant load of dirty dishes we kept accumulating. Once we had finished prep, the men would take them off our hands and allowed us to have a new workspace to move on to the next task. This made the kitchen run more smoothly, and each person had a job to contribute. There was never a shortage of jobs to do.

It was time to serve lunch, and the main table needed to be cleared to make our service line. The menu was based on what we had an abundance of to serve, and what needed to be eaten before it went bad. The intention was to use what we could and try not to waste any donated food. We wanted to provide enough options for our protectors and also put our love into the food we had prepared.

There were about six of us ladies that stayed to serve lunch that afternoon, and we took our place at the serving line. The elders were served first, followed by the women and children, and then came everyone else. I wanted to be able to connect with more water protectors while in camp, but serving the food did allow at least one small moment to connect with a large number of people. Everyone was so grateful and continued to say, "Thank you, sister, for helping with this meal."

It felt so good to be serving this community and giving back in a way that I had never had before. For me, food is medicine and an outlet to share a part of how I love on others, including complete strangers. This time around, I was serving egg salad, and it was comical at times when certain people weren't feeling it.

I would tell them, "It's okay if you don't like egg salad. That doesn't hurt my feelings," and then wink and give a smile. These interactions lasted only seconds, but I loved each one like it was gift. To finally be here among my people and those like-minded, standing together like this was, such a beautiful thing to witness.

Lunch service lasted a few hours, with a few protectors coming back for seconds and thirds. We were delighted to be able to provide that nourishment for them. For some people, this might be the best they had eaten in years. Time to hand the dishes over to our heroic dishwashers, and clear the space for the last of the dinner prep.

The weather continued to be difficult throughout the day, but it did allow things to slow down around camp, and everyone got cozier in confined spaces. After the dog attacks several days prior, the tribe had put a restraining order on the DAPL security team that was in full effect when I arrived. They were not allowed to work on the pipeline, for a period of time at least, and it made things at camp quieter for the time being. Our security team were the only ones keeping watch on the front lines and ensuring that no action was taken by either party. These young brave men were dedicated to this work and stood outside in these horrible conditions all day. We made sure to get several plates of food to them throughout the day; these warriors needed their strength for the long haul.

During our many hours of dinner prep, I met so many strong and beautiful women that shared their personal stories of being called to Standing Rock. Some were mothers, fighting for the future of their little ones. Some were young ladies, fresh out of high school, with the understanding that their future was at stake. And some were future elders, trying to keep the old traditions alive.

What we all had in common was that we felt called to be there. And as strong Indigenous women, we had a purpose to help our relatives and future generations in their plight to protect our Mother. As Native people, we don't claim land to be ours; we understand it is shared with all living things. However, in these instances, we have fight for the legal rights to our land, even when that same land was already promised to our ancestors.

Those promises known as "treaties" continued to be broken for the sake of corporate greed, raping our Mother of any resources she still has. The oil is her blood, and it runs through the land as it run through our veins. She only has so much left to give, and when it is gone, what will we do then? Most of the pipelines laid from the past have already leaked and are at this very moment compromising all of our clean water resources. The water protectors are demanding another way, to say, "Enough is enough," and to get off of fossil fuels. Standing Rock had become a stand not to just keep this pipeline out of the ground, but all future ones to come.

You could feel the love that these women and I were putting in the food as we shared these words and personal stories. This kitchen felt more like a family, filled with all my sisters I hadn't seen in a while. There were smiles all around, and laughter filled our hearts in the hours we spent preparing this meal. Before serving dinner, we prepared a prayer plate for an elder to bless before we served the meal to the camp, taking a small portion of each one of the dishes and giving it to an elder to pray over the food and say thanks to the Creator for this meal. We all got in our service line, ready to serve the biggest group of the day, beginning again with the elders, followed by woman and children, and then everyone else.

I absolutely loved serving the food to the water protectors, and this quickly became my favorite activity. Getting that moment to acknowledge each person that came through our line was very special. Some shared a smile, or just slight head nod, but most said how grateful and thankful they were for our hard work. This was a labor of love, and every minute I spent in that kitchen was worth the reward.

The dinner service continued for several hours. I imagine we served close to three hundred protectors that meal. Luckily, the storm held out for the most part, until the last forty-five minutes of the service. The wind and rain came kicking back through the kitchen, making it difficult for us to keep the prepared dishes dry. But we served until that line stopped and didn't end up closing the kitchen till almost eleven thirty. I had been so wrapped up in my work that I realized then I hadn't eaten all day and had barely had any water. I also considered fasting while being here, which is a common Native American practice done to prepare for ceremonies.

It was getting late, and the night temperatures had me shivering, so I decided it was time for bed and at least an attempt to sleep. I walked back to my car and cleared some space for my sleeping bag. I covered myself in those instant heat packs and changed into the warmest clothes I had. I closed my eyes and lay there, daydreaming about my day spent in the kitchen and processing all the wonderful moments I had already experienced. I fell asleep that night with the understanding that I was meant to be there, and certain the right people would cross my path along the way.

That night consisted of a series of painful leg cramps that continued to wake me up, a direct result of me not drinking enough fluids all day. The car-sleeping situation had me all kinds of sore and uncomfortable. Once again, I had forgotten a pillow, just like I had in California. But I didn't come here to sleep, and there were countless protectors that had been here for months. And some had chosen this path as a way of life and planned to stay the course until the end. A few nights of little rest was a small sacrifice, and I felt so grateful to just be here for any length of time.

It was seven a.m., and the sun was out this morning, shining bright with just a light breeze tickling my face. I changed my clothes and cleaned myself up a bit, preparing for another long day at camp. The kitchen made breakfast easy, and it consisted of donated cereal, energy bars, muffins, and some fruit. Being short staffed in the morning, it was easier to allow the protectors to help themselves to what was offered. And by nine a.m., we had to begin preparing lunch for camp and school lunches for the kids. There was always a job to do, whether or not you were in the kitchen. This was not a vacation, and it was made quite clear that if you came to camp, you came to help.

I was thrilled when asked by one of the kitchen ladies in charge to deliver the kids' lunches. I love any chance I get to connect with the little ones by making them smile or letting them find interest in all the artwork I carry on my skin. Kids seem to love my tattoos, and I enjoy sharing some of those stories behind them.

Walking through camp felt like I was in a community of like-minded people that wanted to see a different future. Everyone was playing their part and sharing what gifts they had to offer. I saw elders sharing knowledge and stories with those that were willing to listen. I saw young men chopping wood to keep the sacred fires going all day throughout camp. The underground media within the camp was doing their part to get the word out, as the powers that be continued to do what they could to stop it. I was among warriors that were sacrificing every day to be here and to be part of the change we all wished to see in this world.

I stayed in the kitchen for the lunch service and then to help with dinner prep all afternoon. But I had intended on taking a walk to reflect on my time there, and to possibly spread my dad's ashes if I was called to. Leaving the kitchen, I heard that canoes from the Kalispell and Northern coastal tribes would be arriving shortly. This was one of those rare opportunities I couldn't pass up and would be of those rare life moments I would never forget. Everyone was heading down to the river to greet our relatives, and the excitement and energy all around was infectious.

The canoe families had come from far and wide, through treacherous conditions, to make it to these waters. They carried with them their ancestors, and the prayers from their homelands to the waters of the Missouri and Cannon Ball River.

The protectors threw their fists in the air and begin to cheer, "Mni Wiconi, Water is Life" as the canoes paddled by and got ready to dock. The anticipation of this moment was building; the crowd was overcome with strong emotions as we awaited our relatives' arrival to these lands. The canoes themselves were quite stunning; the first one I could see were a few Kalispell tribal members paddling a Salishan sturgeon nose design. Shawn Brigman, a friend of mine from back home, had recently carved and designed these exact Salishan sturgeon canoes himself from centuries-old local patterns. The Salishan sturgeon nose canoes were sixteen feet in length and revealed a very sleek look in the water. The Coeur d'Alene Tribe was behind them, arriving in a larger dugout canoe, and the Kalispell Tribe in the smaller dug out. These traditional dugout canoes were made from large cedar trees, ranging in size, and are built to last, while being incredibly heavy. The Northern coastal tribes arrived in the most intricately carved red and black canoes that appeared to be dancing on top of the water. Before the colonization of Turtle Island, these tribes used these canoes for transportation of household and belongings from one settlement to the next. It was a sign of wealth to own a canoe such as this. The materials and crew needed to operate it were indeed a luxury back then.

The newly arriving relatives were greeted with the sounds of the drum and songs to welcome them to a familiar home and to honor their difficult journey. There were smiles all around, and it felt like a family reunion of momentous proportions. The only distraction in this moment was the constant drones that continued to follow us around camp, sometimes getting so close that you could almost smack them away. They were white in color, with a tiny camera in the center, similar to a model aircraft straight out of Star Wars. We paid them no mind and continued on with our traditions and ceremony.

Once the canoes joined together at the meeting dock, the proper formalities and prayers were said. There is always a purpose to the way things are done, and I loved being able to witness moments like this. This was history in the making, and I knew this movement would continue to grow and unite the protectors of this earth.

The weather was ideal for their arrival today, and it allowed me to able to walk around camp and observe a little more. The storm had come and passed and allowed the sun to take its rightful place and welcome our relatives on this day.

An announcement was made all throughout camp shortly after the canoes came in. I could hear a young man saying, "The National Guard is on their way. The elders are calling a camp meeting, head to the sacred fire."

Everyone now trekked from the river back to the main camp, and I was feeling anxious about what this man had said about the National Guard. Within maybe ten minutes or so, a hundred-plus were gathered around the sacred fire. Everyone was asked to turn off their phones, with no videos or photos to be taken at this time. Most protectors already understood this way, but there were always a few that need to be reminded. We were all waiting to hear the latest news and feeling confused about what business the National Guard had being there.

The Standing Rock chairman stepped forward and began to make his announcement.

"It is true, relatives, that the National Guard has been called, and is set to arrive in the morning. They will not intimidate our efforts, nor will I allow them to remove any of us from camp. I am hopeful they are here to keep the peace between DAPL and us workers and come with good intentions. We must remain in peaceful protest, no matter what comes at us in times like these. I have seen some of you young warriors yelling profanities and throwing rocks from the front lines. This behavior is unacceptable and will bring no good to our people or our cause. Our elders want us to remain as peaceful warriors, and we will use the power of prayer to fight this pipeline. I have also been made aware that after the dog attack and pepper spray incident the other day, a few police officers have turned in their badges. We are making a difference in coming with peace in our hearts. We must remain resilient, but with love in our hearts. I promise that when they arrive tomorrow, I will keep them away from camp. No one will be made to leave, and we will continue standing together to take down the Black Snake."

These were powerful words to hear, and looking around the circle, I could feel the impact that these words had on everyone around. They brought a few elders to the front and smudged them first, with a bucket filled with medicine. The medicine was carried around the circle, offering everyone the opportunity to smudge as well. A water protector began passing out tobacco to those who wished to receive it, and I held mine tightly in the palm of my hand. A few more strong warriors stepped up to say a few words and then we moved into a few songs. This was once again another rare moment I would never forget. To be here in this time of history among so many relatives standing in solidarity was overwhelming.

After the meeting commenced, I realized I should check in with my peeps back home. They were concerned about me making this trip. The only place to get any kind of service out here was known as "Facebook Hill." The powers that be had attempted to keep the protectors from sharing the latest details of camp. "Facebook Hill" for many became a popular spot and seemed to be where all the media would congregate. Looking down at my phone, I got at least a few bars by the time I climbed to the top. I had to let everyone know I was okay and would be home in two days' time.

By then, it was around three p.m., and I planned on getting back to the main kitchen to help with the last of the dinner prep and to make myself useful. I couldn't help but be drawn to the fire. The aroma of deer meat stew was coming from the largest pot of soup I had ever seen. It had to weigh damn near fifty pounds because of its sheer size, and it was full to the brim. We had spent a lot of time prepping for this soup and knew it was going to be a crowd favorite tonight, along with the infamous fry bread that never loses its popularity among Native people. Known for its fluffy texture, fry bread was a great addition to soak up broth or served as a dessert with honey or maple syrup. We made sure to always include a salad or some fresh vegetables, for health benefits and to cater to the small group of vegetarians we served. Our main side dish for that evening was potato salad, and to complete the menu, there was always a pot of boiled hot dogs. It became comical the amount of hot dog donations we received—so many hot dogs, and no hot dog buns. We had to get creative and use either hamburger buns or bread. The protectors got very used to hot dogs always being on the menu and found a variety of ways to include them into their meals.

The prayer plate was made before the service began, and then we got several plates ready for the security team to ensure they got their precious fry bread. Weather was more cooperative today, so it made for an easier dinner service to run smoothly and get the people fed. Once again, everyone was very appreciative of our efforts and thanked us as they went down the line. We ran out of fry bread an hour into the service and felt bad having to offer the alternative, tortillas, but we did the best with what we had. Hours later, another successful meal had been served. Once their bellies were full, the rest of us grabbed whatever was left and fed ourselves.

After dinner, I chose to spend some time around the sacred fire just outside of the kitchen. They had a small drum going and people were offering up their songs for anyone to participate in dancing or singing along. Back in the day, when this was the only way for our ancestors to entertain them, the community would come together and share stories, songs, and magic by the fire. Most Native communities still hold that tradition, but for this "urban Indian" I only got to experience this type of connection when I made an effort to leave the city. My tribes are so far away from where I live that I miss out on a lot of shared knowledge and quality time with elders. Not being raised on my reservation, from what I have come to understand, has its benefits and disadvantages. Perhaps I had better options for public school education and housing and missed out on many of the hardships Native communities face. On the other hand, I didn't grow up in the language and ceremonies that would have prepared me for womanhood. The flower girl ceremony is a coming of age ceremony for Yurok girls to become women. This tradition is still strongly practiced among my people, and it lasts for three days. The girl has a lot of preparation to do, including fasting, writing her own song in her language, and morning runs to the river. She is supported by seven chosen star sisters, they come with their songs, and participate in all the three days of ceremony. I couldn't imagine a greater gift than to have this experience coming into womanhood.

It was late and time to turn in. I was not looking forward to another sleepless night in my car, but it was better than a cold night of camping. I made sure to pile on several heat packs in the crucial areas and eventually fell asleep, once my mind allowed me too.

Morning came earlier out here. Being surrounded by thousands of people on very different schedules was something I didn't know if I could ever get used to. I took my time this morning getting dressed and felt like waking up slowly and just observing the camp from inside my car. I watched families tend to their little ones, men chopping wood, and elders practicing their rituals of morning prayer. I made my way over to the kitchen around eight-thirty to help out with the last of the breakfast service, then offered to stay for lunch prep and to deliver the kids' lunches one last time. Since this was my last day at camp, I informed the kitchen that after lunch service, I had to take some time away.

I still needed some time to connect myself to the land and say a prayer with the tobacco I had received during the meeting. I was carrying not just this medicine, but I was also carrying my father. He had to come with me on this journey, and if the time felt right, I wanted to leave a part of him here. Making my way back down towards the river, I found some solitude in a space among tall grasses and gentle breezes. This was the perfect time to journal and store these moments in my writing, including all the details of these rare events. I closed my eyes and imagined my family sitting there with me, lying beside me by the river. They had made the journey with me, and I carried the prayers they had left behind. I offered my tobacco to the water, and I prayed for her protection.

I had planned to spread my dad's ashes, but then the rain came out of nowhere and took me by surprise. This was not a drizzle, but full-on, seek shelter or get completely soaked. The temperatures dropped dramatically at night out in the plains, and you didn't want to be wet when that came. I rushed to my car to retrieve my raincoat and a beanie for my already-soaked hair.

Once the rain subsided, I walked down to the Red Warrior Camp to secure a good spot for the evening's events. A small stage had been set up for an evening concert, and some younger warriors were already sharing their gifts with the crowd. Around ten p.m., the headliners took the stage, consisting of rappers and well-known artists that came in full support of the movement. By then, the sky was blanketed in darkness, and the only light coming through was the stars twinkling like precious jewels in the sky. The view was breathtaking; stars like this can't be seen within the city limits. These are for only those who seek refuge out in the country and in Mother Nature.

By the time the concert ended around eleven-thirty, the temperatures had significantly dropped and it had become uncomfortably cold. Feeling beat from the day's events and having to get up early to catch my flight, I made my way back to my ride. I didn't plan on sleeping much, but an attempt was necessary with an early flight.

I closed my eyes, and actually fell into a very deep sleep, one that allowed me to dream up something very special. It began with me being dropped off in front of a large farmhouse, not sure of how I even got there.

I don't recognize anything about this place or recall ever being here before. I understand that I am meant to go inside, and I proceed down a long hallway and discover what or who was waiting for me. I'm left standing at the entrance of a large kitchen and see all the women in my life that have crossed over at a large table. It appears they have sat down together for a nice meal and are anticipating my arrival. Among them are my mother, sister, and grandmother, but transported back to thirty years ago and how I remembered them when they were healthy and full of life. Then I notice a little girl, at the very end of the table, around the age of five. She has long thick black hair and dark marble-brown eyes. She is dressed up for the occasion and wearing a white lace dress with fancy shoes and stockings. It takes me a moment to process who she is, but then I realize the little girl is me.

My grandmother comes over to greet me and gives me a warm hug followed by a smile. We don't converse at all, just exchange energy and recognition. She leads me over to my mother and allows her to take a good look at me. She reaches out to hold my hand, gives me a good once over with her eyes, and smiles. At first, it seems she is just being friendly, but then I can see the change in her expression when she realizes who I am. She wraps her arms around me so tight, as if she would bind us from ever being separated again. We both understood how long it's been since we were able to connect this way, and this reunion is unexpected but so welcomed. During our embrace, I realize this is a dream and that, in any moment, I will wake up. I don't want to leave my mother's arms; I have prayed for so many years to be held by her again.

Shortly after, I awakened to the sound of my five-a.m. alarm. Time to get up and on the road. My flight was leaving Bismarck at eight, and I had a drive ahead of me to get there. It was still dark when I left Oceti Sakowin Camp, and I felt not at all ready to go. But I was grateful for having the opportunity to at least make the journey and to share this sacred space with other water protectors.

The drive back was perfectly timed with the sunrise; I was able to catch the tail end of the darkness of the night. I imagine at that particular moment that day and night are like two star-crossed lovers that only see each other in passing. One has to leave to allow the other to take the main stage and stay awhile amongst our sky mother. They are only able to catch a glimpse of each other's magic before they must part so that she can begin her slow ascension just above the hillside. The sunrise prepares to take out her shawl of warm bold colors and begins to dance. The colors continue to build on top of each other, sending beams of orange, red, and yellow light across the plains that stretch as far as I can see. She invites the pink cotton candy-like clouds to join in her round dance, along with the winged ones to complete the circle and bring in a new day.

I left Standing Rock with so many gifts that I could have never anticipated. To be able to connect with the land and the ancestors that had laid the groundwork for us to be here was a feeling of pure and absolute joy. The gift of connecting through the dream world has always been appreciated, but on this last night at camp, it coincided with my medicine tracks. My mother was able to hold me one more time, and for time and space to make that reality, I must be blessed. The dream medicine had taken me to another level of healing beyond what I ever imagined possible.

CHAPTER 12
Tattoo Medicine

T FELT GOOD TO BE BACK HOME, and the first thing on my agenda was heading back to Nespelem to sweat with my sisters. My constant travels had left me little time to connect with them, and I needed to sweat to feel grounded in general. Britney was able to make it just in time before I left town, and we agreed this sweat was a great need for us both. Her crane medicine had kept her in solitude other than caring for her mother, and she needed this time to reflect. The travel time was great for catching up. I hadn't seen her since the funeral, and it was important to redirect our energy before we arrived. I couldn't pin point it, but as soon as we left, we both picked up on a strange vibration. The energy that came with it felt different, and as we hit the road, the sensation continued to build.

About an hour into the drive, I had to come to a complete stop for a deer to cross on the road ahead. Normally they move quickly for good reason, if they want to live and not get hit by a moving vehicle going seventy miles per hour. But this particular deer wanted to be noticed and made eye contact. This felt different than before. He possessed no fear of death, and he knew somehow that I would stop in time to keep him safe. Deer medicine teaches us compassion, to be kind and walk upon this earth with a graceful demeanor. Britney and I both found the incident a bit strange but didn't pay it much attention. Until several minutes later a large hawk made his presence known and flew across the windshield of the car. He swooped down from above with his wings spread open, just a few feet away from us. He was so close that I thought he might be interested in catching a lift with us to Nespelem and taking his position as navigator by hitching a ride on the top of my roof rack.

I turned to Britney and said, "Something is different about today, and I feel like this sweat will be incredibly special. I'm not sure what to make of these strange occurrences, or what Creator is telling us, but I'm so glad you could make it, sister."

"I agree. I knew for some reason I had to make it today. Things kept coming up and I felt overwhelmed, but a part of me knew I had to be there," she replied.

We sat there in silence and observation for the remaining part of the trip, paying attention to any more messages or signs that could be received. Once we arrived at our destination, the conversation began again. We grabbed our belongings and rushed into the lodge to greet our sisters. Sharon was preparing the lodge, and Cindy was using her squirrel medicine, chopping wood and feeding the fire. Warm hugs and smiles were given all around, and then I jumped in to help Cindy get the rocks into the lodge for the first round.

I had been able to make it back to sweat after I returned from Hawaii, but it felt like ages since we had seen each other. I briefly got the sisters caught up on my recent trips to California and Standing Rock. I was aware that both Sharon and Cindy had lost family members recently, during my time away, under sudden and unusual circumstances. I left it up to the sisters how much they wanted to share, after I let them know I was there to offer support.

Sharon became my owl medicine by passing on her knowledge and wisdom of the sweat, the language among many other sacred teachings. She was intuitive and had a clear vision of what she wanted passed on to future generations.

Sharon let me set the first four grandfather rocks down into the sweat, starting with the East, then the South, West, and North. Then I carried in three more rocks to represent the seven directions: one for us here on earth, one for down below to represent our Mother Earth, and the last one for the sky and Creator. I was so thrilled being able to help with the sweat now, and it meant a lot to me that my owl felt I was ready.

We entered the sweat with heavy hearts for those we had lost and missed. Sharon asked that Cindy lead the sweat today and pour the water on the rocks. Then she turned to Britney and asked her to be the door person; she wanted us to take on new roles and step up our responsibilities. After smudging and cleansing with rose water, the four of us entered the lodge.

Round one's prayers were said for those sisters that could not make it, and we gave thanks that we could be together again.

When Britney's turn came, she expressed, "Thank you, Creator, for giving me the gift of Donell. Our friendship and sisterhood has brought me here, and I'm so grateful to be here and to be connecting to spirit again."

This meant the world to hear these words; our sisterhood was a gift for me, too. When it was my turn, I wanted to show my gratitude for this special female bond.

"I am so incredibly grateful for all of you, my sisters, and all the strong women I have had in my life thus far. To be back in my Mother's womb, praying with you, is powerful medicine. Thank you, Creator, for the continued gifts of friendship and sisterhood you bestow upon me."

This first round continued to be easiest for me; the heat was building but still very tolerable. After finishing the first round, we each sat down to a light snack of fresh fruit and popcorn, making sure to really hydrate in preparation for the second round, which in my experience was always the most challenging.

Entering the sweat for the second round had proven to be just that. As soon as I sat down, the thickness of the air felt like a heavy blanket laid upon my chest. I had to get my mind right and find that space where the suffering of the heat didn't trigger my fight or flight mode. The breath needs to be intentional and slowed down to calm the mind and keep from igniting a panic attack. There were times in the sweat that I began to feel my heart race and wanted to escape, fearing I would pass out. But those are the most crucial moments to find that stillness within and to embrace the suffering. I am told that in the stillness is when you find the most clarity and peace, and in order to get there, we need to embrace the physical discomfort.

This round I had chosen to say a prayer that Sharon had taught me in her Salish language. Our ancestors can understand our hearts always, but to speak the language is a whole other type of understanding that is sacred to our people.

An elder spoke of this in a documentary I watched about the boarding schools. He said, "The ancestors only understand us when we speak with our Native tongues."

And for him, his Native tongue had been beaten out of him, so he stopped speaking and praying all together. You could see and feel his pain, and I couldn't imagine what that reality was like for him and so many relatives that suffered this same fate and worse. I took on the role of an empath at a very young age, and at times, it's as much of curse as a blessing. The ability to feel everything with such a great intensity, whether good or bad, has its moments of pure joy as well as deep despair. I felt honored to speak these words using my Native tongue and to speak to my ancestors in a way I hadn't before.

While I was speaking these words, Sharon joined with me and began using her owl medicine. She was a messenger, and this prayer grew with a greater intensity because of her continued sharing of wisdom behind the lodge and teaching the language. The salt from my eyes traveled inside the water from within; I felt it roll down my cheeks and understood that this is what healing feels like. I would never forget this moment, and how my journey had brought me here to my new sisters. It was Sharon 's turn, and she was the last to pray in this round. She spoke her truth and said her prayers in her Salish language, holding a sacred space that we could all energetically feel just by being in her presence.

Then she finished her prayers with, "Thank you, Creator, for bringing my sisters back to the sweat and allowing me to teach them the ways of our ancestors, and for them to step up and take new roles in the sweat today."

We called for the door, and the three of us were beyond ready to get out into the fresh air. But not Sharon; she chose to stay in the lodge for another solid ten to fifteen minutes. This was the first time I had ever witnessed her doing so, and I understood that today felt different for all of us.

When Sharon did come back out of the sweat, she stayed very quiet and had a different presence about her. The three of us just continued to chat and gave her any space she might need before the next round. The sunset had just begun to take its rightful position just above the hillside, and for us, that meant round three was ready to begin. Cindy and I brought in seven more rocks, and the four of us didn't waste any time going back into the lodge. The circle began with Britney, and she had asked for the health of some loved ones to improve, along with a better understanding of the situation. I could feel her pain. In the sacred space, my empathetic quality became even more overwhelming within these walls. Britney was such an amazing daughter, friend, and sister, and listening to her prayers affected me in such a profound way.

After Cindy did the four pours of water on the hot rocks, it was my turn to speak. This round, I wanted to pray for the water protectors down at Standing Rock and what I had experienced there.

"Creator, thank you for bringing us to this third round, with my sweat sisters that I hold so dear to my heart. I want to pray for the water protectors down at Standing Rock, that their voices are heard and their ancestors provide them with protection from the powers that be. And I pray for those who oppose our cause to see the truth and understand that we are all connected, that this fight to save our Mother is not just for Native people but a fight for all living things. I pray for our ancestors and the struggle and constant adversity they had to face for us to be here, Creator."

I hadn't finished my prayers, but I was caught off guard by a strange noise just outside of the sweat. It sounded like someone trying to get out, or someone trying to get in. I thought to myself, is Britney okay and is she trying to escape? But she was the door person and could make that happen easily if she chose to. The noise grew louder and took on another sound, now resembling someone rubbing their hands all over the outside of the door. I chose not to speak about it; we could discuss it after the round. I finished my prayers, Cindy poured the water, and then it was Sharon's turn.

Sharon began to pray and speak very loudly, in a way I had never heard her speak before. She had a clear intention about whom she was speaking to and a different understanding of what was going on than we had. The noise grew louder and continued to build, this time with more intensity and a desire to be noticed. My heart began to beat faster while experiencing a release of anxious sweat leaving my body in anticipation of what would happen next. Then the source of the sound began to move, and I could hear something touching and pacing all around the outside of the lodge. It was incredibly fast and made no sound of footsteps, so I assumed it was able to levitate above the ground. Sharon's prayers continued to match the intensity of the thing that wanted our attention, and I felt some fear, but had to let that go.

I understood this was not of this world, and it could have been more than one being we were experiencing. Out of my peripheral vision, I could see a light blue spark of light off to my right side. I thought perhaps some light from the outside had made its way in, but when I looked down it was gone. As Sharon continued to pray, I saw this light several more times. And each time I turned to look, it would disappear and return to the darkness of the lodge. The strange noise lasted during the first several minutes of Sharon's prayer, and then suddenly stopped. Her voice became quieter at that point, and her words were now in English. I know the three of us, with the exception of Sharon, were wondering what had just happened. But none of spoke of it. After Sharon finished her prayers, we just sat with the stillness. Cindy poured the water on the grandfather rocks, and the four of us really took our time breathing in the medicine.

Cindy closed round three, and by that point, we had been in the sweat for quite some time. We called for door, and the four of us all came out to shower and recollect ourselves.

I turned to Britney first and said, "That wasn't you trying to escape from inside the lodge?" I knew that this wasn't the case, but I had to at least ask.

Britney immediately replied, "No, that wasn't me. What came was just on the other side of the door."

We all turned to Sharon, and I could see she was in a different space but felt like she was ready to talk now.

"Sharon, what happened inside during that third round?"

She took a drink of water, and sat with it for a moment, then replied, "We had a visitor, and I didn't address it during the round, in case in might frighten one of you."

"I was very aware that something was trying to get our attention, something not from the natural world. I have experienced some visits from my family that have passed, so it didn't scare me. But it did take me by surprise and felt very different from my other encounters," I replied, and then turned to the other sisters to get their input on what just happened.

Britney chose to share that at first it startled her, and she felt some fear but she understood we were in a safe place and protected. Then Cindy mentioned she had never experienced anything like that before, but also had a similar understanding. Sharon was relieved that the three of us sat well with the experience and had no fear of who was trying to make contact. The simple fact that all four of us had recently lost someone close to us made it hard to decipher who came through during our sweat.

We went back into the lodge for our fourth and final round, anxious to see what other possibilities might unfold. This round was hot, but never seemed to get me too uncomfortable, because I knew it was my last round for the night. I started this round and thanked Creator for bringing me back to my sisters once again and asked that we all have a good week and travelled home safely. In the fourth round, you can pray for yourself, and I still was in need of physical healing. My leg was still limiting me in a lot of activities, and I prayed for some new space and healing to occur. We went around the circle and ended with Britney this time. Sister Cindy poured the last of the water on the rocks, and we sat there this time in silence for a few minutes. Then we called for door and stepped outside into the magic of the sun that now had set. The afterglow in the sky took its sacred space in harmony with Mother Sky, sending beams of purple, pink, and orange hues in its place as a thoughtful goodbye, until we met again tomorrow.

This was a sweat that none of the sisters would ever forget, and as Britney and I got into the car to head back to Spokane, I felt it too. It's normal for me to feel very energized the first couple hours after a sweat, which fuels me for long drive home.

It was obvious we were both still processing what had happened and trying to wrap our heads around what could have possibly come to visit us. I turned to Britney, asking again about what she had experienced and how she was feeling.

"Honestly, at first, I thought someone was trying get in or perhaps was playing a joke, but I thought, why would they do such a thing? And as the noise grew louder and I could feel the energy pressing against the lodge, I got really scared. I was afraid of what could be on the other side trying to get in. I knew Sharon was praying louder to protect us, but I still felt very uneasy."

I mentioned the blue light I had seen several times during that time, and Britney recalled seeing the same exact thing.

"Being the door poor person, I was worried at first that I had let some light in and that the door wasn't fully closed. I would see this light out of my peripheral vision and then look down towards it, and every time, it disappeared."

We had indeed both seen the same light and felt the same kind of energy during that round. It felt good to validate the experiences we had shared, and the drive home continued to feel like magic. We observed the unique cloud formations that took form in shapes we weren't familiar with, similar to a cone or a cylinder. They appeared to be on a mission and moved across the sky in a quick rhythmic dance synchronized with the stars. In fact, everything in that night sky seemed to have a faster movement then normal, as if we were caught in a time relapse stuck on autopilot. Creator was once again in concert, and using space and time introduce new song that I had never been able to hear before. He used the moon as a spotlight for the main stage and the stars transformed into the symphony of many different instruments.

This particular drive felt like a rare moment in time, one that can only be seen when open to its vibration. A cosmic door had been opened that night of our sweat that further allowed us to see something more than what we choose to see. What special gift this night had turned out to be, and getting to share this with Britney and my sweat sisters left a permanent imprint on my spirit.

My journey of continued blessings still felt like it had just begun, and I could feel my ancestors by my side. My role in activism to bring awareness and justice to my ancestors and what they fought for continued to grow along with it.

I joined a group in support of Indigenous People's Day that was formed to get rid of Columbus Day and takes its place. A strong group of community members had come together to get the resolution ready for City Council to make their vote. I appreciated all the hard work that had gone into making this happen in my hometown and had to do my part to support the change.

The night of the council meeting our group joined together outside City Hall to demonstrate our right to speak our voice. This was an exciting time to witness the possible change in the way we celebrate this day, and we felt anxious to get the hearing started. Several tribal members spoke about the true history of this day, and in fact that Christopher Columbus had possibly never even set foot on this continent. In all actuality, it was the Viking Leif Ericson who made it to this country, five hundred years prior to Columbus's birth. And even before that, research shows that fearless Polynesian explorers had sailed to this continent in dugout canoes, not to mention the Native American tribes that inhabited the land up to fourteen thousand years before any of this took place.

The real truth is that Columbus landed in the Bahamas, not in America, and he was greeted by friendly Indigenous tribes consisting of the Taino, Lucayans, and the Arawaks. They offered food and shelter, with no expectations of payment for their hospitality. Columbus saw this as a sign of weakness and led the way to enslaving them for gold and seizing their land, resulting in a mass genocide. Within only two years, half of the original population was dead. He sold young Native girls into sex slavery and even bragged about it in his journals. Columbus was responsible for cruel and unusual punishment from burning the slaves alive, cutting off their hands, ears, or noses, and ordering attack dogs to kill at will. These were just a few of the punishments he chose if the Natives refused to mine gold or didn't meet their quota. His acts of cruelty were so unspeakable that when he returned to Spain, his own family imprisoned him for his crimes against the Native people. But the Queen and King of Spain pardoned him for filling up their treasury with gold and let him go as a free man.

This truth was revealed several times over during the preceding, as community members told their personal accounts of how this holiday was disrespectful to Native American people. How could we possibly be celebrating a man that committed countless heinous crimes against innocent Indigenous ancestors? To continue this tradition of honoring a fake account of our American history, fully being aware of what really happened, was an abomination. The time to change is now, and it was up to the people of this earth that we stopped perpetuating these lies in the young minds of future generations.

What I didn't expect was for a group to oppose the resolution and had no idea that Italian Americans identified so strongly to this day. Several members of the group made the case that Columbus was one of the greatest explorers of all time. They felt pride in that day, being Italian Americans, and wanted us to pick another day to celebrate Indigenous People's Day.

Truth is, the Knights of the Columbus created the holiday back in the 1930s, and they were looking for a Catholic hero. In 1934, President Franklin Roosevelt signed it into law making it a federal holiday. And then the history books followed up with all the bullshit behind 1492 and Columbus's journey to America to make him out to be a great hero. That was the history I was taught growing up, as most of us were never told the real truth because it's disturbing and unsettling. The only way to begin to make this right and to start the healing process was to get the day changed.

The council vote was almost unanimous, with the exception of one who made it clear during the proceedings how he felt about the issue. Our voices had been heard, and this was a day to remember, bringing honor to what had happened and never would repeat itself again. Hugs and cheer filled the room, and then we gathered in a circle and joined hands. A respected elder of the community led us in prayer, and we could feel the healing begin and the wave of change that was to come.

About a week after the event, a mother of a private elementary school asked me to speak about the real history behind Columbus Day. I was thrilled and honored to be asked but did feel some worry about my approach. I wanted these young impressionable minds to understand what really happened, but I had to be careful with my words and what was appropriate for their age. I joked about using sock puppets to soften the blow and perhaps do a puppet reenactment.

These kids needed to understand the life that was here before the colonization, the way we lived, and our connection to our Mother Earth. Things were very different back then and we lived in harmony with the land. It didn't belong to us, we were a part of it.

The morning came, and I chose to wear one of my Yurok basket hats and a Standing Rock shirt so I could discuss that as well. I also brought some other baskets, feathers, and horns that the kids could pass around to get a closer look. The kids came in and were surprised to see me. I heard a lot of "Who's that?" and I wasn't sure if it was my presentation or all my tattoos. But I had their attention right away, and they were eager to listen to what I had to share. I began the class asking what they knew about Columbus Day. I got several responses from the kids.

"He sailed to America in 1492 on three ships."

"He was a great Spanish explorer."

"Columbus came here and found gold."

"Columbus thought he was in India and named the Native people Indians."

I was very impressed with that last answer and didn't expect a third grader to know that already. I thanked each one for their participation and chose to first to educate them on how we had lived.

I greeted them in my Yurok language and then began to tell a short version of the story of my people.

"My ancestors were known as 'Oohl' in our language, meaning Indian people. We lived along the Klamath river, nestled in the heart of the redwood forest. At one time during our history, we had fifty villages that spread throughout our territory. My people were known as great fisherman, basket weavers, dancers, and storytellers. They thrived and lived well along the river. It provided us with our traditional foods of salmon, eel, seaweed, and sturgeon. The forest provided the foods of acorns, berries, and deer. We used every part of the animal we could and showed gratitude for its sacrifice to feed us. It's important to understand our connection to our Mother Earth and all living things. The giant cedars and all the redwood trees are guardians of the forest. They also must be shown respect, and the fallen ones were used to build sweathouses, traditional family homes, and canoes."

I had a few kids raise their hands during this time so I let a few ask away.

"Okay, I am wondering, did you eat dogs?"

I was surprised he was inquiring about this, but it was a valid curiosity, and as far as I knew, I wasn't aware and had never read that we did. I do know some other Plains tribes have for ceremonial purposes, but I can't tell these kids that. They will freak out.

"No, we never ate dogs," I responded.

Then another asked, "Okay, then, did you breed dogs?"

We were starting to get off track, but these kids were so caught up on this dog thing.

"We had dogs, but we didn't breed them that I'm aware of."

I was happy that at least the kids were engaged and asking me questions, but the dog topic did come up a few other times during my storytelling.

It was time to lay down some truth. I had to, but also with the understanding of their age and where I was.

"After we were colonized, and the Europeans came over and took our land, everything changed. The first documented visit was by the Spanish explorer, Juan Francisco de Bodega, who laid claim to the land for Spain in 1775. Then, in 1828, Jedidiah Smith made his way through Yurok territory and the Pacific Northwest. By 1849, the gold rush had made its way to Northern California and caused a lot of a lot of hostility with the Yurok people. This resulted in a loss of at least seventy five percent of our people due to disease and massacres by the white settlers. In the beginning of the 1850s came the boarding schools, where the Native children were forced to leave their families to attend. If the parents didn't comply, they would be sent to jail. These little children, the same age as you guys, had to leave behind everything they knew. The boarding schools cut off their hair, and they weren't allowed to speak the only language they knew. If they practiced any of their culture, they were punished, and many children passed away from illness in these schools and never saw their parents again. By 1900, our language was almost extinct, and it took another seventy years to begin to recover. And some of our ceremonial dances, such as the White Deerskin Dance, didn't occurred from 1912 until the year 2000. This dance was sacred and the White Deerskin symbolized protection for his owner and could only be passed down and never sold or traded. This part of our history is important to understand why things are the way they are today for Native American people."

I wasn't sure how much the kids understood, but I needed to share some of this past with them. I kept it pretty PG, with the understanding they could run home and tell their parents if I said some crazy shit and get the school in trouble. So I walked the fine line of what words I chose and how much detail I used. Then I spoke of our powwows and gatherings around town if they were interested in learning more. The kids' eyes lit up and there was a definite interest among many of them.

The only Native boy in the class raised his hand this time and said, "My grandmother says I come from a strong stock of warriors, and I am Lakota of the Plains people. Sometimes she tells me stories of our people and the animals."

I could see the pride in his demeanor and that he was normally a shy young kid. But in this moment, he was feeling very proud to share who he was and where he came from. I thanked him for his response to my talk and told him he was lucky to have a wise grandmother around. It was time to wrap up my talk, and I wanted to leave the children with an important message. Before I left, I said, "I encourage all of you to talk to your grandparents about where they come from. And I'm sure your grandparents will be thrilled to share what knowledge they have. To know your history is important in understanding who you are."

During this special time I had with these kids, I wanted to evoke the spirit of the Storyteller clan mother of the moon cycle in June. The oral traditions of our people had always been sacred, as well as the way we taught not just our oral history but life lessons through creature teachers. This clan mother teaches us to be honest, humble, and speak from our hearts. The Storyteller's perspective comes from a place of non-judgment, and to see things as the observer. She doesn't speak her opinion if not asked for it. Instead she teaches us to take the time to really listen and respond from a place of love, without projection or criticizing one another's life choices.

Storyteller understood and was willing to face the future with her children, always being mindful that each human being had to find these truths for herself or himself to pass through spirit's evolution. She knew her stories would bring comfort to the weary on the sacred path, and for that reason give them away.

We gathered together after my talk and took a group photo, and a few of the kids gave me a little extra love in the form of a hug.

I felt good about what I had shared and the approach I had used. I reflected on how important it was to me that my voice was heard, and with the right intentions behind it. I thought back to my last healing session with Alex and the curse Nikki had made to not allow this gift to fully develop. As far as I knew, nothing bad had come Nikki's way, as Alex had mentioned after lifting the curse. And I took his advice to heart and planned to not take any glee if and when something did happen. But I felt a desire within me to make a strong statement that symbolized the power behind my voice and how I planned to share it with the world. No surprise here that those ideas took shape and the most meaning for me in the form of tattoos. I imagined something along my throat, so that when I was speaking it held a presence that deserved some attention. I didn't want it to be distracting, but at the same time, it needed to be noticeable. It didn't take long for me to reflect about my time back in California, and how I wanted a tribal design that held significance to my people. I looked down at my coffee table, and there lay the antler I had purchased in Klamath with the sturgeon backbone design. The decision was made for me, and it had found me before I even realized the profound effect it would continue to play in my life. I made the appointment with my buddy Arturo, who took over my canvas after the divorce. In two weeks' time, I would adorn this work of art, culture, and symbol of healing along my throat. Of course it hurt, but that, once again, was another part of the healing process.

I didn't expect another tattoo of healing to come so quickly after my throat but, once again, it chose me as the walking canvas. Back at Standing Rock, I had crossed paths and stayed in touch with a man named Nahaan who was very connected to his Tlingít culture. He not only spoke the language but was also a carver, a spoken word poet, and a tattoo artist. I had always wanted a traditional hand poke tattoo but had never come across the right person to do it. There is a deeper spiritual component to receiving ink this way, and I felt he was the right person for the job. For many Indigenous cultures, tattoos symbolized honorable deeds, gave spiritual protection, and were a sign of beauty.

The night before the tattoo, my father came to me in a dream. I was walking through a large building, with people walking all around and a lot of activity. It felt like an old subway station but without the transit. From a distance, I could see my father leaning up against a pole. I ran over to him as fast as I could. He looked confused, like he didn't know where he was. I noticed that he wasn't wearing a shirt, and then I looked down to see him in a blue and yellow traditional Chilkat blanket. This form of weaving was practiced by the Northwest Coast and Alaskan tribes and is known to be the most complex weaving technique in the world. This wasn't just any design he chose, but in fact he was wearing the exact Chilkat design that I was getting tattooed on my body. I gave him a large hug, and then asked him what he was doing all the way out here. He didn't respond much, and I wondered if his dementia was at fault. I had hoped that he no longer suffered from this disease, that in my dreams he would be set free. But regardless, it still felt like a blessing, and I understood he knew what I was preparing to do.

I told Nahaan of my dream, and he took it as a good sign as well. He mentioned the face in the center of my tattoo represented a good spirit and his ancestors. Before he began the process, he smudged and said a prayer using his Native tongue, followed by a song. This was the medicine I wanted to receive before the process of my ink began, and I felt so grateful for this method of tattooing. This was one tradition among our people that was never fully taken away from us, and to receive a tattoo in the same method my ancestors did should never be taken for granted. One of his girlfriends came over to help with the stretching of my skin and would stay for the entire process. He drew the design on my stomach, and I laid down and prepared myself for whatever pain would follow. The first two hours weren't bad, but the last hour and half were a bit brutal. I just closed my eyes and imagined my family around me and continued to focus my breath with fluid movement and no restrictions. The pain tells you to hold on tight, to hold your breath, but like most things, you have to fight that urge and let go and breathe through it. This creates a space for your body to surrender to the pain, which allows the mind to find some peace within it. Getting tattooed creates a very similar experience to dealing with many forms of pain. It's a lesson on how we handle the discomfort and what tools we utilize to get to the end result, leaving behind a permanent mark on the individual that represents a documented time in their life. After three and half hours, we were done. I couldn't have been more thrilled about my experience and the new artwork that adorned my body. I felt honored to receive this gift, with the sense of my father's blessing behind it.

Feeling famished from hours of tattooing, we agreed to head out for a hearty meal and wanted to discuss further the latest developments at Standing Rock. My fellow water protectors had become an extended family and connected us to each other in ways we never imagined. Just over a week ago, several major injustices had occurred. Things had been heating up as the pipeline moved closer to the Missouri River and the camp. Police in full riot gear, carrying assault rifles, met the water protectors at the front lines. They had come in peaceful protest and were singing songs and smudging with medicines of sweet grass, sage, and tobacco. When asked to leave by the police for trespassing, the people continued to unite and walk towards the blockades. The protectors were pepper sprayed and chased down by rubber bullets shot at them by drones. This resulted in one hundred protectors being arrested, which included elders and journalists. They were facing charges of reckless endangerment, criminal trespass, riot charges, and resisting arrest. Some of the women arrested spoke of being strip searched and forced to cough and squat on arrival at the Mandan jail. This was beyond degrading, and as a woman, I was disgusted by this behavior and couldn't begin to fathom how this law enforcement could sleep at night. These were not criminals; they were the people of the earth, practicing their God-given right to protect our Mother at all costs. Would they treat their own mothers, sisters, and family members with such brute force, for just standing up for what they believe in? This was a clear violation of their rights to protest, not to mention that this was sovereign land cited by the Treaty of 1851 and the care of Sioux. The water protectors couldn't afford to pay their legal fees, and by doing these mass arrests, the state was making a pretty penny on the backs of those who were protecting its resources.

Once again, it all came down to corporate greed and the powers that be doing what was necessary for them to make more money. Meanwhile, the people who fought to protect the land were treated merely as an obstacle that could be easily disposable. This was history repeating itself, and it was a time we could look back and understand some of how our ancestors felt. They had to defend their homes and way of life for centuries from those who didn't understand our connection to this earth.

Nahaan was set to leave and return back to Standing Rock the following week, and I felt some worry for his safety with how things were currently being handled. Sharing our experiences at camp had created a unique bond, one that felt both spiritual and energetic while intertwining our medicine tracks. We hugged goodbye, and I thanked him for sharing his tattoo medicine and the effort that went into creating such a special experience. My tattoos previously had represented my life with James and some memories we shared. However, these last two symbolized a new beginning, a connection not just to my culture but to spirit, leaving behind a permanent imprint of how far I had come in my healing and reminding me that I was strong enough to tackle whatever adversity came my way.

CHAPTER 13
Gratitude Medicine

OVER THE PAST SUMMER and into the fall, I had continued to meet with my Native high school youth group, Nk'wu Nation, to prepare for our traditional dinner. Unfortunately, we had missed the spring of gathering camas, chokecherries, bitterroot, and serviceberries. However, some of my friends and the tribes donated some of these foods to be used for our event.

We were at least able to gather the mushrooms and elderberries at the end of the summer, and I had another fieldtrip planned just weeks before the dinner. We arranged to make the drive out of town to our gathering destination over an hour away to collect water potatoes. My girlfriend and fellow water protector Twa-le and I took the kids out to the Coeur d'Alene Reservation, where she had arranged to meet with our guide Mark, who prepped us to gather for the day.

Mark explained to the group, "This time of year, gathering is known as 'sch'edp,' which means darkness is approaching and it's time to head to the lake to gather the last of the foods. Our ancestors used root diggers called 'pitse' made from service trees, or haw. The handles were made from elk antlers, and woven baskets were used to carry the food."

The root diggers we were using today are made from metal, we planned on using shovels and having buckets to carry the potatoes. We were dressed for battle. The mud comes up to your knees at times, and it was essential to be in the right gear to make the most of our day of gathering.

I knew this would be a difficult task for my injured leg, and the deep mud being the only path for travel would challenge its strength more than ever before. I had faith that I could make it through the day and would deal with the consequences later. There was no way I was not going to participate in such a special tradition that comes only one time a year.

Iaitia and a few other students rode with me on the way out there that day, and Iaitia mentioned that a few of them had been quarreling the last few weeks. I hoped that spending this time together out in nature would settle any misunderstandings and bring some closure. We had made sure to mention to the students how important it was to be in the right heart space when gathering traditional foods. Your intentions needed to be in a good space, because we understand that energy goes into the food. From the beginning of gathering to preparing and cooking the food, this rule of energy applies. It was a privilege to be able to continue this tradition of our ancestors, and we couldn't take that for granted.

Our ancestors had always understood that all plants have spirits and the medicine is the strongest when these living things are shown respect. Whether it was a plant or an animal, some kind of offering like tobacco, corn meal, or pollen was left in its place. There were songs or special prayers performed before, during, and while preparing these sacred foods.

We parked the cars in a pull-in lot surrounded by heavy brush and headed towards the lake, looking for a prime spot to gather. Mark said a prayer for the group, then the kids dispersed down the muddy pathway. Looking out onto the lake, it felt like the perfect day, with the sun shining brightly nestled in the clear blue sky, along with gentle breeze that came in the form of a whisper. I loved being out here, knee deep in mud and digging through the layers upon layers of rich minerals provided by Mother Earth. To reach the water potatoes, you had to dig fairly deep into the mud and turn it over, carefully inspecting it and hoping to find a light to darker pink hue about the size of a Ping-Pong ball. The water potatoes looked more similar to radishes in the mud, but with a softer color, and they were easy to miss. Once you did find one, the work was worth the reward. This task really gave the kids as well as myself a sense of how difficult this way of life had to be. All of our ancestors had to hunt and gather, and now everything is processed and packaged. During these times of hard labor to gather these foods was when I felt the plant medicine already working. It was teaching us to have respect for these foods that Mother Nature provides, along with the lesson of the patience it takes to gather them.

I noticed some healthy cattails growing further down the lake and made my way over to gather a few for the dinner. I could see the flowering stem that holds the pollen was already gone, this late into the season. I am told this green flower can be cooked like corn on the cob, but I have never had the opportunity to try it. The Yurok Tribe and other Northern California tribes used the cattail pollen for special ceremony needs. This medicine could also be a good thickening agent for soups, among other things. I dug around the base of the plant to find the lateral rhizomes or rootlike stems. These could be roasted, or the more labor-intensive approach would be to separate the starch, allow drying, and then make it into flour.

We spent hours out in the mud that day, and few of us got stuck for lengths of time, unable to escape. This mud out here was no joke, and it takes no prisoners without just cause. The kids ended the day with a mud fight, and by the time we left they appeared to be in full camouflage. It took us a great deal of time to get cleaned up enough to get back into the car. The Coeur d' Alene Tribe gifted us a large amount of frozen salmon as a generous donation for our dinner. We came back home successful with quality time gathering medicine and a bounty of food for our dinner.

We were now days away from the event, and the generous food donations continued coming in. We received deer meat from a Colville tribal member who also allowed us to come up and help with drying deer jerky over an open flame. Twa-le and a few other women were so gracious to give us a hearty amount of dried camas. This traditional food looks like a purple flowering lily with an edible bulb. These bulbs when cooked turn their starches into sweet digestible sugars that taste similar to sweet potatoes. When gathering this sacred food, it was important to take the bulb and place the plant back into the earth, leaving the smaller plants behind for another year of growth. I understood the hard work and all the time it took to gather this food, and it meant a lot to be gifted so much. As more ingredients came into play, I began to make a tentative menu for the dinner. We wouldn't know of our entire inventory until the day before the event, so I had to be prepared for whatever I had to work with. I also had no idea how many people to expect, but cooking at Standing Rock had prepped me to serve a small army. The final menu for the dinner was ready, and I made a list for anything else we needed to pick up.

Nk'wu Nation - First Traditional Food Feast

Water potato chips with pumpkin marmalade
Dried deer jerky
Deer steaks with elderberry glaze

Roasted camas with herbs

Wild rice, deer, and cranberry stuffed bell peppers

Baked sockeye salmon, seasoned with Dijon and tarragon

Deer meat stew, with nettles and wild mushrooms

Spaghetti squash with chive butter

Blue cornbread

Chokecherry popcorn balls

Huckleberry honey cake

My morning began at seven a.m., and the first stop was to meet Twa-le and fillet around eighteen whole salmon for the dinner. They had just barely gotten thawed enough to work with, but we had no time left to wait. One by one, we gutted and cleaned the fish, removing the bones and filleting them to be baked. The salmon were freezing cold, and the task became harder with my frozen fingers not cooperating. We managed to get all eighteen salmon prepped in just under two hours. This dinner wouldn't have been possible without the support of food donations by our community and tribal members, along with a few key volunteers who offered their support with the fundraiser.

I packed my car carefully with cookie sheets filled with salmon and headed straight to the high school. Jeremy, the teacher in charge of the group, met me out front with a few kids to help unload my car. The second task became getting down the long hallways of the school into the Home Economics room. I was quickly introduced to the Home Ec teacher, who had been kind enough to let us use the space and offered her students to help with prepping of the food. I needed all the help I could get and was feeling incredibly overwhelmed with all that needed to get done.

In the first hour, I assigned several kids to begin prepping the squash and getting them in the oven. I had six working kitchens, and I planned on utilizing them all. I asked Iaitia to marinate and handle the deer steaks and one of her other friends to assist. She volunteered her entire school day, which meant I could continue to count on her the most. Several kids showed up from the Salish language speaking class to assist, and I quickly sent them to the back to make the homemade water potato chips. I needed to handle the broth, using roasted bones, garlic, onions, carrots, celery, and bay leaf to enhance the flavor.

It felt like controlled chaos, but I found jobs for each of them to do and new ones for those who continued to show up. I tried to remain patient with students that had never cooked a day in their life by showing them the love that goes into the food.

Around twelve-thirty p.m., most of the kids had broken for lunch, while myself and few other students continued in our efforts to get the menu done. *The Spokesman-Review*, our local newspaper, took interest in our story and showed up to do an interview. They spoke with the students about why they wanted to host a traditional dinner and the process it took for us to gather the foods. I spared a few minutes to answer some questions about why this work was important for Native American communities.

"We have the highest diabetes in the nation, and it's no surprise that resulted from the introduction of processed foods," I told them. "In general, Native people are more sensitive to sugar and dairy, as they were never part of our ancestors' diet. The food came from the earth, and we ate in harmony with Mother Nature and the seasons. By returning back to our traditional foods that are also our medicine, our health as a whole will improve, as well as our connection to our culture."

I wanted to give them more of my time but had so much on my plate that time was better spent cooking. The school district sent in a videographer to film the work we were doing and share on their webpage. This was thrilling news for me, as my father had worked for this public school system for thirteen years. I felt like I was carrying on his work, but by sharing my gifts in my way.

Still having no idea how many people to expect, I estimated to cook for seventy to eighty people and hope for the best. The hours were flying by as we drew closer to the dinner being served at six p.m. The last item on our menu, the huckleberry cake, had just finished baking at five-forty-five p.m. The heavy and hot cookware had to be placed on wheeled carts, then carefully taken a long distance to the school cafeteria. This was no easy task, and I crossed my fingers that no one got hurt or dumped the food. The time was here, and I realized I hadn't eaten a thing or even peed since I arrived. The six kitchens were a complete disaster, but I would deal with all that later. Time to feed the people and enjoy the fruits of our labor. Time to celebrate our culture and the youth stepping up their roles in the community.

It looked like we had a great turnout for the dinner. I saw elders, families, and friends gathered and awaiting our arrival. Before we began serving everyone, I made a prayer plate made up of all the dishes being served, then passed it to our speaker, one of the Salish language teachers named Barry, to say the evening's prayer.

"I want to start off by saying how special this traditional food dinner is, and how it's never been done in this school system. I myself graduated from Rogers High School, and to come back for an event such as this is really special," Barry said. "These foods of our ancestors are sacred, and it's important to keep these traditions alive. I want to thank the Nk'wu Nation for providing this meal. May we all be blessed by the medicine and love that went into the food."

Barry went on to say a short prayer in the Salish language and then passed the microphone onto me.

"I want to thank you all for coming, donating, and supporting the Native youth during the process of making this traditional dinner become a reality," I said. "The kids and I spent many days devoted to gathering these foods, and the tribes were so gracious with their donations to this event. I am so proud of these kids, and this community for stepping up to supports our traditional dinner. A lot of love went into this food, and I hope you enjoy what we have prepared for you today. Thank you."

We formed a food service line for our guests, and I had a few kids make some plates for elders. I could see how proud the kids were of all their hard work, as they dished out food for their families. By the end of the line, we had run out of a few popular items, such as the water potato chips and deer steaks, as we approached our total of serving seventy people. I observed the students' smiles and sense of accomplishment while they were serving the community members. That feeling alone was all the validation I could ask for when doing this work.

After everyone had finished their plates, the Nk'wu Nation began to sing at their drum circle. I loved every time I got to see them perform, as it's so rare to witness youth forming their own drum circle these days. After a few songs, we called a round dance so that everyone could participate. The round dance is also known as the friendship dance and is performed at powwows during the intertribal portion. One large circle moves in one direction to the beat. An inner circle is formed that goes the opposite direction, so that we can shake hands to the beat of the drum. This social activity gets people to interact and allows outsiders to participate if they choose to.

The evening's events went on till about eight p.m., and I thanked everyone who came to support the kids. The time had come now to take on the task of six messy and unorganized kitchens that we had left behind. Before I could leave for the day, I had to get them cleaned and set back the way they were when I arrived. Iaitia's mom Mandi was so gracious to get an early start. She had done a large portion of the dishes during the dinner. However, walking back into the Home Ec room, I had no idea where to begin. If you can imagine, around twenty kids had come in that day and made food enough to serve a small army, leaving behind a crazy amount of grease, food scraps, and dirty dishes to clean up, and nothing was where it was supposed to go. Luckily, a few teacher volunteers that had helped the during the whole process offered their services. The three of us made it work and tried to organize the kitchens as best we could for school the next day. I didn't end up leaving the school till ten p.m., feeling exhausted, with my body hurting. I was still dealing with my injured leg, and it had occurred a decent amount of swelling due to the whole day spent running around on it. Alex had told me to honor my body, and up to this point I had really been taking that advice. But I had to be on my feet this entire day and get the task at hand done; I had too many people counting on me. The pain at the time had been masked with busy work, and I gave it little attention. What I was able to witness today with the kids far exceeded anything else, and I would make up for it and now take more time to rest.

At this point, my leg had been injured for almost two solid years, with no running, fancy dancing, or any other high-impact cardio movements. I had come to the conclusion that it would heal itself when I connected to my spirit in a way I never had before. I had given it ample time to make a comeback and tried every known therapy I had available to me. The only thing that I could deduce was that this trauma didn't come from a source on the physical plane, that it was in fact coming from my "pain body," defined by Eckhart Tolle as a collective manifestation of pain accumulating your entire life. This stemmed from past trauma or inherited family history that had left an imprint inside my cells. Mine in particular had continued to feed on past emotional pain I had not released. I wanted to believe in my heart that I had forgiven James and Nikki for the pain they had caused me. However, my authentic self knew that was not the case, and that I might not ever fully be able to. Honestly, my anger had subsided for the most part involving James. I had come to accept that I had a role in his unhappiness. But with Nikki, on the other hand, I still couldn't bring myself to find that closure. The anger fueled by her betrayal still must reside within me, and it was up to me, and only me, to let that go.

I had to take a closer look at the death of my father, as well. Was there part of me that felt angry or abandoned? He had gone to be with the rest of my family and left me behind, a lone wolf without a pack. As I dug deeper, I didn't feel anger but, of course, there was still suffering. I looked into my child archetypes, as defined by Caroline Myss, for more clarity. My wounded child had used these painful experiences to have more compassion for others that were wounded. The nature child within me was fed by connection to our Mother and by the animal medicine that came in human form. But, through my grief and lessons in patience, I have strived to become the magical child more than any of the others, to understand the beauty that lies in all things, and to be able to overcome any and all circumstances with the right intention. I also wanted to follow my dreams as guides and to never take them for granted, for they already understand what I do not yet know myself.

Obviously, there was still some unresolved conflict within my spirit that held an answer to why I was still not able to heal physically. I made plans for one last trip to Nespelem to sweat before I would be leaving for New Zealand.

I chose the right women to braid my sacred energy with for this session and was able to be in the good company of Britney, Iaitia, and my yoga teacher, Lara. She quickly became one of my favorites to learn the practice from and invest my time in. She was a kind and soft-spoken human being with lots to share and did so in such a humble way. Lara knew me when I was married to James and understood why I had needed to take a break from my teacher training during the divorce. She had always been someone I felt comfortable sharing with, even the most personal stories of my life. We had recently connected very randomly, and I shared some of my latest experiences of healing with her. I could feel that she needed this type of medicine for herself, so I offered to take her with me. She was beyond delighted and jumped on board for the next time I was able to sweat.

I loved being able to bring these three other ladies with me to the sweat; it bonded us in a unique way of sisterhood. And the drive went by fast when I had this much company to attend to. Brittany and Lara had plenty to discuss, sitting in the back. They were both philosophy majors, and I knew that, among many other things in common, would bond them quickly. Iaitia sat up front with me so we could discuss the latest developments at Standing Rock and how we couldn't understand how cruel people could be when it came to a matter of corporate greed.

On November 21, 2016, only a few days after the traditional dinner, tensions at Standing Rock had taken an even darker course. It was a shameful day in American history, leaving one hundred and twenty-seven water protectors injured, and seven injured severely enough that they went to the hospital.

At the roadblock of 1806 of Oceti Sakowin camp, the protectors were trapped with nowhere to go, making them easy targets for the DAPL hired hands, who aimed at the protectors' heads and legs with rubber bullets. In addition, DAPL security and police force sprayed them during freezing temperatures of twenty-five degrees with water cannons, rubber bullets, and tear gas. The tear gas made it impossible for the water protectors to get out of harm's way, leaving them completely vulnerable. The videos that leaked showed the protectors trying to take refuge, with no vision and nowhere to escape. They were trapped liked cattle and treated as if completely disposable, with no compassion for human life and the right to be heard. The DAPL claimed the water protectors had started a fire, and that was why they had retaliated with the water cannons. But anyone with a half a brain knows that was horseshit and a ridiculous excuse to behave as they did. The fire was intended to keep them warm while making a stand in freezing cold temperatures. With the bridge blocked by DAPL security, very limited medical staff could be of help, and the ones that were present were beyond overwhelmed.

A disturbing picture of a young woman was circulating my Facebook feed who had been shot in the arm with a concussion grenade. You could see all the way to her bone, and her flesh was torn wide open. I imagined she might possibly lose that arm, and all because she chose to protect the water.

Watching this footage had been beyond disturbing and had me questioning what had happened to our law enforcement protecting us. Clearly, they were owned by the corporations, and people were a mere obstacle to them getting what they wanted. This was what our ancestors had endured, and now we were getting a taste of their struggle to remain resilient and protect our Mother from those who wanted to continue to rape her. This was spiritual trauma that they were creating, which would run the deepest and darkest path of destruction and, from what we had seen, would continue to affect future generations. The men that wore those law enforcements suits did not understand what they were doing or the consequences of their actions. They were lost in the system and immersed in a society whose fundamental values came in the form of dirty paper and superficial objects.

We arrived in Nespelem around five p.m. and made our way into the sweat. Sharon was tending to the fire and prepping for our sweat. She was so pleased to see that I had brought some new sisters with me.

"Sharon, this is Lara, one of my dearest yoga teachers and a friend of mine. This is Iaitia, that I have told you so much about, and I call her my niece. And you know sister Brittany."

Sharon hugged each one of the ladies and replied, "I'm so happy to be finally be meeting some of you that I have heard so much about. I love having new sisters come to the sweat. If this is your first time, I will try to go easy on you. Please continue to drink lots of water, and let me know how you are feeling."

As the ladies got acquainted, I helped with the grandfather rocks and placed them in the four directions in the sweat, then added another three to the four and closed the door. The five of us smudged with cedar and cleansed using the rose water on our upper bodies before entering the sweat. I took my place next to Sharon, who would be running the sweat and pouring the water on the rocks. Iaitia sat next to me, then Lara, and Brittany was once again in charge of the door.

This was our first round, and Sharon began with saying thanks for the new sisters who had made it and the ones that had returned.

Brittany's turn was next. She said, "In this first round, I want to say how grateful I am to be here, and how much this sweat means to me and my spirit. I'm so thankful for Donell bringing us here, and for Sharon always being here to support us and run the sweat."

It was Lara's turn, and her first time in a sweat lodge like ours with only women present. She also mentioned how grateful she was that we had met and that I had brought her to the sweat.

Iaitia was next. This young lady made me cry happy tears on the regular when I witnessed the power of her words on other people, including myself.

"I want to say in this first round how grateful I am for my Auntie Donell, and how she continues to support my growth," Iaitia began. "She is a water protector and chose to go down to Standing Rock and join my Lakota people. I pray for my relatives, the elders, and those who protect the water. I pray for their safety, and well-being during a time like this, when big corporations see dollar signs. It breaks my heart to see people being treated this way, all for the sake of greed and precious resources. I pray for our future, and the future of my grandchildren, and their grandchildren."

Iaitia never ceased to amaze me, and her words had moved me since the moment I met this young lady. I had tears rolling down my face as she continued to pray, and I could feel her strong spirit in full expression.

Now it was my turn. I noticed the rocks this round had never really gotten hot. It made me reflect even more about the cold weather the water protectors were facing down at Standing Rock. In Lakota creation stories, the grandfather rocks were the first creation, with water being the second. The Seneca refer to rocks as "the Stone people" who hold the ancient knowledge and history of our people and must always be respected. This was indeed a lesson for us as well; the first round was meant to be cold as our relatives were suffering. It was my turn to close this round, and I was ready to speak my truth.

"In this first round, I first want to thank all my sisters for being here and sharing this sweat with me tonight. You all mean so much to me, and I do value our time together. Sister Sharon is always here to support and run the sweat, and I am so grateful for her and all she has taught me. Thank you, Creator, for blessing me with these gifts of sisterhood with these wonderful ladies.

"My heart has been heavy with trying to understand the mistreatment by law enforcement of our own people. I pray for my relatives down at Standing Rock who are suffering to protect our Mother. The weather will continue to bring more hardship, and the powers that be have continued to assert themselves in an aggressive manner. I pray for those that were injured recently and that they recover quickly. I pray for the protection of the water protectors against any further action that is not for the greater good. And I really want to pray for the powers that be to see the light and to understand that this affects them, too, and that our Mother is a sacred living being. If we wish to ever live in harmony with her again as our ancestors did, we have to stop this madness. My prayers are for peace, and that love becomes the answer. That is my prayer for the first round."

Sharon closed the round and mentioned how unusually cold this first round had been. She said, "We must respect the rocks, and this round was cold just as our relatives are experiencing right now down at Standing Rock. No sweat is ever the same, and each one has different lessons to teach us, so pay attention to what Creator is telling you, in and out of the sweat."

Sharon decided to move us into the smaller lodge for the second round. We had just enough of us to make it cozy without being too small. Iaitia and I brought in the rocks for this round, and I stumbled upon one shaped as a heart.

"Hey, Sharon, look at this rock." I said.

"Oh, Donell, looks like you have found a love rock. Better watch out when you head to New Zealand. Hey," Sharon replied with a smile that said plenty.

Since the last round was cold, we wasted no time getting in for the second round in the smaller sweat. Britney began this round and went in a circle to Lara, Iaitia, and then myself. This round was hot, and like before, always seemed to be the most difficult on me physically. With the smaller lodge, the intense heat didn't take long for the suffering to begin.

Once the sweat begins taking its course, the suffering comes next, creating a space for healing and for the medicine to take effect. The power of prayer in my Mother's womb is like nothing else I have ever experienced. And during this time, I can feel that continued presence of my family and ancestors, as if they are right next to me.

I used this round to pray for one of my good friends battling cancer, that she had protection and would never feel alone in her fight, that her body would heal itself with the help of medical support, and that she would regain her strength and quality of life back to its full potential. She had been such a warrior from the start, and her inner strength had inspired so many around her. I had made her one of my regular prayers, and I had no doubt she would win this battle.

Sharon mentioned the love rock in this round and asked Creator for me to have a safe journey, and possibly find love on my travels. This was a good round, and the girls really got to experience the heat this time. We called door without hesitation and took a little longer break in between. I headed immediately for the outdoor shower; this round had got me drenched in sweat. The cool water brings such a relief of comfort, and each time I feel reborn. We sat down to a few favorite snacks, and Sharon got to know the new sisters a little better.

Round three turned out to be just as hot as round two, and I was game for that, considering how cold the first round was. I appreciated the intimacy of the smaller sweat, and how close we needed to sit by each other. In here, it felt as if we were sharing the same womb, and that we were indeed sisters and shared the same Mother.

Round four was in full effect, and this round began with Iaitia.

"I pray for our youth, and that they understand the impact of the decisions they make today. Staying away from making poor choices with drugs and alcohol will keep them following the red road. I pray for my fellow classmates that see no future before them and use drugs as an escape from that reality. For those who suffer from depression and want to end their lives, I pray for them. Our ancestors were resilient and fought so hard for us to be here. The least we can do is honor them by taking care of each other, our Mother, and ourselves. This is my final prayer for the fourth round."

Sharon did the four pours of water, and then it was my turn.

"For my final prayers of the fourth round, I want to pray for all the missing Indigenous women and children. I pray for their families, that they find some answers, and some peace. I pray for change, and that this issue will come to light and actually be addressed, so my relatives don't have to live in fear. I pray for the victims of this abuse and any abuse, that they still feel some protection and your love, Creator.

"I pray for my sisters here tonight, and the ones that couldn't make it, that they continue to feel your love and have a safe journey wherever they go. I pray for a safe journey to New Zealand, and that you align me with the right path and people. This is final prayer for the fourth round."

Sharon closed the round and prayed for all of us to have a safe journey home. We exited the lodge, took showers, and changed back into our clothes for the journey back home. I gave Sharon the biggest hug and told her how much I loved her and would miss her. This was to be my last sweat before I left for two months, and I had no idea when I would be back. Everyone was sad to leave this sacred space and our sister Sharon, for it felt like home now to all of us.

I got home just after eleven and crashed hard, with my hair still wet from the last shower, and became one with bed. My dreams on those nights tend to be more vivid, and I am able to go deeper into my subconscious on the nights of my sweats.

This dream began in a familiar way, one that I had experienced many times before over the last ten years. I was in my old room at my father's house, and I could hear strange noises coming from the closet. This part I have replayed countless times, and normally I leave the room. I know there is some kind of spirit or being in there, and in the past, I have been too scared to find out what it was. This time, I get out of bed and head towards the door but decide at the last minute to hold my space and turn around. I am shocked to see what I had been running away from all this time. It's a little boy, maybe around the age of four or five, with dark thick curly black hair and the kindest brown eyes.

He looks me directly in the eyes and says, "I am your son. I have been waiting for you to see me."

I can't believe what he just said. How can he be my son?

I reply, "You look so different from my other son I have met before. How can this be? Do you have a different father?"

"Actually, yes, I do, but I am your son. And I have been in that closet all these years, waiting for you to open it. But you were too scared, and now you are ready to see me."

I really wasn't sure how to process what he was saying. This was something I never expected. Could it be that all those years of dreams, he was right there waiting for me to let go of my fear of being a mother, and of not just of one son but two? It also freaked me out that he said he had a different father. I never planned on having two babies' daddies, but what he is telling me feels right. I hugged my son and told him I would never leave the room again without acknowledging his presence. We spent some time cuddling in bed and sharing stories. He even mentioned how I would deliver him feet first and laid on top of my belly.

"This is how I am supposed to come into this world, Mom, no need to worry," he said.

I don't know how long the dream lasted, but when I awoke, it felt like I had actually connected with my son's spirit. I didn't plan on coming home with a baby in my belly on this trip, so this dream made me feel cautious. I wanted to have a family of my own someday, but I was not quite ready to make that first step. I hoped that perhaps New Zealand would bring a new love interest, and maybe that would lead to another path. The love rock that made an appearance during the sweat was a sign for possible romance and love to come forward. All I knew was that I had to remain open to all possibilities and to be careful what I prayed for. Somehow, it always manifested that I got what I wanted, just not in the timing or the way I wanted it. I have been told, "when praying for something, be specific."

This trip to New Zealand had been a dream of mine for so long, and I waited patiently for years to go at the right time. In a few weeks' time, this dream would become a reality, and I would be gone for the next two months. I would have no one to take care of or to check in with. This was my time to get lost in the experience of true freedom, with no concept of time or day. I came to believe during this passage I would embark on other medicine that would bring me full circle, to heal me from the inside out. New Zealand was that chance to connect with other Indigenous people that understood my values but had their own connections to ceremony and spirituality. The Māori had always fascinated me with their rich culture and strong connection to their land and family. The love that comes from a strong family bond is powerful medicine, one that was strong enough to heal me. And I prayed to receive all forms of love, whether it was family or intimacy or spirit. I was ready to be loved on.

I had made a few contacts through clients and fellow water protector friends on Facebook for a few places to stay during my visit. One contact in particular set me up with a woman in Auckland named Tina, who arranged for me to have a welcoming ceremony on the day following my arrival. Her Māori cultural group was having their end-of-the-year celebration and offered to welcome me to New Zealand in a traditional way. I was beyond honored to have an opportunity like this, to be welcomed to land and their ancestors utilizing their sacred traditions. Other than that, I set no expectations. Just being open to all possibilities was my only goal. No matter what was ahead, I was thrilled to have this chance of a lifetime and I wouldn't take any moment for granted.

Finally, there was some good news down at Standing Rock. It was December 4, and an estimated two thousand veterans arrived to support the efforts of the water protectors. They wanted to call to attention to the brutality that had taken place by a militarized police force against its own people. The vets were prepared to act as a human shield and to stand between the protectors and DAPL security.

Then, in another turn of events, President Obama finally stepped in to have the permit to drill under the Missouri River denied. This was unexpected news when, just four days prior, violent actions had been taken on the water protectors. The people rejoiced with caution and gathered around the sacred fire, while others marched through camp carrying mirrored shields. These were used to send a powerful message of self-reflection to the men who were on the other side. It called them to take a look at themselves, dressed in all this armor, and to realize that it wasn't just unnecessary but was meant to instill fear into those they had originally signed up to protect. This was a small victory, but the fight was not over, and the DAPL could appeal. Another major cause of concern was when our new president would take office in late January and had invested over a million dollars in this project. What would happen then to stand against the oil industry when our own President was financially invested?

There was still so much to consider with continuing this fight, and the winter weather in North Dakota would only get worse. Before the vets left camp and headed back to their homes, another amazing gift was given that heal the scars left behind by the colonizers of the past.

Wes Clark Jr. and Michael Wood Jr. made a call, and by December 7, over four thousand vets had arrived at Standing Rock. These men arranged a meeting with seven tribal councils to then got down on one knee and asked for forgiveness of past war crimes.

As I watched this video for the first time, I couldn't help but get emotional. Wesley Clark Jr. presented himself before Lakota elders, medicine people, and the council. He got down on one knee and began to speak from his heart.

"Many of us, me particularly, are from the units that have hurt you over many years. We came. We fought you. We took your land. We signed treaties that we broke. We stole minerals from your sacred hills. We blasted the faces of our presidents onto your sacred mountain. Then we still took more land and then we took your children and then we tried to eliminate the language that God gave you, and the Creator gave you. We didn't respect you, we polluted your Earth, we've hurt you in so many ways, but we've come to say that we are sorry. We are at your service and we beg for your forgiveness."

The room was filled with tears, as this moment in history was what change is really about, and then the real healing can begin. Chief Leonard Crow Dog, a medicine man of the Lakota, walked over to Wesley and held his hand over his head, saying a prayer of forgiveness for the officer that kneeled before him. Several Lakota leaders accepted the apology, and the veterans formed a line to hug and shake their hands. This was a new day of healing, not just for our people but also for everyone that can feel the connection we have to our Mother and one another.

The vets had succeeded in what they set out to do. They protected the people, in addition to beginning to heal some past scars.

This event gave me some hope that things might turn around at Standing Rock, and the Black Snake would be slain. However, I wasn't sure how much news would be available to me overseas, and that felt unsettling.

The next few weeks went by in a flash, and I arranged my car to be cared for, as well as my plants and mail. I had to pay all my bills in advance for the next three months just in case something came up. I felt fairly confident that all my ducks were in a row and I was ready to leave. I would miss my friends dearly, but this trip had become my right of passage and essential to my healing.

I was up at four a.m. to catch my first flight of the trip, and about to begin an entire day of traveling. Everything went along smoothly until I missed my connection in Vancouver, due to my previous flight being an hour delayed. I was bummed that I had run through the airport like a jackal, with all my gear in tow, to be turned away at the gate. I stared at the plane still there on the tarmac, but they had closed the door and wouldn't let me board. The airline at least put me up in a nice Hilton hotel located inside the airport. Plans had changed, and now my welcoming ceremony would be on the same day I arrived, so I chose to spend the next twenty-four hours relaxing.

The next day, when the five p.m. boarding time finally came around, I was anxious and ready to get my dream into motion. I was feeling beyond joyful, now that this vision that I had prayed to become a reality was actually here. In twelve hours, I would embark upon a new adventure that could possibly change the course of my life.

I arrived in Auckland at roughly six am and felt somewhat refreshed from my deep slumber on the plane. I headed right through customs and to the main terminal.

I had arranged to stay with and be picked up by my client's brother in law, Morri. She told me that Morri would stand out, being six foot seven inches tall. He always stood out. Walking into the waiting area, I saw no one at first that fit this description. I saw several people seated, but no one was trying to connect with me. Then, when this distinguished looking man stood up, it became abundantly clear. Morri was indeed that tall and friendly face that felt very welcoming. After the proper introductions, we set out to drop off my things and get a bite. My only focus of the day was to be ready for my ceremony, and I invited Morrie to come along and observe if he wished. He agreed that it would be a unique experience and confirmed he was in.

From this point forward on my trip, I would embrace the teachings of the twelfth clan mother, Gives Praise. She teaches gratitude in all aspects of our lives, which will then create space for continued blessings. She allows us to look at our hardest and most painful moments with a different perspective. Perhaps these times of great suffering will bring a new awareness of one's self and vision.

> Gives Praise encourages all children of the earth through praising what is best in their natures. She shows us that when we celebrate who we are and give thanks for the lives we are leading, when then open our hearts to continue the healing process of being human. The truth we find in every experience of our spiritual evolution marks a forward step on our individual Pathway of Peace. Giving thanks for every victory we achieve and encouraging others by praising and being grateful for their victories ensures the continued movement of humankind toward unity.

The twelfth clan mother represents the color purple, which happens to be my favorite color. And as I embarked on this journey in her month of December, it made perfect sense to begin my path with her teachings.

I hope through sharing my story, these teachings, and those of my ancestors, you can better understand the medicine. Without continued gratitude, I wouldn't be on this path and making my dreams a reality. This, in fact, might have been the strongest form of medicine I carried all along.

❮ ❮ • ❯ ❯

I am back in my body, and I open my eyes to the sounds of a variety of birds communicating amongst each other. They are of a smaller variety, carrying on and flying from tree to tree just above me. I have no idea just how long I have been asleep, or even what time of day it is. Similar to Snow White, I fell under a deep spell of slumber in the forest amongst the animals, except I didn't need to be awakened by a kiss from a romantic partner. In my fairy tale story, the magic that healed me was the love I had found for myself, not through any validation from an outside source. During this time, and being back into my subconscious, I was able to relive the most painful parts of my past, the life-changing moments that turned the course of my path in an entirely new direction.

By the end of my trip, I found my healing and filled my spirit with the love I received from so many people that crossed my path, I accessed my greatest superpower, my intuition, and continued to follow the medicine tracks. Some are more easily seen than others, and most of the time it is revealed through a vibration or a deep-rooted feeling. This unequivocal trust to feel rather than overthink was necessary to stay the course. This process allowed my body to finally heal, and I was able to run several times during my last week in New Zealand. That was one of many days I cried happy healing tears, tears of gratitude, tears of acceptance, tears of joy.

Through an introspective approach, I came to realize that the greatest experiences and moments I have had so far had to first come from a place of suffering. My relationship with my father would not have been as strong or as special if I had not lost my mother. I don't know that I would have reconnected with my spirit and my culture with such intensity if I had not gone through a painful divorce. And this final gift of complete freedom came with the cost of saying goodbye to my father in this reality. These were all lessons that I needed to learn, to be able to appreciate the process and align myself on my chosen path.

I'm not saying I don't have regrets, but I also wouldn't change any one part of the experience. I retraced my steps back in time to the path that guided me to this new profound place of healing. The one consistency through the entire experience was always having gratitude for the good, the bad, and the in-between. Living with gratitude medicine is a humbling experience. It requires the most patience. My father taught me this medicine from the start; this had been in my tool belt the entire journey. It just had become something I took for granted, to have this understanding of when everything is stripped away, what really matters. Gratitude has the power to heal, to offer perspective, and challenge us when we already are at our lowest point. Gratitude is what carried me to this place of healing and kept me within a short distance of my medicine tracks. We are all storytellers, and we each possess the power to change our story if it is not feeding our spirit. The medicine to heal ourselves resides within us, and once we are able to recognize that, only then do we awake to the magic that is all around us, waiting patiently for us to accept it.

ABOUT
the Author

DONELL BARLOW IS A STORYTELLER, activist, holistic health coach, yoga teacher, and hairdresser. She was raised in Spokane, Washington, by her single father and still lives in the Pacific Northwest.

Donell works with Native youth, teaching them about Traditional foods and overall health and wellness practices. She regularly presents at conferences, events, and webinars, sharing her knowledge of Traditional foods and health. Donell's Native American heritage is Yurok and Ottawa. Her daughter, Dusk, was born in 2018.

Connect with Donell at www.donellbarlow.com.

Made in the USA
San Bernardino, CA
07 July 2019